ARCHBISHOP FULTON J. SHEEN

CHERYL C. D. HUGHES

Archbishop Fulton J. Sheen

Convert Maker

IGNATIUS PRESS   SAN FRANCISCO

Cover photo:
Fulton Sheen Meeting Seminarians
Archives of the Archdiocese of Rochester

Cover design by Enrique J. Aguilar

Copyright © 2024 by Ignatius Press, San Francisco
All rights reserved
ISBN 978-1-62164-723-2 (PB)
ISBN 978-1-64229-319-7 (eBook)
Library of Congress Catalogue Number 2024944408
Printed in the United States of America ∞

CONTENTS

*I dedicate this book to my husband and best friend
of almost sixty years, Bill Hughes*

God is the God of the second chance.

Archbishop Fulton J. Sheen

FOREWORD

When one encounters Venerable Archbishop Fulton John Sheen, one immediately sees that he was a truly exemplary priest who lived his life for Jesus Christ and who witnessed to the faith for the salvation of souls. His life of service to the gospel was rooted in his genuine love of Our Lord's presence in the Most Holy Eucharist and his deep affection for the Blessed Mother. Fulton Sheen wanted anyone and everyone to know how much they are loved by God and are called to follow him as a disciple.

My own admiration for the life of Venerable Fulton Sheen and his amazing witness to the Catholic faith has deepened since my appointment in 2020 as the bishop of the Diocese of Peoria, where he lived as a boy and was ordained to the priesthood. The public announcement of my appointment also included a surprise post on Twitter that I was now the bishop responsible for the cause of the canonization of Venerable Fulton Sheen! Since beginning my ministry as bishop of Peoria, I have seen with ever greater clarity the heroic and faithful witness of this remarkable priest and bishop. What a personal inspiration he has become for me!

As the bishop of Peoria, I see firsthand the impact that Fulton Sheen continues to have on the lives of so many people. Whenever I travel outside the diocese, I only need to mention that I am the bishop of Peoria and I will quickly hear of personal encounters with Sheen and the difference that he has made in people's lives. I have heard countless stories from older folks who have personally met Sheen. Their joy in being able to relive and share their experiences of being in Sheen's presence is uplifting. But there are also many young people—too young to have a living memory of Sheen—who, having discerned a vocation to the priesthood or consecrated religious life, readily give credit to Sheen for giving them the courage to say yes to their vocation. Their exposure to him came through his writings, his videos, and the various recordings of his talks that have been preserved. I have seen a new generation of devotees to Sheen grow as their parents and grandparents continue to speak of the powerful witness of Sheen's faith. It's not only in the United States that I find such love for Sheen; I have witnessed it around the world. In visits to Italy, France, and Tanzania, I have seen souls on fire for Christ because of Fulton Sheen! His ministry of bringing souls to Christ is as alive and active today as ever!

In his book, *The Priest Is Not His Own*, he wrote: "The work of conversion is accomplished by the Holy Spirit through the use of human means."[1] As such, in every personal encounter there exists the possibility of influencing others by our love and our witness of faith. Sometimes this occurs in the ordinary interactions of daily life. As people learn the details of Sheen's life and are inspired by his holiness, it often prompts them to reflect on their own lives. As they discover the depth of faith and the spiritual wisdom that are found in his writings and talks, it is not uncommon for people to experience a deepening of their own faith and the desire to bring others to Christ. He had a way of making the faith "real" for those who heard him. Archbishop Fulton Sheen has provided a treasure trove of material that continues to call many people to conversion and to live their life with and for Jesus Christ.

I believe that the Church has received a great gift in the legacy of Fulton Sheen. This legacy is not a cold and static recognition of his accomplishments in the last century. Rather, his legacy is alive in the present moment—drawing on the past and calling us forward into the future. Fulton Sheen's influence as a priest and his heroic witness of the faith is found today in the lives of all of us who have been touched by him. He inspires us to respond to the Holy Spirit by creatively spreading the good news of Jesus Christ in our day as he did in his. Cheryl Hughes has captured this reality in this insightful book on Sheen's life. I am confident that your encounter with Archbishop Fulton Sheen in the pages of this biography will open you to the inspiration of the Holy Spirit—to a deeper conversion of heart and soul. And inspired by the same Spirit, may you accompany this great priest by bringing God's love and mercy to the world!

Most Reverend Louis Tylka
Bishop of Peoria

[1] Fulton Sheen, *The Priest Is Not His Own* (San Francisco: Ignatius Press, 2004), 108.

PREFACE

You are a priest for ever according to the order of Melchizedek.

—Psalm 110:4

To understand the great Archbishop Fulton J. Sheen as the celebrity priest and most noted convert maker of twentieth-century America, it is important first to situate him within his priesthood. Everything he accomplished in his life had its roots in his priesthood. When Fulton John Sheen was ordained a priest on September 20, 1919, he was fulfilling a lifelong ambition and a call from God: he became a priest in the Roman Catholic Church, once and forever a priest in the order of Melchizedek.

Melchizedek was a Canaanite king and high priest of Salem (Jerusalem) who offered a sacrifice and blessed Abraham after Abraham's victory over the combined armies of four kings, the first war mentioned in the Bible (Gen 14:1–20). Melchizedek is one of those individuals in the Bible who is a mystery, a shadowy figure. "He is without father or mother or genealogy, and has neither beginning of days nor end of life, but resembling the Son of God he continues a priest for ever" (Heb 7:3). Melchizedek's death goes undocumented in the Torah, leading early rabbis to surmise that his life and priesthood continued forever. According to early rabbinic thought, nothing that is not mentioned in the Torah exists; if Melchizedek's death is not in the Torah, it never happened. This was an idea later perpetuated by the author of the New Testament Letter to the Hebrews. Melchizedek is a pagan, yet he invokes a blessing in the name of "God Most High", the same God as worshiped by God's Chosen People. Melchizedek's blessing of Abraham indicates that he is greater than Abraham in stature, as he who blesses is greater than the one who is blessed. Melchizedek also receives from Abraham one-tenth, a tithe, of Abraham's victory

7

spoils. The high priest makes a sacrifice of bread and wine in thanksgiving for Abraham's victory, not the usual Near-Eastern blood sacrifice. Melchizedek's sacrifice of bread and wine is the only one in the Bible until the institution of the Eucharist at the Last Supper by Jesus. Of course, the bread and wine at the Last Supper became the true Body and Blood of Jesus under the appearance of ordinary bread and wine. In all this, Melchizedek, the first priest mentioned in the Bible, is a type or prefiguring of Jesus, the last priest to be named in the Bible. It is into this priesthood, the priesthood of Jesus and the priesthood of Melchizedek, that Fulton John Sheen was ordained on the last day of summer in 1919.

During his ordination by Bishop Edmund Dunne, the anointing and laying on of hands by the power of the Holy Spirit made the young Sheen a new man, an ontologically new person. Sheen was eternally changed in essential ways. He became a Catholic priest, with the lifetime obligation to conform himself ever more fully to the person and priesthood of Jesus, the true High Priest. In the Rite of Ordination, after the anointing of the new priest's hands, Psalm 110 is usually sung, including this verse, "The Lord has sworn an oath he will not change: 'You are a priest forever, according to the order of Melchizedek.'" The bishop then tells the new priest, "Receive the oblation of the holy people to be offered to God. Understand what you will do, imitate what you will celebrate, and conform your life to the mystery of the Lord's Cross."[1] Fulton Sheen freely and joyfully gave up himself to put on Christ, to guard and present the mysteries of the faith, teach its truths, offer the sacraments, comfort and strengthen the people of God, and bring converts into the light of Christ.

Whatever else Sheen became after his ordination day, he always remained foremost a priest of Jesus Christ. Later he would become a great celebrity, first on radio during its golden era, and then on television in its infancy. He would bring many converts into the Church. Sheen's face was on the cover of magazines, and he was recognized everywhere. The priest from Peoria, Illinois, had global recognition, even in the most remote places on earth, down to hidden cannibal villages in Africa. Children wrote to him asking questions or requesting prayers. In addition to his live media exposure, his more than sixty books, many pamphlets, magazine articles, and newspaper columns made Fulton Sheen a household name. He became personally known to Hollywood stars and European royalty. But he also befriended the down and out, the diseased, and the disabled. High and low, the masses wanted Sheen, but first he belonged to Jesus— and to the Virgin Mary, to whom he had dedicated his priesthood. Everything he did in life he did through, by, and for his priestly vocation. Fulton Sheen would advise seminarians and priests, "At every moment of our priesthood, we are or should be in contact with the Divine Intercessor."[2] It was the power of his vocation that accounted for the power of his ability to attract the many people he brought into the Church.

Bishop Robert E. Barron, of the Word on Fire media apostolate, writes that "the priest of Jesus Christ is ... a mystagogue, one who bears the Mystery and initiates others into it. At the heart of the Christian faith is a configuration with the all-grounding and all-encompassing mystery of Being itself, which is God."[3] It is the priest who bears the power given him by the Holy Spirit to mediate between heaven and earth, reconciling creation with the Creator. He forgives sinners in the name of Jesus; he offers the sacrifice of the Mass, one of the greatest mysteries of all. In the Mass, the priest is acting in the person of Christ, *in persona Christi*, and at the same time he is also the willing victim offered in the sacrifice. Christ's willing sacrifice of himself on the Cross is a unique sacrifice in the history of mankind. In offering the sacrifice, Christ is the High Priest; in being that which is offered, he is also the victim. Pope Benedict XVI explained the priest's role as an *alter Christus*: "The priest is in Christ, for Christ and with Christ at the service of mankind. Precisely because he belongs to Christ, the priest is radically at the service of all people: He is the minister of their salvation, of their happiness, of their genuine deliverance, growing in maturity as he progressively takes on the will of Christ through prayer and through "heart to heart" contact with him."[4]

---

[2] Fulton Sheen, *The Priest Is Not His Own* (San Francisco: Ignatius Press, 2004), 38.
[3] Robert E. Barron, "The Priest as Bearer of the Mystery", *The Furrow* 46, no. 4 (April 1995): 204.
[4] Pope Benedict XVI, "The Church's Alter Christi", General Audience (June 24, 2009).

Fulton J. Sheen kept his "heart to heart" contact with his Lord in his prayer life, especially in his daily Holy Hour before the Blessed Sacrament. It was a time when Sheen was utterly in the presence of the Lord to the exclusion of everything and everyone. They were alone together for an hour. The Holy Hour was a form of prayer that Sheen recommended especially for priests, but also for laity. He even convinced some Protestants of the efficacy of the Holy Hour. Sheen's entire life as a priest was an extended prayer to God, grounded in his Holy Hour. By the example of the Blessed Virgin Mary, Sheen came to understand that "there comes a moment in the priest's life when he recognizes that he does not belong to his family, his parish, his diocese, his country. He belongs to Christ, the missions and to the world; he belongs to humanity. The closer the priest gets to the mission of Christ, the more he loves every soul in the world."[5] Sheen would title one of his books *The Priest Is Not His Own*.

Sheen's Holy Hour was in addition to his required daily praying of the Liturgy of the Hours, or the Divine Office. The Liturgy of the Hours consists of set hymns, psalms, readings, and prayers and is broken up into the Office of Readings, Morning Prayer, Daytime Prayer, Evening Prayer, and Night Prayer. The Mass is the Church's most perfect prayer, and all priests are recommended to offer Mass daily. For Sheen, the Mass was not just an obligation, but a great joy. To the prayers required by his vocation, Sheen added the Rosary and the Litany of Our Lady. From his ordination onward, Fulton Sheen's daily life was punctuated by prayer, those prayers that are required of every priest and those of his own choosing.

Everyone who knew him recognized him as a holy man, a holy priest. Timothy Cardinal Dolan said of Sheen, "He was pre-eminently a man of intense faith, whose love of Jesus, before whose Eucharistic presence he would unfailingly spend an hour every day of his priestly life, animated everything he did."[6]

For Fulton Sheen, it was a matter of *kenosis* and *pleroma*, emptying himself of self and filling himself with the Lord. In Philippians 2:7, Saint Paul writes that Christ emptied himself to take the form of a

---

[5] Sheen, *Priest Is Not His Own*, 273.

[6] Congregatio de Causis Sanctorum, *Beatificationis et Canonizationis Servi Dei Fultonii Ionis Sheen* (Vatican City: Libreria Editrice Vaticana, 2011), 1.97 (hereafter *Positio*).

slave. Christ was teaching that the Christian must be the servant of all, a slave in service to the people of God, the role most suited to those in the priesthood.

Sheen once left a tip and a note for a waitress who had served him. The note read, "Dear Molly, Tonight you served me, may I serve you forever in heaven. Fulton J. Sheen."[7] To strengthen himself, Sheen filled himself with Jesus in the Sacrament, which he prolonged with his presence before the Lord in his daily Holy Hour. His was a penitential life, a Lenten life of prayer, fasting, and almsgiving. He was continuously in prayer; he was known for his abstemious eating habits; he gave away or donated all his considerable personal earnings, his things, and even the coat off his back. Sheen once admitted to a small group of friends that he wore a hair shirt. "He wore an itchy sheep's vest, a hair shirt, as penance", according to one present at the dinner party.[8] Despite his notable pride and vanity, Sheen struggled to be worthy of his priesthood and to keep those vices under control— hence the hair shirt. He was acutely aware of his shortcomings, yet he persevered to the very end serving the people of God in the Church and bringing others into communion with Christ. The life of Fulton Sheen is an example of what Saint Paul wrote about: "I have been crucified with Christ; it is no longer I who live, but Christ who lives in me" (Gal 2:20). Fulton John Sheen became an existentially new creation at his ordination, a priest forever in the order of Melchizedek. Everything he did or was for the rest of his life followed from and was enabled by the indelible mark of his priesthood.

[7] Ibid., 1.238.
[8] Ibid., 1.140.

Fulton J. Sheen: In the Beginning

Man and Priest

Seeing Fulton Sheen on television was an unforgettable encounter with a remarkable individual. In person, he must have been even more riveting. He was a good-looking man, not Hollywood handsome, but striking nonetheless. It was his eyes that first captured one's attention. His arresting and deeply set blue eyes were steely and direct with a certain twinkle in them, as if he had an important secret to share with his audience. Bill Osterlund, who met Archbishop Fulton Sheen in 1974 in Council Bluffs, Iowa, said looking at Sheen "was like looking into God's eyes".[1] Then there was Sheen's distinctive voice. He spoke with a precise accent that was impossible to place; it was his own, influenced, no doubt, by years spent abroad and a facility with many languages. He was always impeccably dressed in the ecclesial garb of his rank in the Roman Catholic Church. He was a priest, monsignor, then bishop, and finally archbishop. As a monsignor, he wore a black cassock with piping of amaranth, a rose-red, with amaranth buttons and sash above his waist. When he became a bishop, he added the violet zucchetto, or skullcap, his voluminous ferraiolo, or long cape, that tied at the neck became violet, and, of course, he wore a bishop's gold or silver pectoral cross. He was an impressive sight, the likes of which most of his television audience had never seen and would never see anywhere else. With his eyes, voice, and attire, it was impossible to realize he was a slight man of short stature. He was less than five feet eight inches tall and usually under 130 pounds, but his physical proportions were inverse to

---

[1] "A Sheen Moment", *Archbishop Fulton J. Sheen Foundation Newsletter*, Summer 2022, 3.

the enormous influence he wielded for mid-century Americans of all religions or none. *Time* magazine would put him on its cover, and the Television Academy would recognize him with an Emmy as the best television personality for the year 1952.

More importantly, for an undetermined number of individuals, he was the occasion for their conversion to Roman Catholic Christianity. He would never claim to be the reason anyone converted, because conversions, he would say, are the work of God. "I never keep a record of converts lest I fall into the error of thinking I made them. The Good Lord would never let me have another. He would punish me for my pride."[2] Nevertheless, his conversions were numerous and sometimes notorious. He was so well known as a maker of converts to the Catholic Church that *Newsweek*, *Time*, *Life*, and *Look* all published stories about him and the many he brought into the Church. In his introduction to Mark Zia's book about Archbishop Sheen, Andrew Apostoli wrote, "Through his preaching, teaching, and writing, it is estimated that Bishop Sheen converted approximately forty-two thousand to the faith, in addition to the many personal conversions."[3] This will be the story of Bishop Sheen and eight of his better known "celebrity" converts: Heywood Broun, journalist, critic, playwright; Ada "Bricktop" Smith, Black entertainer and nightclub owner; Louis Budenz, editor of the Communist newspaper, *The Daily Worker*; Clare Boothe Luce, journalist, playwright, U.S. congresswoman, and ambassador to Italy; Fritz Kreisler, violinist and composer; Elizabeth Bentley, Soviet spy and government informant; Bella Dodd, teacher, lawyer, and Communist organizer; and Virginia Mayo, actress. While largely unknown today, these converts were famous (or infamous) in their day, and their conversions were the stuff of media attention. At the time, their conversions were considered quite a victory for the Catholic Church in America and another coup for Fulton J. Sheen.

It is important to understand what sustained Sheen throughout his long life. He became a celebrity with a status akin to that of beloved entertainers or sports figures of the day; he earned and raised millions of dollars on television and from books, pamphlets, talks, and

---

[2] Kenneth Stewart, "Monsignor Fulton J. Sheen", *PM Magazine*, June 23, 1946, 9.
[3] Andrew Apostoli, introduction to *The Enduring Faith and Timeless Truths of Fulton Sheen*, by Mark J. Zia (Cincinnati: Servant Books, 2015), xi.

events across the country and around the world; he was influential in society and in the Church; for decades his face was one of the most widely recognized in the country. For all the glitz and glamour associated with Fulton Sheen, he was at the core of his being a priest in the Roman Catholic Church. He was a man in love with his God and his vocation, the Virgin Mary, and the people of God—and all were the people of God. It was this firm faith and the spirituality engendered in Sheen that fed his drive to find the lost sheep, to save souls, to preach the Word of God, to feed the hungry, and to clothe the naked.

His was a very Lenten life. Lent is the Church's forty-day penitential period of preparation for Easter, in which the faithful are asked to fast, give alms, and pray in repentance for their sins. Hope, of course, is in the Resurrection of Jesus from the tomb; but first there is the Cross. Fulton Sheen did not just observe the Lenten obligations for the official forty days of Lent; he cheerfully lived them throughout the year, year in and year out. His was a *kenotic* or self-emptying spirituality in imitation of Jesus, while at the same time filling himself up with the Eucharist and the love of the Virgin Mary.

The Young Sheen: PJ, Fulton, and Spike

Aside from the fact that he was a very intelligent little boy, nothing about Fulton Sheen's earliest years marked him as destined for the level of ecclesial stardom he achieved in his lifetime or the sainthood that he may achieve in this century. He was born on May 8, 1895, in El Paso, Illinois, a farming community that had a population of less than fifteen hundred at the time. His grandfathers on both sides had been immigrants from Ireland, but his paternal grandfather had married a Protestant woman and left the Catholic Church. Sheen's father had also married a Protestant woman, Ida Clara von Buttear, and they had a daughter, Eva. Ida died while Eva was a baby, and the widower, Morris Newton "Newt" Sheen, converted to Catholicism to marry the twenty-nine-year-old Delia Fulton, who was Irish Catholic on both sides of her family. So strong was the anti-Catholicism of the day that baby Eva's Protestant grandparents sued in court for custody of the infant in order to save her from "popery", a case the court found compelling. The von

Buttears, with the blessing of the United States legal system, managed to adopt Eva away from the Sheens; Fulton Sheen's Protestant half-sister virtually disappeared from the Sheen family.

Delia and Newt Sheen went on to have four sons: Fulton, Joseph, Thomas, and Aloysius.[4] Their eldest son was baptized Peter John Sheen: Peter for his father's father and John for his mother's father. After his Baptism at Saint Mary's Church in El Paso, Delia Sheen placed her four-day-old infant son on the altar of the Blessed Virgin Mary and consecrated him to her care. Though baptized "Peter", he quickly became PJ and later "Fulton", after his maternal grandfather. PJ was a colicky baby who cried and cried unless he was held and consoled by his mother's father. In the family, baby PJ became known as "Fulton's baby" because only John Fulton could soothe his grandson and stop his incessant crying. Over time, everyone came to just call the baby Fulton, the name he would carry for the rest of his life. After his birth, he lived with his family over the El Paso hardware store owned and run by his father and Uncle Andrew.

Little Fulton was five years old when the store was burned down by a cigarette hastily tossed aside by a young clerk who did not want to be caught smoking. The Sheen family moved to Peoria, Illinois, a somewhat larger town about thirty miles away. It was time for Fulton's baby to start school, and there were no Catholic Schools in El Paso. Fulton Sheen's father had but a third-grade education, and his mother had only completed the eighth grade. Nonetheless, what was good enough for them was not good enough for their children. They wanted their sons to have the benefit of the best education possible. Peoria boasted an excellent Catholic school, Saint Mary's, operated by the Sisters of the Sacred Heart. Upon his enrollment in Saint Mary's, Peter John Sheen officially became Fulton John Sheen. Exactly how this happened is somewhat of a mystery, and accounts vary. In his autobiography, Sheen wrote that it was his grandfather who enrolled him in Saint Mary's under that name; other accounts say that little Fulton himself was responsible for the name change. No school records remain from Fulton's Saint Mary's days, but everyone seems to agree that Fulton and the three brothers who followed him were all academically gifted.

[4] Joe became a lawyer, Tom a doctor, and Al a businessman.

With Catholic schooling and growing up in a devotedly Catholic family, Fulton Sheen appears to have been a devout child from the beginning. At the age of eight, he became an altar boy in the large Saint Mary's Cathedral next to his school. When he was twelve, Fulton was confirmed and took the Confirmation name John, after the Beloved Disciple, and from that time forward he signed his name Fulton J. Sheen. The impressive cathedral was the parish church for the Sheen family. Presiding at the cathedral was Bishop John Lancaster Spalding, bishop of Peoria from 1877 to 1908. Bishop Spalding is considered to have been one of the most dynamic and influential Church leaders of his day. Spalding's legacy includes his part in cofounding Catholic University in Washington, D.C. Unfortunately, another part of his legacy was a sexual scandal that involved a putative relationship between the bishop and a young woman for whom he was the guardian. Of course, nothing of the scandal was known to the Sheen family or the public at large. Bishop Spalding greatly impressed the young altar boy when he told Fulton to tell his mother, "I said when you get big you are going to go to Louvain and some day you will be just as I am."[5] The Catholic University in Louvain, Belgium, was noted for its philosophy and theology departments. Eventually Fulton would earn two graduate degrees from Louvain and go on to become a bishop, though what possessed Bishop Spalding to make such a prediction to a grammar school boy is a complete mystery. The boy from El Paso would have to put forth a great deal of time and effort before the prophecy became true.

In 1909, Fulton entered the local Catholic boys' high school named after Bishop Spalding. In high school, he continued to excel in academics. Sometime in his childhood, Fulton had suffered with tuberculosis, which may have accounted for his small stature, weak lungs, and delicate stomach. High school sports held little interest for him, although he played some handball and ran track. He would later be an avid tennis player who played twice a week into his later years. Fulton acted in drama club plays. He was well liked by his classmates and affectionately called Spike because of his high, wavy hair.

---

[5] Fulton J. Sheen, *Treasure in Clay: The Autobiography of Fulton J. Sheen* (Garden City, N.Y.: Doubleday Press, 1980), 12.

After school and on weekends, Fulton worked at a local men's clothing store, where perhaps he picked up his penchant for sartorial splendor. He also worked summers and holidays on the two farms the family owned and tenanted out. Young Fulton plowed and harvested. He did not take to farming as an occupation, however, and although he worked hard at it, he was largely inept. One farmer remarked, "That eldest Sheen boy is never going to amount to nothing. He can't even back a wagon into the corn shelter!"[6] Despite his dislike of farming, Fulton was always a conscientious worker, following the excellent example of his parents' work ethic. Nineteen-hour days were common throughout his life. "The habit of work was one I never got over, and thank God I never did", he wrote.[7] It was just that he did not like farming. Somewhat relatedly, he was never able to enjoy a chicken dinner, as it was his job to kill the birds for the family. He estimated with exaggeration that he had wrung the necks of 22,413 chickens, writing, "At night, I do not have nightmares: I have 'night-hens.'"[8] Bill Ryan, one of his father's friends, told the senior Sheen, "Newt, that oldest boy of yours, Fulton, will never be worth a damn. He always has his nose in a book."[9]

Fulton not only disliked farming, but he felt demeaned by having to wear the farmer's overalls. Vanity and pride were stumbling blocks he would have to fight until late in his life; they often got the best of him. But, as far as he was concerned, overalls, "from the point of view of fashion, [are] about as low as you could get."[10] Fortunately, for the sensitive and vain young man with a religious bent and an inquisitive mind, he was soon to leave farming and the overalls behind and go full tilt into the books he loved. He had decided quite young that he wanted a vocation to become a priest. In fact, he would pray a daily Rosary for the gift of a vocation.

At his First Communion, he had been given a lovely Communion book that contained a litany to the Virgin Mary, and from that time

---

[6]Joseph F. Sheen, "My Brother's Vocation", *Missionary Youth*, 1954. See also Thomas C. Reeves, *America's Bishop: The Life and Times of Fulton J. Sheen* (San Francisco: Encounter Books, 2001), 26.

[7]Sheen, *Treasure*, 20.

[8]Ibid., 172.

[9]Ibid., 18.

[10]Ibid.

on and throughout his life, he prayed the Marian litany every night. At his Confirmation when he was twelve, he dedicated himself to the Virgin Mary and resolved to become a priest. It was a resolution he would not share with anyone for years. In 1913, he graduated from high school as the valedictorian of his class of seven and went on to enroll in Saint Viator College in Bourbonnaise, Illinois. In college, he excelled in the classroom and on the debate team. His good friend and classmate Charles Hart wrote, "On the debating platform of St. Viator's there has not been known his superior if ever his equal, in any point that contributes to effective debating." The collegiate newspaper maintained, "No one has shed greater 'sheen' upon the Class of 1917 than this golden-tongued fiery young Demosthenes, who has shown his quick wit, versatility and power of mind so often on the debating platform. In stature he is rather abbreviated, slight of build, quick, business from the word go, with shining eyes that catch you and flood you with his striking personality."[11] Collegiate effusiveness aside, this adulatory description of Fulton J. Sheen and his rhetorical skills would be repeated in one form or another throughout all the years of his life.

His college years were happy ones. Fulton was a popular student noted for his sunny personality, hard work, quick wit, and silly pranks. As in high school, he participated in plays; he felt comfortable on the stage. For his last three years, he had a regular column in the college newspaper and wrote twelve essays, including one supporting natural law and one on the Intelligent Designer. Upon his graduation, he was awarded a full-tuition, three-year scholarship for graduate school to get a Ph.D. in philosophy. He sought the advice of his debate coach, Fr. William J. Bergan. Fr. Bergan advised him to give up the scholarship and go directly to seminary. Fulton Sheen took Fr. Bergan's advice and never looked back. Sheen would be forever grateful to Fr. Bergan for this advice and for Fr. Bergan's advice as his debate coach on public speaking: "Be natural."[12] Sheen was to become one of American Catholicism's most notable and persuasive speakers. Audiences found him so natural that each felt that Sheen was directly addressing him in an intimate way.

---

[11] *The Viatorian* 34 (June 1917): 291–92, quoted in Reeves, *America's Bishop*, 24.

[12] Kathleen L. Riley, *Fulton J. Sheen: An American Catholic Response to the Twentieth Century* (New York: Alba House, 2004), 3.

Seminary, Louvain, and Academic Excellence

Later, in writing about the priestly vocation, Fulton Sheen noted that there are three stages in coming to the priesthood. It all begins with the holiness of God, not with the young man's desire. It is God who calls and, because he is God, it is a call that cannot be ignored. The second stage is the great feeling of unworthiness in the face of such a call and the desire to be purged of all that makes the man unworthy. The final stage is the response to the call. Sheen's biographer Thomas C. Reeves tells us, "Fulton Sheen entered the seminary seeking purgation and praying for the grace to be sent."[13] That he would title his autobiography *Treasure in Clay* indicates his ongoing awareness of his unworthiness—a conviction that he could never completely purge. However, he took comfort from the observation "[God] did not call angels to be priests; he called men. He did not make gold the vessel for His treasure; he made clay."[14] Not as angels, but as ordinary men, in 1917, Fulton and his friend Charles Hart both entered the Saint Paul Seminary in Minnesota. In part, his educational expenses from grammar school up until seminary were subsidized by his father's brother, Daniel R. Sheen.[15]

Archbishop John Ireland, the first bishop of Saint Paul, had established the seminary in 1894 with the belief that a priest should be "a gentleman, a scholar, and a saint".[16] Fulton Sheen, farm boy, would become a gentleman and a scholar and is on his way today to becoming a saint—but first he had to get through seminary. He steeped himself in Neo-Thomistic thought and papal encyclicals and pronouncements. He worked so hard he suffered from ulcers to the point where he had to go to the Mayo Clinic, where part of his intestines was removed. He would suffer from a delicate stomach for the rest of his life. He ate little and at banquets would stir the food on his plate, especially when the entrée was chicken. His one weakness was sweets. He loved cookies and candy, especially if they were chocolate.

[13] Reeves, *America's Bishop*, 26–27.
[14] Sheen, *Treasure*, 39.
[15] Thomas J. McSweeney, "Sheen, Fulton John", in *The Encyclopedia of American Catholic History*, edited by Michael Glazier and Thomas J. Shelley (Collegeville, Minn.: Liturgical Press, 1997), 1285.
[16] Reeves, *America's Bishop*, 28.

While sitting in a seminary seminar, Sheen had what he understood was a mystical experience. He described it as an "illumination of soul, a light that suffused my intellect, bringing with it an overwhelming conviction of the certitude of the Faith.... I was momentarily possessed of the absolute and irrefutable character of Faith."[17] His experience reconfirmed for him his vocation to the priesthood. It may have also been this experience that led to his keeping a daily, continuous hour of adoration of the Lord present in the Blessed Sacrament of the Eucharist. The keeping of a daily Holy Hour was something he would recommend henceforth to young priests, seminarians, laity, and even non-Catholics. The Holy Hour was a time of prayerful meditation that energized him for the other eighteen hours of his work day. It was a practice grounded in love. He wrote, "Very few souls ever meditate; they are either frightened by the word, or else have never been taught its existence. In the human order a person in love is always conscious of the one loved, lives in the presence of the other, resolves to do the will of the other, and regards as his greatest jealousy being outdone in the least advantage of self-giving. Apply this to a soul in love with God, and you have the rudiments of meditation."[18]

Meditation before the Eucharistic Christ was essential to Fulton Sheen. He wrote that meditation allowed the individual access to the will of God and helped cast off self-deceit: "Meditation allows one to suspend the conscious fight against external diversions by an internal realization of the presence of God. It shuts out the world to let in the Spirit.... It turns a searchlight of Divine Truth in the way we think, act, and speak, penetrating beneath the layers of self-deceit ... so that we may see ourselves as we really are, and not as we like to think we are."[19]

Sheen was someone who was consecrated to the Virgin Mary at birth by his mother and reconsecrated by himself to the Virgin at his Confirmation; it was not lost on him that there was a Marian apparition at Fatima the year he entered the seminary. The Virgin's call for prayers for the conversion of Russia, then in the beginning throes of

[17] Sheen, *Treasure*, 229.

[18] Fulton J. Sheen, *The Holy Hour: Readings and Prayers for a Daily Hour of Meditation* (Washington, D.C.: National Council of Catholic Men, 1946), 3.

[19] Fulton J. Sheen, *Lift Up Your Heart* (Garden City, N.Y.: Garden City Press, 1942), 151.

a Communist revolution, would add direction to Sheen's mission in life. Communism would be a topic of his preaching and writing for years to come, but he still had some important hurdles to overcome before he could turn his attention to preaching. Before entering the seminary, he had earned a bachelor's and a master's degree in philosophy from Saint Viator's. He still felt a draw to earning a Ph.D. After his ordination in Peoria's Saint Mary's Cathedral, he and his fellow classmate Charles Hart, now both young priests, enrolled in graduate work at Catholic University of America in Washington, D.C. Fulton Sheen apparently loved almost every minute of his graduate studies. However, he was not just a student, but also a priest. He said the daily 6:00 A.M. Mass as chaplain of Saint Vincent's Orphan Asylum. On weekends, he said Mass at whatever local parish needed a priest. He was so short and young looking, he was told by one monsignor to get back to the sacristy immediately with the other altar boys. He was twenty-four years old.

It was at this time that he won his first convert. He was asked by a parishioner to visit an ailing relative. When he arrived at the relative's door, she spat on him and ordered him to leave. Five months later, the woman phoned Fr. Sheen and requested that he visit her. Since their original encounter, she had been diagnosed with a terminal disease and was concerned for her children. Fr. Sheen told her that God was trying to scare her into the Catholic Church, so he began instructions with her and told her she was not going to die anytime soon. She was received into the Church and, indeed, lived several more years. He wrote of his first conversion, "It illustrates how much Divine Light in the soul, rather than the efforts of the evangelist, produce the harvest."[20] That same Divine Light would shine in the souls of hundreds of other men and women who would come to Fulton Sheen for instruction and reception into the Catholic Church.

At Catholic University's 1920 graduation, Frs. Fulton Sheen and Charles Hart were awarded two degrees each: bachelor of canon law and a bachelor of sacred theology. The doctor of philosophy degree was still in the future. Fr. Hart would stay on at Catholic University, earning his doctorate and teaching philosophy there until his death in 1950. Fr. Fulton J. Sheen had a greater ambition: the University

[20] Sheen, *Treasure*, 266.

of Louvain, Belgium, was beckoning. The young priest was seeking "answers to errors of modern philosophy in light of the philosophy of St. Thomas", and Louvain was the mecca of Neo-Scholastic training.[21] Modern philosophy, wrote Reeves, put forth "various forms of empiricism, positivism, pragmatism, and materialism" that the Neo-Thomists sought to counter with "rational arguments for the existence of God complemented [by] revealed truth".[22] The Neo-Thomists at Louvain also posited the existence of objective right and wrong, natural law, human free will, and the importance of personal moral responsibility, all topics that would later be found in Fulton Sheen's preaching, speaking, and writing, and all topics whose importance in the eyes of society would recede with each passing decade.

Fulton Sheen had always been a serious and good student, but at Louvain he would really excel. He firmly believed that faith depended upon reason: "People who get religion without using their brains usually end up believing some crackpot is God, because he says so. The Church won't take you without your thinking things through to the full extent of your ability."[23] It was the individual ability of the one seeking entrance that would determine the depth and detail of instruction he would need before Sheen would receive him into the Church.

The Bishop of Peoria, who had been underwriting Sheen's educational bills since he joined the seminary, approved of Sheen's desire to attend Louvain but would not cover the costs, so it fell to Newt and Delia to at least partially fund their son's doctoral studies at Louvain. His bills were also funded by the largesse of the wealthy family of a fellow Louvain student and good friend, who would become Msgr. Hickey.[24] Sheen's brother Tom joined Fulton in Belgium to study medicine at Louvain. The young Sheen men were often short of funds but somehow made it through their European years of study.

Louvain classes were in Latin and French, so Fulton went to Paris in the summer of 1921 to improve his French language skills before

[21] Ibid., 23.
[22] Reeves, *America's Bishop*, 43.
[23] Gretta Palmer, "Why All These Converts? The Story of Monsignor Fulton Sheen", *Look*, June 1947, 38.
[24] *Positio*, 1.637.

going on to Belgium. While he was in Paris, his landlady, Madame Citroen, showed up at his door one evening with a bottle of poison declaring her intent to commit suicide over her unhappy life and poor financial situation. He asked her to allow him nine days to make a novena of prayers for her conversion and to give her instruction. With his school-boy French and her little bit of English, Fr. Sheen brought her into the Church and reconciled her with her husband. Even the maid was so impressed by her mistress' conversion and the apparent strength of Fr. Sheen's prayers that she, too, resumed her practice of Catholicism. Madame Citroen's husband reunited with his wife and began to practice his Catholic faith again; such are the ripple effects of a single conversion. Sheen always maintained that it is God's answering of prayers that makes converts. He would tell his would-be convert to "pray for the Light and that you will be strong enough to reach the Light".[25]

One cold January morning on the Feast of the Epiphany when a very young Fr. Fulton Sheen was on holiday from Louvain and opening Saint Patrick's Church in London, an inebriated, disheveled young woman all but fell in the door when he opened it. She had been on the steps of the church all night, so Sheen brought her inside and made her a cup of tea to help her sober up and get warm. It turned out that she was having relationship problems with three different men. Fr. Sheen noticed that the woman looked like the woman on a billboard across the street, and she admitted that she was the star of the musical comedy then playing. She also told the young priest that she had been a Catholic but no longer practiced. Sheen asked her to go home to get some rest and to return to him in the afternoon. She agreed to return on the condition that he not ask her to go to confession. She returned as promised, and he invited her into the church with the purported object of showing her some famous paintings. As they walked down the aisle, he pushed her into an empty confessional, where she fell to her knees. He went into the confessor's side and heard her confession. Sheen would later write, "I pushed her in. I did not ask her to go, for I had promised not to ask her. Two years later I gave her the veil in a convent in London, where she is to this day."[26] His methods might be occasionally

[25] Palmer, "Converts", 40.
[26] Sheen, *Treasure*, 265.

unconventional, but Fulton Sheen never passed up an opportunity to bring a soul to God.

Back in Louvain, Fr. Sheen not only worked hard at his studies, he also increased the level of his daily devotions, while at the same time nursing a prayerful ambition to someday become a bishop. He began each day at 5:00 A.M. and continued working until midnight. He recalled studying Einstein's theory of relativity for over one hundred hours.[27] Not all was study in these years, though. Fulton and Tom Sheen traveled about Europe, enjoying the sights and developing a taste for opera, beginning with Puccini's La Bohème. Fr. Sheen would later record that he saw twenty-one operas in an eight-month period.[28] While on his travels, he was in Rome when Pope Benedict XV was succeeded by Pope Pius XI and was able to have a private audience with the new pope—evidence that somebody, somewhere, pulled a few strings for the twenty-seven-year-old American priest.

Success was crowned with success when on July 23, 1923, Fr. Fulton Sheen's doctoral degree was granted by the University of Louvain with great distinction. So outstanding was his dissertation, "God and Intelligence in Modern Philosophy: A Critical Study in the Light of the Philosophy of St. Thomas Aquinas", that the newly minted Ph.D. was invited to continue for a postgraduate degree known as the agrégé. The earning of the extremely rare agrégé degree would automatically make the recipient eligible to be a member of the Louvain faculty. Only ten students in the previous forty years had been invited for the agrégé.[29] To sit for the agrégé, a scholar must be invited, pass an examination before professors from other universities, and write a distinguished book. Thomas Reeves wrote, "If he could win the degree, [Sheen] would be the first American to do so."[30]

Fr. Fulton J. Sheen liked nothing better than a challenge to his intellectual abilities. Rather than stay in Belgium, he went to Rome to work on his book and prepare for the grueling agrégé examination. In Rome, he also took voice lessons that taught him to speak from the diaphragm and with lungs full of air. He returned to Louvain for his examination in the spring of 1925. The oral examination lasted approximately six hours, after which the panel of examiners would

[27] Reeves, America's Bishop, 46.
[28] Ibid., 48.
[29] D. P. Noonan, The Passion of Fulton Sheen (New York: Dodd, Mead & Company, 1972), 12.
[30] Reeves, America's Bishop, 50.

meet to determine the appropriate grade: satisfaction, distinction, great distinction, very highest distinction. At the traditional celebratory dinner that evening, the type of drink offered (beer, wine, or champagne) depended on the level of the candidate's grade. For Fulton J. Sheen, the champagne flowed, and he remarked, "The champagne never tasted so good that night!"[31]

On July 16, 1925, Fr. Fulton J. Sheen was awarded the *agrégé en philosophie*. His dissertation was almost immediately published as *God and Intelligence in Modern Philosophy* by Longmans, Green & Company. Its introduction was written by G. K. Chesterton, the famous English author and critic who had converted to Catholicism in 1922. Fulton Sheen had met Chesterton on a summer assignment teaching dogmatic theology at St. Edmund's College in Ware, England. The British convert to Catholicism, who was an expert apologist for the Church, had weekly radio broadcasts on the BBC.[32] The young man from Peoria was impressed by Chesterton and would count him as one of the major intellectual influences in his life. The great Chesterton was obviously impressed by the newly minted Ph.D. and *agrégé* from the United States and did Sheen a great favor in lending his name to Sheen's first book. The following year, the University of Louvain awarded the Cardinal Mercier International Philosophy Award to Sheen. He was the first American to ever win the prize, made even more precious because the prize is awarded only once a decade. It was a high distinction for the young priest from Peoria, Illinois. The relatively new Catholic magazine *Commonweal* called *God and Intelligence* "one of the most important contributions to philosophy which has appeared in the present century".[33] The Jesuit magazine *America* called the book "brilliant".[34]

Over the course of his life, Fulton Sheen would make about thirty pilgrimages to Lourdes. On the fifth anniversary of his ordination, he decided to go to Lourdes to pray a novena (nine days of prayers) of thanks to the Virgin for his vocation. Despite being nearly penniless, he checked in to one of the best hotels in town and began his novena.

---

[31] Sheen, *Treasure*, 27–28.

[32] McSweeney, "Sheen", 1288.

[33] Edward Sutherland Ernest, "A Champion of Reason", *Commonweal*, January 13, 1926, 264–65.

[34] William I. Lonergan, review of *God and Intelligence in Modern Philosophy*, by Fulton J. Sheen, *America*, June 19, 1926, 238.

If he was going to rely on the Virgin Mary for a hotel room, it might as well be a good one. As the end of his stay approached, he was not sure how he was going to pay his hotel bill or how he was going to afford a train ticket back to Paris. He was depending on Our Lady of Lourdes. At about 10:00 P.M. on the last night, an American, Thomas Farrell, introduced himself to Sheen. Farrell asked if he spoke French and, if so, would the young priest be willing to accompany him and his family to Paris to help them communicate? The young priest jumped at the opportunity to help his fellow Americans and to avoid washing dishes to work off his bill; Farrell paid for his hotel stay and return trip to Paris. The Farrells became Sheen's lifelong friends.

Upon finishing his studies in Europe and not quite sure what was coming next, Sheen determined to visit Mary's shrine at Lourdes one last time, fearing that once he returned to the United States, he would never have the opportunity to visit it again. He prayed to the Virgin to give him a specific sign: he asked that after he offered a Mass and before he reached the exit gate, he would be met by "a little girl aged about of twelve, dressed in white, who would give me a white rose." He wrote, "At about twenty feet from the gate I could see no one. I remember saying 'You better hurry, there is not much time left.' As I arrived at the gate a little girl aged twelve, dressed in white, gave me the white rose."[35] His consecration by his mother to the Virgin when he was an infant, his rededication to Mary at his Confirmation and again at his ordination, and the sign of the little girl with the white rose were all reasons for his firm belief that the Virgin of Lourdes would watch over her servant in his priestly career and would bring him back to her grotto at Lourdes. It seems remarkably cheeky and uniquely American for the young Sheen to challenge the Mother of God, "You better hurry up!" But Fulton Sheen had completely dedicated himself to her service and was confident of her loving support.

A Test of Obedience for Young Dr. Sheen

Offers of teaching positions poured in; the now-celebrated scholar was in great demand. He was seriously considering offers from Oxford and Columbia when Bishop Edmund M. Dunne, his superior from

[35] Sheen, *Treasure*, 318.

Peoria, called him home to become the associate pastor at Saint Patrick's parish in Peoria. It must have been a shock to Sheen and those who knew him that he would be assigned to a poor inner-city parish where few of the parishioners even spoke English. At Saint Patrick's, Sheen had the good fortune to be the curate for Msgr. Patrick O'Connor Culleton, an older priest who appreciated his new associate's energy and drive. Participation at Mass at Saint Patrick's had been flagging, but with the invigoration of Fulton Sheen's talents, the pews began to fill once again. His lively preaching during Lent and Advent brought many people back to the Church and won several converts. The new priest in the parish visited every single home to meet and pray with his flock personally; he even visited those in the neighborhood who were not on the rolls of Saint Patrick's or even Catholic. But he had to take the bad with the good, for he found himself occasionally the object of hatred, and at least one monkey wrench was directed at his head. After he approached a rather tumbledown house, he was let in by an elderly woman who told the young priest that she had been raised in the Catholic Church. While they were talking, the woman's son came in, dressed as an automobile mechanic, and he let fly the monkey wrench he was holding. Sheen ducked and, with great presence of mind, asked the son how much it would cost to put a new carburetor in a Hudson automobile. After chatting for several minutes about cars, carburetors, and prices, the young man became more relaxed and amiable. He and his mother returned to the parish with regular attendance, thanks to Fr. Sheen's quick reflexes and quicker wit.

On another occasion, Saint Patrick's parish received a donation of $10,000 from a woman in the parish who could not possibly have had $10,000 to her name, so the pastor asked Fr. Sheen to go around and visit her. The woman invited him inside and he met her brother, a man who had spent thirty years in prison for robbery and murder. The money was clearly ill-gotten, so the woman, not knowing what to do with it, had given it to the Church. Sheen asked the brother if he wanted to confess his sins, and he responded that he had not been to confession in seventy years and that to confess now would be a form of weakness. "Why should I now, at the end of my life, be a coward and ask God to forgive me?" But the next day Sheen heard the man's confession and brought him the Blessed Sacrament; the following day, one day after his welcome back into the Catholic Church, the man died. Sheen would write of him, "He was not the first thief the Lord saved on his last day."[36] According to Sheen, "No life is too far spent to be recouped; no lifelong idleness precludes a few minutes of useful work in the vineyard of the Lord, even the last few hours of life, as was the case with the penitent thief."[37] This particular repentant thief and murderer would not be the last he would meet in his career of bringing souls to God. Saint Patrick's parish would forever hold a special place in Fulton Sheen's heart. He would always visit there when he returned to Peoria. It was at Saint Patrick's, not in Saint Mary's Cathedral, in 1951 that the newly ordained Bishop Sheen would say his first pontifical Mass.

His sojourn in Peoria lasted only eight months before Bishop Dunne sent the brilliant priest to teach at Catholic University. Sheen was appointed to the Chair of Apologetics in the School of Sacred Sciences. His brief time as a parish priest was a test of obedience to see if the much fêted and credentialed Sheen would submit to his bishop and accept the lowly position of a curate. But like almost everything else Fulton Sheen did, he excelled, even in Peoria among the people of Saint Patrick's. Bishop Dunne told him, "Run along now [to Catholic University]; you have my blessing."[38]

Sheen's humble beginnings working on the farms, being mistaken for the altar boy as a young priest, and serving the poor people of Saint Patrick's were important for the formation of his character. He was always vitally interested in every person he met—he never treated anyone like a stranger. He believed every person was a soul loved by God and that God had somehow chosen him to bring those thirsting souls home to the Catholic Church. The high and the low were all God's children. Whether they were dressed in silks or rags, Fulton J. Sheen loved them all; their conversion became his mission in life. He would say that everyone loves a rose, "but it takes a great heart to love a leaf".[39] Sheen, indeed, had a great heart.

[36] Ibid., 277.
[37] Fulton J. Sheen, *Simple Truths: Thinking Life Through with Fulton J. Sheen* (Liguori, Mo.: Liguori/Triumph, 1998), 62.
[38] Sheen, *Treasure*, 42.
[39] Sheen, *Simple Truths*, 73.

2

Professor, Radio Personality, Convert Maker

Classroom Walls

Fr. Fulton Sheen joined the faculty of the Catholic University of America in 1926, a position he held for twenty-five years. He was a popular professor who taught only graduate students, usually in two classes a year and an occasional seminar. The rules for good teaching he set for himself at the suggestion of one of his favorite Louvain professors were (1) "Always keep current: know what the modern world is thinking; read its poetry, its literature; observe its architecture and its art; hear its music and its theater; and then plunge deeply into St. Thomas and the wisdom of the ancients, and you will be able to refute its errors"; and (2) "Tear up one's lecture notes annually."[1] Another rule he made for himself was always to stand and never to sit when giving a lecture, homily, or presentation, for "fires cannot be started seated."[2] He might not have known where his career was going to take him, but young Fr. Sheen knew he wanted to "start fires", so he wrote prodigiously and threw himself into the world of academics. He was a founding member of the American Catholic Philosophical Association, becoming its secretary and, later, its president. Yet there was always the pull of life outside of the university that stirred his greater efforts. The classroom was too small to contain him.

---

[1] Thomas C. Reeves, *America's Bishop: The Life and Times of Fulton J. Sheen* (San Francisco: Encounter Books, 2001), 76.
[2] Ibid.

Religion and the Earliest Days of Radio

In 1927, he was invited to give the homily at the solemn pontifical Mass on the Feast of Saint Thomas Aquinas at the National Shrine of the Immaculate Conception in Washington, D.C. One member of the congregation, reporting on the homily for the university newspaper, wrote, "Doctor Sheen's panegyric combined a beautiful literary style with remarkable precision and clarity of thought and his remarks made a great impression on all of his hearers."[3] Fr. Sheen quickly become a popular public speaker, on campus and off. In 1926 and for the next five years, he served as the Lenten homilist at the Paulists' Saint Paul the Apostle Church in New York City. Thanks to the Paulist Fathers, he made his radio debut when his Lenten homilies were first broadcast in 1928 on New York's WLWL, a locally popular radio station. The church was full to capacity, both upstairs and downstairs, so chairs were put out for the overflow crowd. The enthusiastic crowds inspired the Paulists to broadcast Sheen's sermons to reach an even larger audience. The radio audience grew throughout the Lenten season and into subsequent Lents. Archbishop Patrick Hayes of New York then invited the young professor to give the annual Advent sermons on Sunday mornings at Saint Patrick's Cathedral. Sheen's name was heard everywhere Catholics gathered. The vain and prescient young priest even hired a newspaper clipping service to keep track of his fast-spreading fame.

It was radio that gave Fulton Sheen his initial boost into the national consciousness, although he was not the first radio preacher to reach into the homes of Americans. In 1921 a vesper service was broadcast from Calvary Episcopal Church in Pittsburgh, conducted by Rev. Edwin J. Van Etten. The first Catholic priest to make use of the airwaves was Fr. Charles Coughlin, who began his radio ministry on October 3, 1926. By 1930, Coughlin's show moved to the Columbia Broadcasting System (CBS). Coughlin's *Golden Hour with the Little Flower* was immensely popular but became controversial as the radio priest grew more extremist in his political and social views to the diminution of his religious content. As he grew more and more alarming to both his broadcasters and to the Catholic Church, CBS

---

[3] *The Tower*, March 9, 1927, quoted in Reeves, *America's Bishop*, 62.

was no longer willing to provide the fiery Coughlin airtime, so, after only a year, the priest had to develop his own alternative. He earned millions of dollars through donations to his independent television network. Coughlin felt so powerful that he started his own political party in 1934, the National Union for Social Justice. His audience peaked in 1932, but, with his ranting anti-Semitism and other offensive, incendiary rhetoric and thoroughly materialistic point of view, he became such an embarrassment to the Catholic hierarchy that his bishop pulled him off the air and silenced him. Fr. Coughlin ended his days in an obscure parish doing pastoral work and seeing to the mundane needs of his parishioners.

At the same time as Fr. Coughlin was becoming popular on the radio, fundamentalist Protestant preachers were also discovering the medium to great effect. Radios were becoming less expensive and more common in American homes. From 1930 to 1935 the number of U.S. households with radios doubled to eighteen million. The radio was the source of American leisure entertainment, ripe for the flourishing of religious content. Paul Rader of the Chicago Gospel Tabernacle was an early radio preacher. Even Aimee Semple McPherson, a Canadian evangelist, took to the radio airwaves. Later, Charles E. Fuller quickly became America's best-known fundamentalist preacher with his *Old Fashioned Revival Hour*, which was produced weekly from Los Angeles, reaching almost twenty million listeners from coast to coast.

Both Fr. Coughlin and the fundamentalist preachers who dominated the airwaves were considered too hot and too out of the mainstream by CBS and the National Broadcasting Company (NBC), the two main national broadcasting platforms. Together, NBC and CBS decided to offer limited free airtime to mainline Protestant, Catholic, and Jewish programs that promised to be constructive, nonsectarian, and free of acerbity. Each faith group was to choose its most outstanding speakers who could "interpret religion at its highest and best".[4] It was the prefect entrée for Fr. Fulton J. Sheen, a media man if there ever was one.

---

[4] Kathleen L. Riley, *Fulton J. Sheen: An American Catholic Response to the Twentieth Century* (New York: Alba House, 2004), 62. See also Spencer Miller, Jr., "Radio and Religion", *Annals of the American Academy of Political and Social Science*, no. 177 (January 1935): 137 (for the broadcasters' principles).

Fulton Sheen and *The Catholic Hour*

Sheen came to national radio through *The Catholic Hour*, sponsored by the National Council of Catholic Men (a subsidiary of the National Catholic Welfare Conference [NCWC]). The series opened on NBC on March 2, 1930, over WEAF in New York City. The expressed purpose of *The Catholic Hour* was "to promote a better understanding of the Catholic Church and its doctrines and to contribute to the growth of friendly relations among the several religious groups in the United States".[5] The weekly program ran on Sunday evenings from 6:00 to 7:00, Eastern Standard Time. The first program was introduced by Patrick Cardinal Hayes, the archbishop of New York, and featured a talk by Bishop Joseph Schrembs of Cleveland. Cardinal Hayes said that night, "We feel certain that [*The Catholic Hour*] will have both the good will and good wishes of the majority of our great countrymen. Surely, there is no true lover of our country who does not eagerly hope for a less worldly, a less material, and a more spiritual standard among our people."[6] The cardinal was undoubtedly addressing the consternation aroused by the excesses of Fr. Coughlin and the unrelenting criticism of the Catholic Church by many of the fundamentalist radio preachers. The hope for *The Catholic Hour* was to present the Catholic Church in a positive, American light and to diminish the anti-Catholic bias that was evident across the land. The programs, aimed mainly but not exclusively at a Catholic audience, were to be uplifting, informative, and entertaining. Each program would be leavened with music by the Paulist Choristers and various orchestras.

It was not until the second program, on March 9, 1930, that Fr. Sheen made his national debut and immediately became the star of the show. His presence was so dominant on *The Catholic Hour* that Sheen became synonymous with the show. Most people thought it was Sheen's show, and in many ways it was. For the next twenty-two years, Fulton J. Sheen would be the primary and most frequent speaker on the weekly *Catholic Hour*. His addresses would be widely quoted and, at the inspiration of the Paulist Fathers, printed for

[5] Reeves, *America's Bishop*, 79.

[6] Quoted in "N.C.C.M. Inaugurates Weekly 'Catholic Hour'", *NCWC Review* 12, no. 3 (March 1930): 15. Later printed as a pamphlet distributed by *Our Sunday Visitor*, October 1936.

distribution. In 1934 over one million pamphlets on his series of talks on the "Eternal Galilean" were given away.

Sheen was already well known to the National Catholic Welfare Conference from his Lenten homilies at the Paulist church, but also from his regular articles in the NCWC newspaper, beginning in early 1930. His series of articles on the "New Paganism" gained Sheen considerable praise both locally and in Rome. He was a known and safe quantity with style and substance, and nothing at all like the unfortunate Fr. Coughlin. Sheen was required to write out his twenty-minute talks for *The Catholic Hour* and to have them approved in advance. He chose as his first address topic the existence of God and the divinity of Christ, calling it "Man's Quest for God". In his autobiography, Sheen noted that *The Catholic Hour* program ran opposite the very popular *Amos 'n' Andy*. The worst criticisms he had, he wrote, came from Milwaukee and Oklahoma City with the suggestion that they take Sheen off the air and replace him with two men who could imitate Amos and Andy talking about religion.[7] This could not have been a very serious suggestion and is perhaps an apocryphal story, as Sheen enjoyed a good story with himself as the butt of the joke.

Sheen's presence made *The Catholic Hour* an immediate hit. His first series on the show ran from March 9 to April 30, 1930, to extremely positive reviews. There were over a thousand letters of appreciation, many of which came from non-Catholics. At the end of the first year of the show, the American hierarchy assessed the apologetic goals of the program, finding them "to use all resources to cause the Church, its doctrines and its teachings to be better known to America in order that she may be better understood in places where there is misunderstanding and prejudice".[8] They were resources well spent. The radio program *The Catholic Hour* and its most eloquent presenter, Fr. Sheen, continued to receive accolades both nationally and internationally. In August 1934, *Catholic Action* announced, "The Holy Father, recognizing Dr. Sheen's notable service as a pulpit and radio

[7] Riley, *Fulton J. Sheen*, 64. *Amos 'n' Andy* was a popular radio situation comedy starring two Black characters who were played by white men, Freeman Gosden as Amos and Charles Correll as Andy.

[8] Charles A. McMahon, "The First Year of the Catholic Hour", *NCWC Review*, no. 13 (March 1931): 9.

orator, has elevated him to the dignity of Papal Chamberlain with the title of Very Reverend Monsignor.... Dr. Sheen was received in special audience by Pope Pius XI, who gave him a special blessing on the Catholic Hour radio broadcast and to its listeners, together with a particular blessing for his own apostolic work in this field."[9]

By 1938, *The Catholic Hour* and its star speaker, now Msgr. Fulton J. Sheen, was heard over fifty-seven stations across the country, eliciting more than eight thousand letters for Sheen in the month of February alone. Sheen did not shy away from political and social issues of the day, but always addressed them in a way that was grounded in Catholic thought. Nor did he shy away from attacking Communism as a serious threat to the United States and American democracy. In fact, anti-Communism was one of his favorite topics. When Pope Pius XI blessed Fulton Sheen, he enjoined him to speak out against Communism at every opportunity. It was an admonition that Sheen took to heart.

Sheen's Anti-Communism and the Unready Convert, Louis Budenz[10]

The year he entered the seminary, 1917, was the year of the beginning of the Russian Revolution and the appearance of the Virgin Mary in Fatima, Portugal, asking the world to pray for the conversion of Russia from atheistic Communism. Sheen, with his dedication to the Blessed Virgin Mary, took cognizance of those facts and became an ardent spokesman for democracy against Communism. With his characteristic academic approach to understanding any topic, he read every piece of Communist literature he could get his hands on. He read Marx, Engels, Lenin, and Stalin. He read the Soviet Constitution and all the current propaganda available. Sheen was perhaps the best versed opponent of Communism in the United States. His 1936 talk and pamphlet *Against Communism* naturally drew the attention of the Communist Party in the United States and did not go unchallenged.

[9] "Catholic Hour Speaker Honored and Broadcast Blessed by Holy Father", *Catholic Action* 16, no. 8 (August 1934): 13.

[10] The facts of Budenz's life come largely from his autobiography, Louis Francis Budenz, *This Is My Story* (New York: McGraw-Hill, 1947), which has since gone out of print.

The editor to the *Daily Worker*, Louis Francis Budenz, wrote a response to Sheen's December 14, 1936, attack on Communism, posing provocative questions for him and challenging him personally. Budenz, in many ways, was not unlike his interlocutor. Intelligent and intellectually curious, Budenz was a Midwesterner from a deeply Catholic family from Indiana. His mother was an orphan whose people came from Ireland; his father was of German and Irish descent. So dedicated was Budenz's father to the Blessed Virgin Mary that for over fifty years he put flowers on her altar every December 8, the Feast of the Immaculate Conception, in gratitude for the bank position that allowed him to better support his wife and five children. His mother, Mary, would remind her children when they quarreled, "Remember, you began the day with the sign of the cross."[11]

Louis attended Catholic schools and colleges before earning his law degree from the Indianapolis Law School in 1912. Unlike the Sheen household, the bookish Budenz family was well educated and immersed in culture and ideas. Their study overflowed with books; the family took in theater and discussed politics. They were Jeffersonians, following the beliefs of Duns Scotus and Thomas Aquinas, who propounded democratic ideals long before John Locke; they followed the thought of the Jesuits Robert Bellarmine and Francisco Suárez in defending the Catholic Church from those who would accuse it of supporting the divine right of kings and authoritarian rule. Pope Leo XIII, in his 1892 encyclical *Rerum novarum*, forcefully set forth the dignity of man as a laborer, firmly aligning the young Louis Budenz with the plight of the common man. The encyclical argued persuasively for a just wage and decent living conditions for all workers and for the right of the laborer to form collective institutions for his own benefit and the mutual benefit of his fellow workers.

Even though *Rerum novarum* was issued when Louis Budenz was a baby, it was in many ways his personal manifesto, even as he drifted further left throughout his career as a writer and labor organizer. The encyclical expressed the sorry plight of working people at the mercy of rapacious companies and at the same time gave a blueprint for the remediation of that plight. Louis Budenz's first involvement in

---

[11] Budenz, *My Story*, 5.

the labor movement came in 1913 as the associate editor of the official paper of the Brotherhood of Carpenters and Joiners. The following year he became the assistant director of the Central Catholic Verein (union) in Saint Louis. He was convinced that his actions on behalf of laborers and labor unions were directed by his calling as a Catholic. In 1919, Fr. John A. Ryan, a progressive reformer and faculty member of Catholic University, wrote the document "Bishops' Program of Social Reconstruction", which laid out the principles of justice and charity that called for legislation establishing a minimum wage, a limit to child labor, unemployment benefits, health and old-age insurance, and public housing. Budenz seemed poised to follow in his footsteps and those of Catholic converts like Orestes Brownson, who founded the first Workingman's Party. Catholics were beginning to look outward to society and see a larger role for themselves, not just inwardly to their parishes' sacraments and devotions, for Christ called on Catholics to be a leaven to society.

While still in high school, Budenz had attended the conference sessions of the United Mine Workers of America. Throughout his twenties and thirties, he became associated with various unions, their strikes, and their newspapers. He was an organizer of strikes for hosiery workers, silk workers, and auto workers. He was arrested for his activities twenty-one times and acquitted each time. Eventually, he began to believe that the Catholic Church was not doing enough for the working man and woman; he wanted more action. He became a socialist, supporting Senator Robert M. La Follette of Wisconsin of the Progressive Party for president in 1924. Then he moved even further left.

Budenz broke with the Catholic Church for a common reason: he married a divorced woman. The couple had one daughter. As a well-informed Catholic, he knew his 1916 marriage was invalid according to canon law; the Church did not recognize divorce. The couple was therefore living in an adulterous union. But, as is typical of many who leave the Catholic Church for any reason, Budenz began to find fault with the Church and rationalizations for why the Church he had once loved no longer deserved his allegiance: for example, the apparent slowness of the Church's push for social and political reform, such as housing for the poor and support of labor unions, and especially World War I, which he vehemently opposed. Someone who leaves the Church always finds reasons why the break is necessary and honorable. It is always the Church's fault, never his own. Few people leave the Church for doctrinal or liturgical reasons; sin is the most common cause of falling away from the Catholic Church. Fulton Sheen wrote of the phenomenon of leaving the Church or refusing to convert to it: "Oftentimes what appears to be a doctrinal objection against the faith turns out to be a moral objection. Most people basically do not have trouble with the Creed, but with the commandments; not so much with what the Church teaches as with how the Church asks us to behave."[12] Yet, even Budenz would later agree, "I knew in my heart that [my leaving the Catholic Church] was solely to defy the Catholic moral law."[13]

Louis Budenz, because of his labor activities, came into the orbit of the Communist Party, which recognized his talents for organizing and writing. It took time for him to accommodate himself to the Party. He felt that the Communists had the correct ideas about economics, but that they had gone about instituting their ideas incorrectly. What they needed and what he felt he could add to their laudable efforts for the betterment of the working men and women was an "American", democratic approach. This was a fallacious position Budenz would persist in holding for years: that it was possible to meld Communism with American values and approaches. He was blind to the fact that the Communist Party in America was being directed from Moscow. For years, he thought there could be true compatibility between Communism and the United States, a sort of Communism with an American face and sensibility. Later, he would refer to his entire period of affiliation, informally and later formally, with the Communist Party as "self-delusion", remarking, "The wake of victorious Socialism was not a mirage for me then."[14] Much to his chagrin, it was a mirage that took him more than a decade to recognize.

Budenz eventually left his wife and soon thereafter developed a relationship with Margaret Rodgers, with whom he was to have four daughters. It would be more than ten years before the couple would

---

[12] Fulton J. Sheen, *Treasure in Clay: The Autobiography of Fulton J. Sheen* (Garden City, N.Y.: Doubleday Press, 1980), 278–79.

[13] Budenz, *My Story*, 157.

[14] Ibid., 124.

formally marry in the Church. In the meantime, in 1933, Budenz joined the Communist Party and began working for its paper. Although he carried a signed Party membership card, he did not publicly proclaim himself a Communist until October 2, 1935. When the central governing committee of the New York Party thought that making Budenz's Communist Party membership public would be of benefit to the Party, Earl Browder, secretary of the Central Committee, ordered it to be announced in the *Daily Worker*. The announcement did not create much surprise, but it did take away from Budenz any possibility of denying his affiliation.

In addition to his column for the *Daily Worker*, his Party assignment was to recruit new members from across the various labor movements in the country. He considered himself a good recruiter. He would be dispatched from New York to Saint Louis or Chicago to help the Party in those cities and to report back to New York on the purity of their commitments and the effectiveness of their activities. Once back in New York, he became a member of the Central Committee, still headed by Earl Browder. In his memoir, Budenz wrote of the various gentlemen with innocuous English-sounding names like Jones and Richardson, but with strong Eastern European accents, who would show up in New York Party offices only to disappear a few years later. Only later did he come to recognize that these men had been sent from Moscow to help shape the Communist Party USA (CPUSA) according to the dictates of the Kremlin. The Party in the United States would be all in against Hitler, only to have to change its tune after the Hitler-Stalin Non-Aggression Pact of 1939, and then again oppose the Nazis when the U.S.S.R. joined the Allies. It was opposed to President Roosevelt until Moscow decided it was expedient for the Party in the United States to back him against Hitler. As the editor of the *Daily Worker*, Budenz had the challenging job of making the Party line coherent and compelling, whatever it was and however it had changed. As an expert apologist for the Communist Party in America, Louis Budenz was bound to come up against that expert American Catholic apologist and anti-Communist, Fulton J. Sheen.

In his Christmas 1936 editorial, Budenz again explained that the Soviet Union stood for peace in the world and the brotherhood of man, supporting the Communist Republicans in Spain. He wrote:

It is the Soviet Union which has pointed to the sole path that leads to peace—the joining of hands in pacts to halt the war aggressor by the peace-loving democratic peoples of the world.... How strange it is to see, in a world so set up, that the Catholic spokesmen in so many instances belabor Communism!... Monsignor Fulton J. Sheen of the Catholic University at Washington has been perhaps the most persistent of these spokesmen. As late as December 14—almost on the very eve of Christmas—he again speaks out against the Communists who fight for peace [in Spain]."[15]

He added, "Come, come, Monsignor Sheen."

Budenz then posed a number of questions to Sheen's refutations of Communism. In short order, Monsignor Sheen sent Budenz a reply in the form of "Communism Answers a Communist". Sheen had carefully combed the Soviet press reports for damaging stories of Soviet "crimes and crudities" and quoted from official Soviet governmental documents. Budenz proposed to print Sheen's rebuttal in the *Daily Worker*, a proposition that was vehemently rejected by the Central Committee. Budenz took Sheen's piece home to study and was dismayed to find so many damning examples of Soviet perfidy and oppression. Sheen asked, "Why do so many oppressive laws and regulations exist in the Soviet Union?" Why did the Soviets call the Catholic Church, and specifically the priesthood, the enemy of young people? Sheen wrote, "I am rather surprised that a Communist is not more familiar with Communistic literature and should have to ask for texts, but there they are."[16] Sheen's manuscript concluded, "The more I read about Communism, the more I am convinced that its greatest propagandists know practically nothing factual about it. They talk of Russia either in general terms or in the stereotype language of its propaganda. That is why I believe many Communists are in good faith, and here I include you, Mr. Budenz."[17]

Sheen's response to the Budenz Christmas attack on him was never published in the *Daily Worker*, but it was printed by Sheen in pamphlet form and sold sixty-five thousand copies at a nickel apiece. In his pamphlet, Sheen invited the public to take a stand with him

---

[15] Ibid., 153.

[16] Fulton J. Sheen, *Communism Answers Questions of a Communist* (New York: Paulist Press, 1937), 45.

[17] Budenz, *My Story*, 159.

against Communism: "We know your [communist] tactics from your documents; we know your purpose from your writings; we know your failures through Mexico, Spain and Russia. No! We will not join with you. *We prefer to be loyal to our God and to our Country*."[18]

A few months later, in the spring of 1937, Msgr. Sheen invited Louis Budenz for dinner at the Grill Room of Manhattan's Hotel Commodore. Sheen must have looked into Mr. Budenz's past and found out he was an ex-Catholic and an ex-altar boy. After a fairly brief chat on the various articles of the Soviet Constitution, of which Budenz was ignorant, Monsignor Sheen pushed away the things on the table, as if to clear the playing field. "What [Sheen] did took me totally by surprise", Budenz said. Sheen proclaimed, "Let us now talk of the Blessed Virgin!"[19] The effect in Budenz of the introduction of the Virgin Mary into their conversation was electric. He replied, "Very well." As the monsignor spoke to him of Mary, what Louis Budenz had left behind in the Catholic Church came crashing down on him. Monsignor spoke of the revelations at Lourdes and Fatima and Our Lady's prayer for the conversion of Russia, but Budenz was recalling those bouquets of flowers left by his father on the Virgin's altar every December 8 and his mother's Rosaries. As Monsignor spoke of the richness of the blessings that come through the intervention of Mary, Budenz was fairly stunned: "Immediately, I was conscious of the senselessness and sinfulness of my life as I then lived it. The peace that flows from Mary, and which had been mine in the early days, flashed back to me with an overwhelming vividness."[20] That the monsignor would talk of Mary was shocking in itself, but then Sheen told his Communist adversary, "I shall always pray for you because you have never fully lost the faith."[21]

The two exchanged a few notes after their dinner. Budenz was shaken to remember the beauty of the Virgin, but nonetheless threw himself into even greater efforts to further the Communist cause in America. From Europe, Sheen wrote to Budenz, "I shall remember

---

[18] Sheen, *Communism Answers Questions*, 47.

[19] Budenz, *My Story*, 162. On a 1947 *Catholic Hour* presentation, Fulton Sheen recalled saying, in a dinner conversation with Louis Budenz, that he wanted to talk to Budenz about his soul and the Blessed Virgin. See Fulton Sheen, "Communism and the Conscience of the West", YouTube video, https://www.youtube.com/watch?v=9awHSzqTWoU.

[20] Budenz, *My Story*, 163.

[21] Ibid., 163–64.

you, particularly, at the Shrine of Our Lady of Lourdes, that you may once again recover not only the faith which was once yours, but also the peace which surpasses all understanding, and which only Christ can give."[22] The two men were not to meet again for another eight years. "The 'why' of this [lapse of time] must be laid to the perversity of the human soul when once it had been led into a camp of error through the delusion of being led by reason", wrote Budenz.[23]

Whatever Budenz had thought of Msgr. Sheen at the time of their exchanges, Sheen was developing his own skills and rhetoric to bring in those lost sheep who had strayed from the Church and those who had not yet found a home there. Sheen's popularity on *The Catholic Hour* gave him a following and a prestige that made seekers flock to his convert classes. It was like Sheen to make an abrupt statement, as he did to Louis Budenz: "Let us now talk of the Blessed Virgin", or "Let us talk about your soul", as he said later to Heywood Broun. This approach would unsettle Sheen's would-be convert, moving him away from some rational or extraneous line of argument to focus on the individual in a very personal and intimate way. It would be obvious to the individual that Monsignor really cared about him and wanted nothing but the very best, the salvation of his soul. It was a technique that most often worked to make the person open to the movement of the Holy Spirit within his soul, making him receptive to the truths of the Catholic Church, and giving him a strong desire to receive the sacraments of the Church as the means of salvific grace, where one comes to know and love the Lord. Sheen would say that his role in the process was to open the door; the Holy Spirit did the work. Sheen's statement "We are not yet what we can become"[24] applied to the case of Louis Budenz in 1937; the Holy Spirit had more work to do with Budenz.

A More Willing Convert: Heywood Broun

Heywood Broun, in contrast to Louis Budenz, was more than willing when he encountered Fulton Sheen. The conversion of Broun

---

[22] Ibid., 165.

[23] Ibid., 166.

[24] Fulton J. Sheen, *Simple Truths: Thinking Life Through with Fulton J. Sheen* (Liguori, Mo.: Liguori/Triumph, 1998), 36.

proved what Sheen wrote: "Grace will move you only when you want it to move you, and only when you let it move you."[25]

When Sheen opened wide the door for Heywood Campbell Broun, a renowned sportswriter, columnist, theater critic, novelist, playwright, failed socialist candidate for Congress, newspaper editor, and actor from New York City, Broun was ready. Heywood Broun was known for writing on social issues from the point of view of the political Left and always being on the side of the underdog—the little guy struggling against the larger forces of society. He would champion Sacco and Vanzetti, the executed Italian anarchists, and the African American Scottsboro boys who were unjustly accused of raping two white women.

Aside from his keen intellect, Broun was much the opposite of Sheen. Broun was a large man, overweight, slovenly in his dress, a heavy drinker, and twice married. "Those of us who seldom looked presentable were grateful to Broun", his biographer wrote of him.[26] Broun in his disheveled glory resembled "an unmade bed" or a "one man slum".[27] But like Sheen, he was also a very kind person and generous to a fault. He was a beloved raconteur and a popular member of the Algonquin Roundtable. A little older than Sheen, he was born in Brooklyn on December 7, 1888, and died in New York City on February 18, 1939. His father was a successful printer of Scottish Presbyterian descent; his mother was a well-educated German American. Broun attended private schools in New York City before going on to Harvard in 1909, where he was an indifferent student—so indifferent was he that he flunked French his senior year and never received the much-coveted Harvard degree. He valued his Harvard days for the friends he made, like John Reed and Walter Lippmann, the speakers he heard, and the late-night discussions of life and politics.

Heywood Broun had wanted to be a writer since his high school English teacher talked him into the editorship of the school newspaper. His first job out of Harvard was a young man's dream job. For $20 a month he covered baseball games for the *New York Morning Telegraph*, whose sports editor was the famed Dodge City sheriff, Bat Masterson. He left the *Telegraph* for the *New York Tribune*, where he

[25] Sheen, *Simple Truths*, 9.
[26] Richard O'Connor, *Heywood Broun: A Biography* (New York: G.P. Putnam's Sons, 1975), 35. Many of the facts of Broun's life come from O'Connor's biography.
[27] Sheen, *Treasure*, 260.

talked his way into an unpaid position as a foreign correspondent in China, supporting himself with his poker table winnings in addition to a small expense account. Back in the United States, he became the *Tribune*'s theater critic. Broun was usually a gentle critic who loved the theater and actors. In his 1930 socialist bid for the U.S. Congress, his slogan was "I'd rather be right than Roosevelt!" It was perhaps at the very least an insincere attempt by Broun, as he complained that socialists were atheists while he was a believer. His loss at the ballot box left him completely unfazed. He immediately threw himself into *Shoot the Works*, a musical comedy written by, produced by, and starring the indefatigable man himself. Two years later, Broun was even the star of his own radio program, *The Red Star of Broadway*, sponsored by Macy's. He was a man of many talents and interests with a prodigious output of creativity. Along with his many activities and his regular columns for various New York newspapers, he continued to write short stories, novels, and columns for magazines. He was often at odds with his editors, and Broun was fired from nearly every New York paper. But so popular and interesting was he as a journalist, that over his career his income went from the $20 a month he had made as a sports reporter to $4,000 a month, a rich sum during the Great Depression, when the average workingman's salary was $25 a week.

In search of a domestic life, Broun proposed to a petite Russian ballerina, who accepted his proposal and then turned around and broke off the engagement. Broun almost immediately married Ruth Hale, a feminist writer and cofounder of the Lucy Stone League, which urged women to keep their maiden names after marriage. The marriage lasted for sixteen years and produced one son, Heywood Hale Broun. The year after their Mexican divorce in November of 1933, Ruth Hale died with Heywood at her side. Despite the divorce, he thought of her as his best friend, and she felt the same toward him. It was Ruth who had wanted the divorce, feeling that marriage was stifling and somehow denied her independence and personhood. Soon after her death, Broun married a widowed chorus girl, Maria Incoronata Fruscella Dooley, who went by her stage name, Connie Madison. Importantly for Broun's later conversion, Connie was a Catholic.

As early as January of 1930 there were rumors circulating in Broun's social circle that he was considering converting to Catholicism. His not-so-religiously-sympathetic biographer wrote, "The incense, the votive candles, the priestly ritual at the altar, the bells, the robes, the sonorous Latin would appeal to [Broun's] theatrical sense.... The most generous interpretation of his reported intention [to convert] was that he had, during a bout with delirium tremens, suffered a St. Paul-like delusion and had been frightened into the nearest rectory."[28] His friends were insensitive to Broun's religious impulses; their set was too intellectual and sophisticated, as well as too busy and self-absorbed, to take seriously the possibility of one of their own swimming the Tiber. Broun himself wondered if one could be a political liberal and a Catholic at the same time. He approached two different priests and put this question to them. Perhaps he was even looking for a reason not to convert, but each priest gave the same answer, of course: the answer to Broun's question was yes, and they encouraged him to seek instruction and join the Church. One priest recalled their lengthy conversation: "The one adamant point upon which he felt he could not yield an inch was his devotion to the labor movement."[29] He told the astonished Broun, "Don't you realize you are a little naïve, Heywood? You like to call yourself a radical, but the doctrines of the Church to which I belong imply so many deep changes in human relationship that when they are accomplished—and they will be—your own notions will be nothing more than outmoded pink liberalism."[30] In fact, the priest told him, "As regards radicalism, I have also discovered that no social philosophy is quite as revolutionary as that of the Church."[31] In the same conversation, Broun admitted that "there was no conflict but rather basic harmony between his labor views and the labor views of the Catholic Church."[32]

Broun was obviously concerned that his friends would say of him that by converting to Catholicism, he was selling out labor and the many liberal causes he and they had espoused. As the founder of the Newspaper Guilds of America and as president of several guilds (Toronto, Saint Louis, New York, San Francisco), he feared the

---

[28] O'Connor, *Heywood Broun*, 210.
[29] John L. Lewis et al., *Heywood Broun as He Seemed to Us* (New York: Random House, 1940), 46.
[30] Sheen, *Treasure*, 100.
[31] Reeves, *America's Bishop*, 111.
[32] Lewis et al., *Heywood Broun*, 46.

perception that if he became Catholic, he would be undercutting or denigrating the legitimacy and importance of those guilds. Broun also feared that his friends would say that Connie forced his conversion, that he was scared into it by a fear of death, or that perhaps he had actually been religious all along and had hidden it, pretending to be indifferent so as to protect his liberal credentials and radical causes.[33] It is somewhat surprising that such an intrepid person, who did not hesitate to take on powerful individuals like the governor of Massachusetts and the president of Harvard or to espouse various radical causes, would be so concerned about the opinions of his friends on so personal a matter as his faith. After his conversion, he even refused to discuss the reasons for his actions, saying, "A man's religion is his own business."[34] His friends and fans felt he owed them an explanation, which he refused to give. He felt that nobody should have to discuss the things that are closest to him. The only reason Heywood Broun would ever give for his conversion was that "Catholicism would provide him with spiritual security.... He had always been obsessed with the pursuit of the brotherhood of man, which he now (after his conversion) believed could reach full fruition only under the fatherhood of God."[35] Fulton Sheen would later write, "To believe in the brotherhood of man without the Fatherhood of God would make man a race of bastards."[36]

Heywood Broun called on Fulton Sheen, inviting the monsignor to his Connecticut home, Sabine Farm, for a weekend to discuss his entry into the Church. "Sheen had the reputation of converting or bringing back to the altar rail hard cases, doubting intellectuals, [and] Manhattan sophisticates.... Msgr. Sheen's celebrity as a missionary to the elect naturally attracted Broun, who liked to go first class when it came to important things."[37] Sheen would recall their original meeting quite differently. Sheen described seeing Broun in his rumpled clothing in the dining room at the Plaza Hotel in New York. Sheen's companion asked him if he had ever tried to convert Broun, and, if not, he encouraged him to give it a try, so he telephoned Broun,

[33] O'Connor, *Heywood Broun*, 212.
[34] Ibid., 214.
[35] Ibid., 211.
[36] Fulton J. Sheen, *Life of Christ* (Garden City, N.Y.: Doubleday, 1977), 199.
[37] O'Connor, *Heywood Broun*, 212–13.

telling him he would like to see him. When Broun asked what he wanted to talk about, Sheen said, "Your soul." Broun agreed to meet the following Saturday, explaining, "I am interested in the Church for the following reasons: I am convinced that the only moral authority left in the world is the Holy Father; second, I made a visit to Our Lady of Guadalupe in Mexico and was deeply impressed by the devotion to the Mother of Christ. Finally, I do not want to die in my sins."[38] Probably both accounts are accurate. Sheen first encountered Broun at the hotel to talk about his soul, and then Broun invited Sheen to Sabine Farms for more detailed instruction.

While Heywood Broun had always had the premonition of an early death, he was not ill at the time of his conversion—so dying in his sins was not an immediate concern. During the period of his instruction, Broun would tell Sheen not to go into details, as "I am not going to live long, just long enough to be absolved of my sins."[39] In general, Sheen would spend ten hours a week giving personal instruction in the faith, and he must have gone into some detail with Broun, despite his protestations. Heywood Broun took over ninety hours of instruction because, while he did not want details, he did want to be thoroughly informed of what he was getting into.[40] He was baptized and received into the Catholic Church on May 23, 1939, by Msgr. Fulton Sheen in Saint Patrick's Cathedral in New York. He received the Sacrament of Confirmation from the newly elevated Archbishop Francis J. Spellman on Pentecost Sunday, May 28. Broun recalled the immediate effects of his conversion.

> The first was great peace of soul and a feeling of being home at last; the second, a realization that much of liberalism was extremely illiberal.... I discovered that freedom for them [my liberal friends] meant thinking as they did.... It has dawned upon me that the basis of unity in radicalism is not love, but hate. Many radicals love their cause much less than they hate those who oppose it.... I have also discovered that no social philosophy is quite as revolutionary as that of the Church.[41]

[38] Sheen, *Treasure*, 260.
[39] Ibid.; Lorene Hanley Duquin, *A Century of Catholic Converts* (Huntington, Ind.: Our Sunday Visitor, 2003), 109.
[40] Reeves, *America's Bishop*, 110.
[41] Ibid., 111.

A little more than six months later, over three thousand mourners would gather in Saint Patrick's Cathedral for the funeral of Heywood Broun, on December 18, 1939, and hear him eulogized by Msgr. Sheen. Broun died from pneumonia. As he feared, he indeed died young, at the age of fifty-one, but shriven of his sins as he desired. If the Gospel means anything, it means there are second chances for sinners: as Sheen wrote, "The essence of the Gospel is the blessing of the second chance."[42] He found the spiritual security he was looking for in the Catholic Church, led there by the grace of the Holy Spirit and the open door of Fulton Sheen. Broun's conversion and his public funeral did a great deal to burnish the celebrity of Msgr. Sheen as a convert maker, but much of that role was still in the future for the rather young professor from Catholic University and radio personality of *The Catholic Hour*. In the meantime there was growing conflict nationally and internationally as World War II was looming.

[42] Sheen, *Simple Truths*, 41.

3

Tensions Home and Abroad for American Catholics

Anti-Catholic Bias in America

It is difficult today to imagine the time in mid-twentieth century America when Catholics were looked upon with suspicion by their fellow citizens and their Church was thought to be alien, authoritarian, and subversive to the American polity and way of life. Catholics were thought to be un-American, giving their loyalty to the monarchical pope in Rome, not to the man in the White House. The fact that young Catholic men made up 35 percent of the United States' World War I fighting force while being only 6 percent of the population was not enough to assuage the determined prejudices of many Protestant Americans.[1] The revival of the Ku Klux Klan in the 1920s was directed as much against Catholics as it was against Black Americans. Klansmen had to be white, Protestant, and male. As Jay P. Dolan wrote, "The historian John Higham labeled these years [the 1920s] 'the tribal twenties' because of the rabid nationalist and racial fervor that ignited violent attacks against immigrants and Catholics."[2] The nomination of the Catholic Alfred E. Smith for President in 1928 was fought with a savage bigotry and hatred that wounded the Catholic community in the United States and increased the number of citizens who viewed the Catholic Church as a menace to the country. There were forces at work at the time when Fulton J. Sheen was coming into prominence that made him the right man at the right

[1] John Tracy Ellis, *American Catholicism* (Chicago: University of Chicago Press, 1956), 139.
[2] Jay P. Dolan, *In Search of an American Catholicism* (New York: Oxford Press, 2002), 134.

49

time. His mission was not so much to proselytize over the airwaves and in speeches, books, columns, and pamphlets, although he did that well; the hierarchy saw in him an instrument for the "Americanizing" of the Catholic Church: not to democratize the doctrine of the Church, but to make Catholics and Catholic culture more familiar and friendly, less foreign, and more accessible. On *The Catholic Hour,* Fulton Sheen would be speaking to Catholics and to non-Catholics, to Protestants and Jews, and to those of no faith at all. It was a tall order. Harvard Professor Arthur Schlesinger Sr. wrote, "I regard the prejudice against your [Catholic] Church as the deepest bias in the history of the American People."[3] John Tracy Ellis believed that much of what plagued Catholics and Catholicism in the United States was self-inflicted, but much of it was also in perceptions beyond the control of anyone in the country. The role of Msgr. Fulton J. Sheen is crucial to understanding the mid-century American Catholic Church as it made its way through the perilous times.

The number of Catholics in the United States had increased to eighteen million by 1920, making it the largest Christian denomination in the country. Catholic involvement in urban politics fed the fear of a Catholic takeover of the country. By 1936 the number of Catholics in the United States had climbed to twenty-one million. Catholic dioceses and organizations were not shy about public displays of belief and devotion. The Society of the Holy Name had over one hundred thousand marchers in its 1924 parade though Washington, D.C. There were more than one hundred fifty thousand in attendance for a 1926 parade marching down Chicago's Michigan Avenue to attend a Mass in Soldier Field Stadium. President Calvin Coolidge summed up the fears and bigotry of the Anglo-Saxon Protestant majority when he said, "America must be kept American."[4] At the time, the entire immigrant population was about 13 percent of the overall population.[5]

---

[3] Ellis, *American Catholicism,* 151.

[4] President Calvin Coolidge, First Annual Message to the U.S. Congress, December 6, 1923, https://www.presidency.ucsb.edu/documents/first-annual-message-20.

[5] For comparison, the 2020 foreign-born citizen and noncitizen population in the United States was 14.4% out of 244 million people. "U.S. Immigrant Population and Share over Time, 1850–Present", Migration Policy Institute, accessed April 18, 2024, https://www.migrationpolicy.org/programs/data-hub/charts/immigrant-population-over-time.

Many of those immigrants were Catholics from Ireland, Germany, Italy, Poland, and Mexico, who had brought with them their language, culture, and religion. They first inhabited the coastal cities before moving inland, making immigrant islands of foreign cultures in various urban neighborhoods in large cities. Catholics built churches and schools wherever they lived and settled into a rather parochial life. It would take World War II to move them out of the cities and into the suburbs, along with their Protestant fellow citizens. Catholic parishes tended to be segregated by their nations of origin. The Germans, Poles, Irish, Italians, and Mexicans maintained national parishes where their native tongues were spoken. Masses were in Latin, but the readings and homilies would be in German, Polish, Irish, Italian, or Spanish. Some parishes insisted on teaching the children in their parochial schools in their foreign languages. It is easy to see how the rest of the American citizenry would view Catholics as foreign and insular. Catholic bishops like Chicago's George Mundelein fought against Catholic insularity, mandating English-only in Catholic schools and trying to use the seminaries as the locus for Americanization of the priesthood. Naturally, there was serious pushback from clergy and parishioners, but over the decades, Catholics would assimilate, beginning with the emergence of mass labor movements and the rise of a mass culture and utilizing a vibrant Catholic press and the radio airwaves, especially when radio ownership became widespread. It would be the radio that would catapult Fulton J. Sheen into the national consciousness.

The well-educated, economically successful Catholic laymen and clergy in the 1920s and 1930s were at the forefront of Americanizing the rest of the Catholic population. Dolan wrote, "Looking back on this period, Catholic publicist Frank Sheed commented on the 'euphoria' that 'reigned among Catholics.' The number of converts was increasing; a brilliant crowd of novelists, poets, philosophers, and theologians appeared on the scene; and Catholic publishing became a thriving industry. 'The intellectual activity was enormous,' ... and 'we were happy in the Church and confident of its future.' "[6] When a vocal minority gets confident, the majority takes notice and gets nervous.

[6] Dolan, *In Search of an American Catholicism*, 151.

American Catholics and the Spanish Civil War

One area of international conflict that aroused anti-Catholic sentiment in the United States was the American Catholic hierarchy's support for the Nationalists under General Francisco Franco during the Spanish Civil War (1936–1939) against the mostly Communist Republicans (sometimes called Loyalists). The general belief among the American public at large was that the Vatican favored fascists; its support for Franco reinforced this belief, even though the Vatican had repeatedly condemned both fascism and Communism in the nineteenth and early twentieth centuries. Pope Pius XI himself wrote two encyclicals in opposition to fascism, *Non abbiamo bisogno* in 1931 and *Mit brennender Sorge* in 1937. He also wrote *Divini redemptoris* against atheistic Communism in 1937. The Spanish coalition of Communists, anarchists, and intellectual liberals overthrew the Spanish monarchy in 1931 and eventually formed Spain's very unstable Second Republic. The largely Communist Republican coalition was aggressively anti-clerical, for example burning fifty-seven of Barcelona's fifty-eight churches (sparing, unintentionally, only Gaudí's Sagrada Família) and murdering bishops, priests, and nuns across the country. Of course, the Catholic Church would stand against such violence and butchery committed against herself. There were attempts in 1932 to restore the monarchy that miserably failed, making the Republicans even more violent in reaction. By 1936 a full-scale civil war was raging in Spain, with atrocities on both sides. Yet only the left-leaning Republicans were intent on destroying the Church, its institutions, and its devout people. Republicans were especially vicious toward priests, seven thousand of whom were murdered in horrific ways: eyes gouged out, crucified, burned at the stake or in pits. Fulton Sheen tells the story of a Spanish priest tortured by the Republicans. After they had chopped off his hands, the priest raised his bloody stumps, making the sign of the Cross and blessing his tormentors.[7]

What made the Spanish Civil War so much worse was the intervention of foreign governments and individuals on both sides. Germany

[7] Thomas C. Reeves, *America's Bishop: The Life and Times of Fulton J. Sheen* (San Francisco: Encounter Books, 2001), 103.

and Italy supplied Franco's forces, and the Soviet Union, France, and Mexico supported the Republicans. The German air force, in support of the Nationalists of Franco, was responsible for the bombing of the civilian population of Guernica, ultimately giving the world Picasso's famous anti-war painting. Seven brigades of international left-leaning men, like the almost three thousand men of the Lincoln Brigade from the United States, joined the war on the Republican side, supported and outfitted by the Soviet Union. The most famous American supporter of the Republican cause was Ernest Hemingway, who wrote *For Whom the Bell Tolls*, a pro-Loyalist novel later made into a Hollywood film starring Gary Cooper and Ingrid Bergman. The socialists of France sent twenty-eight thousand troops to Spain on the Republican side, the most troops from any one country. While the Republican government was never officially Communist, it was the Communists within the Party that held sway and managed to keep the war going longer than it might have through the support of the Soviet Union. The death toll of both combatants and noncombatants was extremely high. Hugh Thomas suggested "total deaths from all causes of about 500,000, including 200,000 among combatants (110,000 on the Republican side and 90,000 on the Nationalist) and 130,000 executions (55,000 by the Republicans and 75,000 by the Nationalists). In addition, another 100,000 people were executed by official Nationalist tribunals after they took power in 1939."[8]

In the United States, there were partisans on both sides of the Spanish political divide, each side arguing that the United States owed it to Western civilization to intervene in the Spanish Civil War on one side or the other. The split of opinion ensured that the United States would remain neutral in the Spanish Civil War and would not supply either side with aid or war *matériel*. Within the Catholic community, the hierarchy and official organizations of the Church favored the Nationalists, but the laity was more split, with 39 percent favoring Franco, 30 percent favoring the Republicans, and the rest neutral.[9] Msgr. Fulton Sheen was firmly in the camp that supported

---

[8] Quoted in Charles R. Morris, *American Catholic: The Saints and Sinners Who Built America's Most Powerful Church* (New York: Vintage Books, 1997), 233.
[9] Reeves, *America's Bishop*, 102.

the Nationalists in Spain. Later, he would say that he was supporting Spain, not Franco, from the Communists: "Simply because one is anti-communist, it does not follow that he is a fascist." Franco and the Nationalists were, he said, "the lesser of two evils".[10] There was at least freedom of religion in Fascist Italy, while the Italian Communists, following the lead of the commissars in Russia, were expressly atheistic, with the aim of destroying all religion. Fulton Sheen was always more concerned with what he perceived as the evils of Communism, but his sometimes enthusiastic but more often tepid support for Franco brought him enemies on the Left.

George Seldes claimed to represent the "progressive and democratic majority in America" in writing his 1939 critique of the Catholic Church in America. With the support of the Catholic hierarchy for Franco in the Spanish Civil War, Fr. Coughlin's virulent anti-Semitism, and the Vatican's concordat with Mussolini, Seldes saw the Church as having reactionary and totalitarian tendencies, and he warned the Church that she must choose democracy over fascism. Of course, he addressed the hierarchy, as he hoped to separate the laity from its leaders. Sheen had long recognized that the Communist Left always called its opposition "fascists", an insult meant to delegitimize those who spoke against it. Seldes took seriously the prophecy of Henry Cardinal Manning that the future of the Catholic Church lay in America and feared that an ascendent American Catholic Church would work to undermine liberal democracies worldwide. Sheen's response to criticisms like those of Seldes, even though most of the criticism was not directed specifically at Sheen, was to give his audiences moral guidance, some platitudes, and charming stories. He always tried to be positive and to avoid the sometimes-complex details of Catholic thought and belief. As Kathleen Riley wrote, "[Sheen's] underlying motive was to defend religion."[11] Especially as World War II loomed, a constant theme of Sheen's was the compatibility of Catholicism and American democracy. He preached piety, patriotism, and the peace of Christ.

---

[10] Kenneth Stewart, "An Interview with America's Outstanding Roman Catholic Proselytizer and Philosopher", *PM Magazine*, June 16, 1946, 6.

[11] Kathleen L. Riley, *Fulton J. Sheen: An American Catholic Response to the Twentieth Century* (New York: Alba House, 2004), 112.

Sheen's Personal Philanthropy

Between the world wars, most Americans were not particularly
caught up in politics, as they were dealing with the aftereffects of
the Wall Street crash of 1929 and the lingering devastation of the
Great Depression. They were Fulton Sheen's audience on the Sunday evening *Catholic Hour* and avid readers of his weekly columns.
He did not sermonize or lecture to them. His approach was more
conversational and personal. People believed they knew the monsignor and felt that he truly cared about them. If he mentioned on
the air that he liked chocolate, the following week his office would
be flooded with chocolate candies, cookies, and cakes. If he asked
for dimes for the missions, thousands of dollars' worth of dimes
would arrive taped to envelopes or cards. Children would mail him
pennies. His was a very personal apostolate. He tried to answer all
the six thousand letters a day he received and had to employ a small
army of secretaries to help him. Undoubtedly, most replies used
form letters, but he also answered many directly, dispensing advice,
prayers, and checks. The amount of money he gave out increased
throughout the years, especially after his ascendency on television.
But it was well known that whatever money Fulton Sheen had, he
would give away.

On one of his many trips to Lourdes, Fulton Sheen met Mrs. William J. Babington Macaulay, the wife of the Irish minister to the
Vatican. Mrs. Macaulay was the former Genevieve Florence Gar-
van, whose first marriage had been to Nicholas Frederic Brady, an
American industrialist and philanthropist of great wealth. For their
generous philanthropy to various Catholic institutions, Pope Pius XI
named them Papal Duke and Duchess Brady. In 1936, Sheen introduced Mrs. Macaulay to Eugenio Cardinal Pacelli, soon to be Pope
Pius XII. Msgr. Sheen and Mrs. Macaulay became fast friends. He
convinced her to keep a Holy Hour daily, which she did for the
last seven years of her life. When she died, she left Sheen $68,824 in
her will. Her late first husband, Nicholas Brady, is quoted as saying,
"What are rich people but trustees of God for the deserving poor."[12]

---

[12] Mark Meredith, "Nicholas Frederic Brady (1878–1930)", House Histree, updated January 4, 2022, https://househistree.com/people/nicholas-frederic-brady.

She embodied that belief and, in her bequest to Sheen, benefited generations of mothers and babies in Mobile, Alabama. It would be Fulton Sheen who would preach her requiem Mass in Saint Patrick's Cathedral in New York, and, oddly, not Bishop Francis Spellman, who received the same amount from Mrs. Macaulay's will.

Within a week of receiving her largesse, Sheen gave most of it to the Sisters of Mercy to build the Saint Martin de Porres Hospital, a maternity hospital for Black women in Mobile, Alabama, who were not allowed to deliver their babies in the city's white-only hospitals. Mobile's Bishop Thomas Joseph Toolen wrote to his friend K. I. Jemison that Saint Martin de Porres was "the only hospital in the city for colored and is very much appreciated by them".[13] According to Sheen biographer Thomas Reeves, his gift to the Sisters of Mercy for their hospital was inspired by Fanny Washington, his devoted cook and housekeeper in Washington, D.C. He gave other funds from the Macaulay bequest to open the Immaculate Heart of Mary Mission Church in Hillsview, Alabama, and other chapels across the south—but especially in Alabama. Sheen traveled around Alabama for a week in the summer of 1943 in a trailer with a local priest, talking with people wherever he could find them. There is a charming picture of a smiling Sheen in full monsignor regalia, complete with flowing ferraiolo, speaking on a street corner in Alabama sometime in the late 1930s and standing behind a sign that says "Questions cheerfully answered".[14] Sheen's largesse continued to flow to Alabama, especially to its Black communities. For years he sent his book royalties and speaker's fees to Bishop Toolen. When the much-enlarged Saint Martin de Porres Hospital in Mobile was rededicated in 1950, Sheen was on hand. Most of the $600,000 for the renovations and additions was raised by or donated by Monsignor Sheen. It was this keen concern for the common person, with all questions cheerfully answered, that endeared Sheen to so many people and drew prospective converts. People did not have to meet him personally to feel connected to him and moved by his holiness.

[13] Letter from T.J. Toolen to K.I. Jemison, January 24, 1959, Archdiocese of Mobile Archives.

[14] Fulton J. Sheen, *Treasure in Clay: The Autobiography of Fulton J. Sheen* (Garden City, N.Y.: Doubleday Press, 1980), 59.

A Strictly Radio Conversion: "Bricktop" Smith[15]

Ada Beatrice Queen Victoria Louise Virginia Smith was a dancer, singer, and nightclub owner who converted to the Catholic Church in 1943 after listening to Fulton Sheen on the radio. It would be years before she would meet him in person, yet he changed her life by connecting with her over the airwaves. Born in Alderson, West Virginia, on August 14, 1894, to an ex-slave woman, baby Ada had red hair and freckles from her Irish grandfather on the side of her mother, who was quite light skinned with "really blond hair and blue eyes".[16] The daughter's red hair would earn her the moniker "Bricktop". When her father died young, the widowed Mrs. Smith moved her family of four children to Chicago. Ada was starstruck at the early age of five when she made her stage debut in *Uncle Tom's Cabin* at Chicago's Haymarket Theater. Nine years later, avoiding the truant officer, she became a paid chorus girl at the Pekin Theatre. As soon as it was legal, Ada left school for good and traveled with the Theater Owners Booking Agency and the Pantages vaudeville circuit across the country. She kept up this peripatetic life throughout her teens, eventually making it to Harlem at the age of twenty, where she landed a job at Barron's Exclusive Club. Barron Wilkins took one look at Ada's red hair and christened her "Bricktop".[17] It was Ada who convinced Barron's to hire the then-unknown "Duke" Ellington. While in New York, Bricktop began to make a name for herself so that through friends of friends she was offered a job in Paris at Le Grand Duc nightclub.

Bricktop, or "Bricky" to her friends, sailed to France on the *America*, landing on May 11, 1924, at the age of twenty-nine. When she arrived in Paris, it was bustling with American writers, entertainers,

---

[15] The facts of Bricktop's life come largely from her autobiography, *Bricktop*. Bricktop (Ada Smith DuCongé) and James Haskins, *Bricktop* (New York: Atheneum, 1983). Used with permission.

[16] Ada "Bricktop" Smith, "Brick Top Discusses Her Career, Her Colleagues, and the Jazz Scene" (interview by Studs Terkel), *Studs Terkel*, WFMT, May 6, 1975, https://studsterkel .wfmt.com/programs/brick-top-discusses-her-career-her-colleagues-and-jazz-scene.

[17] Patrick Monahan wrote that it was not Wilkins but Connie Immerman, the owner of Connie's Inn in Harlem, who gave her the name of "Bricktop". Patrick Monahan, "To Bricktop on Her Belated Birthday", *Paris Review* (blog), August 15, 2011, https://www.theparis review.org/blog/2011/08/15/to-bricktop-on-her-belated-birthday/.

and artists. On her first day at Le Grand Duc, upset over the small size of the Paris nightclub in comparison with the grand Harlem establishments she was used to, she found herself consoled by busboy and aspiring author Langston Hughes, to whom she remarked, "My, this is a nice little bar. Now where is the cabaret?"[18] She was more of an entertainer in the broader sense than a singer. She could sing a bit and dance well, and Cole Porter said she had "talking feet and legs",[19] but it was her repartee and warm personality that made her a favorite cabaret performer. She was one of only a few Black female entertainers in Paris at the time, and she became immensely popular. She became close friends with the other famous Black female entertainer in Paris, Josephine Baker. The regulars at Bricktop's performances included American expatriates F. Scott and Zelda Fitzgerald, Ernest Hemingway, Paul Robeson, and John Steinbeck. One evening, she threw Steinbeck out of her club for being "ungentlemanly", and the next day he sent a taxi full of roses to her as an apology.[20] F. Scott Fitzgerald bragged, "My greatest claim to fame is that I discovered Bricktop before Cole Porter."[21] The up-and-coming Duke Ellington also came to her shows, as did Fred Astaire and his sister Adele. Cole Porter, a frequent guest and perhaps her best friend, composed his "Miss Otis Regrets She's Unable to Lunch Today" just for Bricktop, and it perfectly suited her limited singing style and range. Cole Porter had a table at Bricktop's club that was always reserved just for him. His "Miss Otis" would become her signature song.

By 1926, Bricktop was tired of working for others and ready to become a club owner herself. She ran afoul of the infamously strict French licensing laws with her first nightclub venture, but managed to keep open her second club, the eponymous Chez Bricktop, named at the inspiration of Cole Porter. Bricktop's, the club, was an immediate and long-lasting success. Its opening night was a private party hosted by the prince of Wales. "Once Cole discovered me," she recalled, "then all the royalty came."[22] Her mother had told her

[18] Bricktop and Haskins, *Bricktop*, 85.
[19] Ibid., 101.
[20] Albin Krebs, "Bricktop, Cabaret Queen in Paris and Rome", *New York Times*, February 1, 1989.
[21] Bricktop and Haskins, *Bricktop*, 98.
[22] Smith, "Brick Top Discusses Her Career".

and her siblings, "Think big and you'll do big."[23] So Ada Bricktop Smith thought big. A large measure of her club's success was due to its charismatic owner, who served, as she herself wrote, as a "hostess-entertainer ... [in] a club that gave the illusion of being private and the special property of its clientele".[24] Inebriated with her success, Bricktop married a New Orleans jazz saxophonist, Peter DuCongé, in 1929, but because of his infidelities, the marriage did not last long. The couple separated but never divorced, remaining friends until DuCongé died in 1967.

Chez Bricktop, and Bricktop herself, continued to thrive in Paris for several more years. The clientele largely consisted of wealthy white patrons. Chez Bricktop was a space shared by both black and white American expatriates, where racial divides were not as clear cut as in the United States.[25] As she said of her club, "It was always chic."[26] She kept an orderly club. Once she interrupted her song to evict two men who were getting into fisticuffs. "Hey you guys," she shouted, "get out in the street if you want to fight. This ain't that kind of a joint." She then continued the song.[27] She credited Cole Porter with her success: "Without Cole Porter I wouldn't have been anything. He and his friends formed a sort of protective cocoon around me. I got so used to it that I sometimes forgot about what the outside world was like."[28] The singer Mabel Mercer was a regular performer at Chez Bricktop. Django Reinhardt wrote a song entitled "Bricktop" in her honor. The club was so essential to the expatriates in Paris at the time that Woody Allen paid homage to it in his film *Midnight in Paris*, where Zelda Fitzgerald calls out, "Let's go to Bricktop's!"[29]

But when the Depression began to get the best of Paris and the winds of war were blowing in Europe, Bricktop closed her establishment. For a while, she made patriotic radio broadcasts on behalf

[23] Ibid.

[24] Bricktop and Haskins, *Bricktop*, 214.

[25] Jeffrey H. Jackson, *Making French Jazz: Music and Modern Life in Interwar Paris* (Durham: Duke University Press, 2003), 67.

[26] Bricktop and Haskins, *Bricktop*, 125.

[27] Robert McAlmon, *Being Geniuses Together: A Binocular View of Paris in the '20s*, revised by Kay Boyle (New York: Doubleday, 1968), 316–17.

[28] Bricktop and Haskins, *Bricktop*, 127.

[29] *Midnight in Paris*, directed by Woody Allen (New York: Gravier Productions, 2011).

of the French government. She was reluctant to leave Paris and the cocoon that had enveloped her there. Although by October of 1939 the American consulate was warning American citizens to leave France, somehow Bricktop continued to think she might be useful if she stayed on in Paris, despite the danger of approaching Nazis and knowing that some of her friends carried "suicide pills" around with them.[30] It was the Duchess of Windsor and Lady Elsie Mendl who convinced her to go back to the United States and bought her a ticket home. She left France on Cunard's *Washington*, which departed on October 26, 1939, one of the last ships to leave France. She had been an expatriate for sixteen years and was coming home broke. She packed her bags and returned to the United States in a state of near nervous collapse.

Back in New York, Bricktop began listening to Fulton Sheen's *Catholic Hour*. The monsignor was recommended to her by a friend, one of her employees in Paris, whom she recalled as a surly young man who could not get along with anybody. When she met him again in New York, though, she was amazed at the man's transformation. He told her that he had converted to Catholicism, and when she asked what that had to do with his changed personality, he replied, "You'd be surprised."[31] Sheen's broadcasts must have struck a chord. While she never received any catechetical instruction directly from Sheen, she gave him the credit for her conversion. Hers was strictly a "radio conversion". She was baptized by a New York priest on December 5, 1943.[32]

New York was not as congenial to Bricktop as Paris had been between the wars; she found racial prejudice in New York she had not experienced in almost twenty years abroad. After running a boardinghouse in Saratoga for a few years, she tried opening a club in Mexico City, funded by her friend Doris Duke. The club thrived at first but then foundered. Bricktop decided to return to Paris, only to find that it was not the same place it had been before the war. With American GIs and tourists flooding the place, prejudice came to the City of Light in a way that was uncomfortable for a Black woman from West Virginia, and she lasted less than a year in post-war Paris.

[30] Bricktop and Haskins, *Bricktop*, 204.
[31] Ibid., 220.
[32] Reeves, *America's Bishop*, 173.

She knew people in Rome who had been her patrons in Paris before the war who assured her that Rome had nothing like Bricktop's—no small intimate clubs. So she went to Rome in 1951 and set up shop. She was successful there as the proprietor of Roman Chez Bricktop.

One evening she was told that Bishop Sheen, who had become aware of her charitable activities for the Church, wanted to meet her. An appointment was made, but Bricktop was not feeling well and did not show up for the meeting. She called him the next day to apologize and to ask if he could still see her before he left Rome. "He told me to come the next day *and to be on time*", she recalled, so she walked around the block a few times before knocking on his door so as not to be early. She would describe their meeting as "beautiful".[33] A few years later, Bricktop found herself lacking in funds, so she approached Sheen, who was once again in Rome. Happy to renew their acquaintance, Fulton Sheen invited her in and, when she told him of her financial straits, he got out his check book. He asked her how much she needed: "Five hundred, five thousand? What?" He wrote her a check for $500 and gave her a book with the inscription "My child in Christ, Bricktop, who proves every walk of life can be spiritualized". Later, Bricktop came to Sheen's New York office with a $500 check in repayment. Sheen was amazed. Reeves wrote, "It was the first time in his long lending career that anyone had repaid him."[34] The friendship between Bricktop and Bishop Sheen became an enduring one. In a eulogy at her funeral, James Hastings, who had collaborated with Bricktop in writing her autobiography, remarked that the bishop "had confessed to a periodic need for a 'Bricktop fix'".[35]

Like Sheen's other children in Christ, Bricktop was changed by her conversion in fundamental ways. It was something she noticed in herself: "I was finding rewards in just living ... that I had never known before. My religion was making life happy for me again. Every day I found myself drawn to it. I like the mystery of the Catholic Church, the insistence on blind faith in God. I found richness in the solitude of going to church, and the stresses of everyday life just

[33] Bricktop and Haskins, *Bricktop*, 263.
[34] Reeves, *America's Bishop*, 174.
[35] "300 Attend Service for the Singer Bricktop", *New York Times*, February 5, 1984, nytimes.com/1984/02/05/obituary.300-attend-service-for-the-singer-bricktop.html.

didn't seem as important anymore."[36] Sheen had written, "God made you to be happy. He made you for your happiness, not His.... God does not love us because He needs us. He loves us because He put some of His love in us. God does not love us because we are valuable; we are valuable because He loves us."[37]

Bricktop was serious about her new life in the Church. She sought out priest confessors wherever she lived. Her life as a saloonkeeper had not been a chaste one, but after her conversion, she took a vow of chastity. She prayed, "Lord, never let me be a foolish old woman." There was nothing more pitiable to her than an older woman caught up with a younger man. "Some good-looking fellow would walk into my life and show interest in me, and I'd go running to church.... In my church I found the strength to keep my dignity," she wrote.[38] Sheen would say that Bricktop's conversion consisted in her "being re-created, re-made, and incorporated into the risen Christ, so that [she] live[d] His life, [thought] His thoughts, and will[ed] His love".[39]

Bricktop had always been free with loans and gifts to her friends; that was generosity. But with her conversion, she practiced charity as a virtue. Sheen pointed out that conversion begins with conversion to Christ, then to the Church Christ founded, and then to the world. For Bricktop, charity was personal, but no longer directed only at her friends. "After I converted to Catholicism," she wrote, "I became more aware of how necessary it was for those who had to help those who hadn't, and in Rome I became deeply involved in charity work."[40] She especially embraced the children of post-war Italy. She noticed that the orphan camps run by the Communists were always well funded with excellent facilities and plenty of food. Those camps run by the Church, though, were poorly funded, leaving the children in need of clothes, shoes, and food. Bricktop decided to help. She took the money for every customer's third drink and deposited it in a box to buy milk and shoes for the children. She put a small card on the tables of her club that read, "The only thing a dead man holds in his hands are the things he gave away." Soon her

---

[36] Bricktop and Haskins, *Bricktop*, 227.
[37] Fulton Sheen, *Preface to Religion* (New York: P.J. Kennedy & Sons, 1946), 20.
[38] Bricktop and Haskins, *Bricktop*, 227.
[39] Sheen, *Preface to Religion*, 65.
[40] Bricktop and Haskins, *Bricktop*, 262.

patrons were bringing her donations of money and clothes for the children and the unwed mothers who were also under her special care. Bricktop became known as the "Holy Hustler".[41]

Her famous guests in Rome included Elizabeth Taylor, Richard Burton, Frank Sinatra, Louis Armstrong, Martin Luther King Jr., King Farouk, and the Duke and Duchess of Windsor. So many famous actors and actresses made Bricktop's a stop on their Italian holidays that she came to refer to her club as "Hollywood on the Tiber". Bricktop retired from the European cabaret life in 1961 and moved back to the United States, which had become a much more congenial place for a Black woman entertainer than it had been after the war. But she was not completely retired; she continued to perform in the States and abroad well into her eighties. She played herself in Michael Schultz's 1974 film *Honeybaby, Honeybaby* and again in Woody Allen's 1983 mocumentary film *Zelig*. Her recordings of Cole Porter songs were never released to the public, but there are videos of her on YouTube. Bricktop's only released recording is "So Long Baby", made in the 1970s with Cy Coleman.

Her "radio conversion" held to the end of her life while she continued to generously support various Catholic charities. She appeared at Catholic fundraising events into the early 1980s. Bricktop and Fulton Sheen remained friends; she was even invited to an intimate party to celebrate the anniversary of his priesthood. She was awarded an honorary degree by Columbia University, both Boston and Chicago declared "Bricktop Days", and New York City honored her with a "Certification of Appreciation for Just Being Herself". Ada "Bricktop" Smith died on January 31, 1984, in New York City at the age of eighty-nine. Fulton Sheen may have had only an indirect or distant influence on the conversion of Bricktop to Catholicism, but it was a profound and lasting conversion for his "Child in Christ".

The Coming World War

While Bricktop Smith was longing for peace of mind and soul during her gay Paris days, singing and dancing away the nights, Europe was

[41] Ibid., 261.

lurching into what would become the Second World War. Fulton
Sheen foresaw the war that would come, along with its Cold War
aftermath. The signing of the Hitler-Stalin Non-Aggression Pact of
1939 raised alarms for him: "America has suddenly turned against
communism ... not because of a universal moral judgment based on
the intrinsic wickedness of communism, but because of a particular judgment that communism signed a treaty with someone whom
most Americans hate, namely Hitler."[42] It pained Sheen to witness
the moral confusion and willing blindness of his fellow Americans
over the existential threat posed by Communism. He wrote, "The
anti-God regime is always the anti-human regime. What more clearly
proves it than the Red Fascism of Communism and the Brown Fascism of Nazism, which by denying the spirit of God as the source of
human rights, make the State the source? But if the State is the giver
of rights then the State can take them away. It is ever true that the
loss of God is the beginning of all tyranny."[43]

When the Soviets broke with Germany and joined the Allies,
Sheen decried our new association with the Communistic country
as bad ethics, even if it was good politics, and he believed the West
would come to rue the day it allied itself with the Soviet Union.
Sheen called for the primacy of ethics: "I beg my fellow citizens to
be less concerned with politics and be more concerned with ethics."[44] Of course, once the United States was at war with the Axis
powers, the Catholic Church in America, and Fulton Sheen along
with it, gave the war effort unqualified support. Despite the small
brouhaha over President Roosevelt's appointment of Myron Taylor
as the country's first representative to the Vatican that unleashed a
wave of anti-Catholic criticism, when the United States joined the
war, the Catholic Church provided an abundance of evidence of
the patriotism, dedication, and sacrifice of American Catholic citizens. As far as Sheen was concerned, it was a war to preserve democracy and Christianity. Christianity can survive without democracy,
but " 'democracy cannot live without religion, for without religion
democracy will degenerate into demagogy by selling itself to the

---

[42] Fulton J. Sheen, *Peace: The Fruit of Justice* (Huntington, Ind.: Our Sunday Visitor, 1940), 14.
[43] Ibid.
[44] Fulton J. Sheen, *Simple Truths: Thinking Life Through with Fulton J. Sheen* (Liguori, Mo.:
Liguori/Triumph, 1998), 99.

highest bidder,' meaning that the sole source of right and wrong will be determined by public opinion polls."[45] Catholic men flocked into the recruiting offices. Catholics would make up 35 percent of America's fighting forces, even as they were but 20 percent of the population. As a priest, Fulton Sheen was focused on the religious and spiritual aspects of the worldwide conflict. He looked upon it as an opportunity for people to draw closer to God: "Moments of great catastrophe are often the eves of great spiritual renaissance."[46] Always the college professor, he would lecture on the Catholic theology of just war, in which there is a good end, right intentions, and the employment of justifiable means. The cause of the Allies was righteous, according to just war theory as Sheen presented it: "We are defending a Christian civilization; we are fighting for religious freedom; we are fighting for justice."[47]

Fulton Sheen was also fighting with the National Council of Catholic Men, the Church sponsor of his appearances on the weekly *Catholic Hour*. The Council was upset with Sheen's persistent attacks on Communism that continued even after the Soviet Union joined the Allies. He was criticized by those in academia who censured his programs' religious content and even his grammar. Sheen was piqued. He refused to answer letters from the Council's secretary; he turned in his prepared talks too close to show time to be revised; he ad-libbed on the air; and he told others that the Council was trying to take him off the air altogether. On the fifteenth anniversary of *The Catholic Hour* in 1945, Sheen called it *his* fifteenth anniversary, as if he and the program were one. In many ways he was correct, for without Sheen *The Catholic Hour* would not have been so popular and would likely have failed in its mission to reach out to Catholics and non-Catholics as well to make the country realize that its Catholic citizens were true Americans and not aliens with a foreign political allegiance, while at the same time introducing Catholic thought and morality to the population.

[45] Fulton J. Sheen, *Whence Come Wars* (New York: Sheed & Ward, 1940), 71.

[46] Fulton J. Sheen, *The Catholic Hour*, April 13, 1941, quoted in Joseph Pronechen, "Prophecy of Venerable Fulton Sheen Offers Hope to a Troubled America", *National Catholic Register*, March 29, 2021, https://www.ncregister.com/blog/fulton-sheen-and-our-troubled-times.

[47] Fulton J. Sheen, *The Catholic Hour*, January 11, 1942, quoted in "Moral Law Means Strong Morale", *Catholic Bulletin of Foreign News*, February 21, 1942, 3.

Throughout the war, Sheen was traveling weekly from Washington, D.C., to New York City while maintaining his teaching schedule at Catholic University. On weekends and holidays, he traveled across the country giving talks and retreats. He met regularly with convert classes in both Washington and New York. He even held convert classes especially for African Americans in both cities. After his New York Sunday homilies at either Saint Patrick's Cathedral or Saint Paul the Apostle's church, Monsignor Sheen would announce that he would meet anybody who desired instruction in the faith.

A Communist Comes Home to the Church

Louis Budenz, still the active Communist, was waiting in the wings for Fulton Sheen. Budenz had kept his eyes closed to what he knew to be the truth. He wrote, "I hid from myself what I knew to be the case, that this very materialism [of Communism] had to rely on terror as its only law. It wiped out intellectual integrity."[48] Budenz had continued to hope for cooperation between the Communists and the Catholics and was shocked to find out that the Communists planned to destroy the Church by any means necessary. A man Budenz only identifies as "Comrade B" lectured to him: "We mean by [separation of church and state] the subjugation of the church by the state, the complete control of religion by the Socialist state so that finally we can abolish it.... The Socialist state must pursue religion into the home, if necessary, to wipe it out there—by persuasion if possible, by force if required. We shall probably have to destroy it by force."[49] This was a reality that Louis Budenz could no longer ignore. All his hopeless naïveté came back upon him, yet he was still not willing to give up on the promises of Communism: "In 1940 I was not yet ready for any anti-communist conclusions."[50] For a few years he would consider himself part of the Communists, but not fully *with* them. With the conversion of his fellow journalist, Heywood Broun, some years earlier, and the open hostility of Communism to religion, Budenz had resolved to extricate himself from the Party and to rejoin the

[48] Louis Francis Budenz, *This Is My Story* (New York: McGraw-Hill, 1947), 171.
[49] Ibid., 185.
[50] Ibid., 209.

Catholic Church: "It was as though I had performed my assignment for the Party and was now intent upon putting my own personal house in order." He was motivated by more than the intellectual self-deception required to present the Party line in the *Daily Worker*; he felt a moral weariness. "There was a balm for such a moral illness, I knew—and it lay in the Catholic Church and its Sacraments."[51] It was during the 1941 Christmas season that he stopped into a Catholic church to pray for five minutes for a Catholic-Communist reconciliation and wound up on his knees for over an hour. "Looking at myself frankly for the first time in years, I went further and pledged that if the grace were given to me to return to the Church, I would do so at all costs. 'To thee, O Most Sacred Heart of Jesus in the Blessed Sacrament and to Mary the Immaculate, I pledge that if this comes about I shall be a daily communicant for the rest of my life, to make amendment for my years of sin.'" However, he admitted, "I was still in the fog."[52]

Louis Budenz and his family moved out of New York in 1943 into the suburbs of Westchester County to remove themselves as much as possible from the ready and persistent view of the New York Party members. They agreed among them that he would rejoin the Church, and again he pledged to do so at all costs. He now thought of himself as a Catholic trying to moderate a Communist Party whose overall utopian goals he still supported. He persisted in that support until it became obvious that the Soviet Union had scheduled the United States for "future Soviet destruction".[53] He wrote, "I was able to grasp the realities of the Soviet Union's concerted and unrelenting determination to crush both religion and our nation."[54] The only solution for him was to return to the Church, but how to extricate himself from the many tentacles of the Communist Party? And the Communists were one problem; his wife was another.

Margaret's only church association had been, loosely, with the Unitarian Church, and she had casually told her spouse that she could never become a member of the Catholic Church. What Budenz came to realize was that Margaret really had no understanding of the

[51] Ibid., 231.
[52] Ibid., 232.
[53] Ibid., 312, n.
[54] Ibid., 315.

Catholic Church and that her conception of the Church was completely wrong. When they moved to Crestwood in Westchester County, Margaret announced that she wanted to take their three daughters to the Episcopal Church, which she thought was ritualistic enough and close enough to Unitarianism to make her feel at home. They also had Communist friends at the church, the Episcopal clergyman and his wife, whom Budenz had recruited into the Communist Party. Perhaps Margaret thought that the rituals of the Episcopal Church would be close enough to those of the Catholic Church to suit her husband's aesthetic sensibilities. Budenz, for his part, attended Sunday Mass at the local Catholic church. His Mass attendance began to have a transformative effect on him, something his wife noticed. She told him that going to Mass seemed to bring him a peace that the Episcopal service never did. In October of 1944, Margaret suggested that she join Budenz in stopping by Saint Joseph's Church. He wrote, "It was there that the 'miracle' as we called it, occurred. During the course of our prayers, Margaret sensed at once the Real Presence and realized the difference from other churches. Thereafter she went to Mass with me, and after the Christmas Mass of 1944 said simply: 'I would like to be a Catholic.'"[55]

Once the decision had been made, there were many things to consider: how to keep the information from the prying eyes of the Communist spy network, whom to tell and how, and would the Church even accept them, considering their many offenses against God? And, of course, they were still Communists. So they vacillated. The final straw that made them break from the Communist Party came when William Z. Foster, the general secretary of the Communist Party USA, told Budenz, "Until the Soviet regime governs the earth, a state of war will exist.... The two chief enemies of the Soviet Union and progress are American imperialism and the Vatican. They are eternal foes of Socialism and have to be fought endlessly.... The cornerstone we have to get rid of first is the Catholic mythology and the Catholic organization."[56] As if the scales finally fell from his eyes, moments later, Budenz told his office mate, "Foster has just taught me a lesson I should have learned long ago."[57] He hurried home that

[55] Ibid., 333.
[56] Ibid., 339–41.
[57] Ibid., 341.

night to tell Margaret his intention to completely break from the Communist Party.

Louis Budenz naturally turned to Monsignor Fulton Sheen, sending him a letter requesting a meeting with him at his earliest convenience. When Margaret asked him why he wanted to talk to Sheen, he replied, "He told me that he was interested in my soul."[58] They met Sheen on September 7, 1945, in the Roosevelt Hotel and arranged for Margaret to take instruction from him.[59] The monsignor would fly to New York from wherever he happened to be lecturing on the appointed day—all three of them recognized the great need for secrecy and speed during the preparation period. Louis Budenz, Margaret, and their three daughters all joined the Church on October 10, 1945. For Louis Budenz, it was a welcome homecoming too long delayed. He went to confession, and Margaret and the girls were baptized. Then, Louis and Margaret were officially married in the Church. Even before they had received their First Communion on October 11, Budenz had announced to the world his reception back into the Church:

> With deep joy, I wish to announce that by God's grace I have returned fully to the faith of my fathers, the Catholic Church. My wife, the companion at every step of my spiritual journey, and my three daughters have become Catholics with me.
>
> Reason and faith have led to this happy step. From St. Peter to Pius XII, the Papacy has brought light to mankind, and despite all the pulls and tugs of history has continued its divine mission.
>
> The voice of Catholicism is the guide to the winning of the real peace. The privilege of returning to the sacraments is one to be deeply prized; it is, after a long journey, the true returning home.
>
> Communism and Catholicism are irreconcilable. Communism, I have found, aims to establish a tyranny over the human spirit; it is in unending conflict with religion and true freedom.[60]

As Budenz left the Mass where he had received his first Communion in three decades, he said, "I feel as though I had just escaped

---

[58] Sheen, *Treasure*, 266.

[59] In Washington, Sheen usually met with prospective converts in his home. For large numbers he would use a church hall or Catholic school auditorium.

[60] Budenz, *My Story*, 349.

from prison."[61] He may have been out of prison, but breaking from the Communist Party meant that Louis Budenz, with a wife and three children, was out of a job. It was a relief but also a worry to leave the *Daily Worker* and the daily barrage of Communist propaganda. Budenz writes, "When I finally left the Party, the Communist official statement said that I was 'frightened'" (by the coming war between the United States and Russia).[62] But it was not fright but disgust and anger that made Budenz leave the Party—most of all directed at himself for his self-delusion, as he served as an important arm of that hateful propaganda. How many had he misled in his articles and editorials? How had he undermined the safety and security of the United States, and, moreover, what damage had he done to the Catholic Church? He would spend the rest of his life atoning for these sins. But first he needed safety and security for his family.

Msgr. Sheen arranged for the Budenz family to leave New York immediately for the University of Notre Dame in Indiana. After the years-long turmoil of leaving the Communist Party and helping to bring his family into the Church, Budenz was mentally exhausted. The quietude of the Notre Dame campus cosseted the family over the next year, giving Louis Budenz the opportunity for silence from the world as he had known it and to plan their future. That year he taught economics at the University of Notre Dame. Then he taught at Fordham University and briefly at Seton Hall University and Providence College, where his papers are housed. But his main occupation was as an ardent anti-Communist, writing, lecturing, and testifying against his former bosses and colleagues. He estimated he had spent over three thousand hours testifying before the F.B.I. and was later a witness in the Alger Hiss investigation by the House Un-American Activities Committee and before Senator Joseph McCarthy and Senator Millard Tidings, who chaired the committee to investigate the loyalty of government employees. In 1947, Budenz gave five radio talks on *The Catholic Hour* on the Church and labor. Louis Budenz became the darling to the anti-Communist right and a vilified anathema to the left.

[61] Ibid., 350.
[62] Ibid., 367.

Budenz was not everyone's darling. There were those who opposed him and other ex-Communist treason hunters. Joseph Alsop wrote in *The Atlantic Monthly*:

In a short year and a half of appearances before Congressional committees, Louis F. Budenz has brought the charge of treason against no fewer than twoscore citizens of this republic. White-haired, pale-faced, looking like a conservative elderly lawyer in his dark, expensive suit, the eminent ex-Communist speaks with confident authority: "This man was a party member; that woman was under discipline; him we called one of ours." In some sense, it has become his avocation; and there is every reason to expect that he will continue mass-producing treason charges so long as the Senatorial demand continues.[63]

Budenz was accused by Alsop and others of defaming loyal government employees with inuendo and hearsay that lacked hard evidence: "[S]olid proofs are no longer demanded by press or Congress, as they were when Whittaker Chambers denounced Alger Hiss. Instead, the accuser speaks; the next morning's headlines announce the accusation; and the accused is marked thereafter as a traitor to his country."[64] It is true that in one year Budenz earned $70,000 in speakers' fees going around the country talking about the Communist menace in the federal government. It is also true that Communists tried to be very careful to hide their affiliation with the Party. While there were many people falsely accused of treason, others were eventually confirmed to have been working for the Soviets. "By 1957," Daniel Levin cites, "140 leaders and members of the Communist Party of the United States of America had been charged under the law, of whom 93 were convicted."[65] Louis Budenz died of a heart attack at the age of eighty-one in 1972, a staunch anti-Communist and ardent Catholic to the end. His experience of conversion (or "reversion") to the faith of his fathers was intensely personal but at the same time universal: like so many other converts, he found he had discovered answers

---

[63] Joseph Alsop, "The Strange Case of Louis Budenz", *Atlantic Monthly*, April 1952, https://www.theatlantic.com/magazine/archive/1952/04/the-strange-case-of-louis-budenz/640455/.

[64] Ibid.

[65] Daniel Levin, "Smith Act", in *Encyclopedia of American Civil Liberties*, ed. Paul Finkelman (Boca Raton, Fla: CRC Press, 2008), 1488.

to questions he had not even asked himself. They would be questions and answers with consequences that demanded the assent of the will and intellect to the truths as revealed by God and treasured by the Catholic Church. For many years, his intellect had been feeding him the errors of materialistic, atheistic Communism, but his intellect was clouded by pride in his various choices and by the vain hope held out by the Communists of an idealized world. By the time his intellect began telling him it was necessary to leave the Party, his will was too weak to act until, by the grace of God, he could no longer ignore the reality that his intellect recognized.

Fulton Sheen believed that conversion is an act of grace from the Holy Spirit, as it clearly was for Budenz. Most conversions, wrote Sheen, are initiated out of a personal crisis that leads to "on the one hand ... a profound sense of one's own helplessness, and on the other ... an equally certain conviction that God alone can supply what the individual lacks.... The grace of God comes to us in just the degree that we open our souls to it; the only limit to our capacity to receive Him is our willingness to do so.... The latch is on our side and not on God's, for God breaks down no doors."[66]

[66] Fulton J. Sheen, *Peace of Soul* (New York: Whittlesey House, 1949), 55.

4

Communism, Secularism, and World War II

A Young Man on His Way Up

Fulton J. Sheen inherited his parents' Midwestern work ethic. He famously worked a nineteen-hour day. D. P. Noonan said of him, "Sheen in his day accomplished ten times as much work as any businessman on Madison Avenue." Fr. Charles McBride, one of Sheen's assistants, commented, "He never sleeps at all. Well, maybe five or six hours."[1] By 1940 he had published twenty books and stacks of pamphlets and sermons. His speaking engagements earned him high fees, eventually as much a $5,000 a night after he became a television star, and, when his engagements exceeded 150 a year, he was making a great deal of money. It is true that he pampered himself with limousines and a custom-designed home with a private chapel in a fashionable section of Washington. Certainly, his cassocks were tailor-made for his slight frame. But it is also true that he lived a very ascetic life for such an important clergyman. D. P. Noonan called Sheen's "an unglamourous existence".[2] He was an extremely conscientious and hard worker in all that he undertook. He disciplined his body with abstemious eating habits and regular exercise and took little sleep. He neither smoked nor drank. In 1951 he reported that "every cent I received while on the *Catholic Hour* was always turned over to the National Council of Catholic Men."[3] Whatever he earned he gave away—if not to the Council of Catholic Men, then to the needy.

---

[1] "The Many Roles of Bishop Fulton J. Sheen", *New York Post*, October 14, 1955.

[2] D. P. Noonan, *The Passion of Fulton Sheen* (New York: Dodd, Mead & Company, 1972), 107.

[3] Fulton J. Sheen to Martin Work, March 14, 1951, Archdiocese of New York Archives. See James C. G. Conniff, *The Bishop Sheen Story* (New York: Fawcett Publications, 1953), 30.

73

People would send him jewelry, which he always took to a jeweler he knew, Herbert Trigger, to sell so he could give the money away. Money just seemed to flow into and out of Sheen's pockets. One of his nephews recalled "seeing people stuffing money into Sheen's coat pockets as he walked through a Chicago hotel".[4] He said he never liked money and gave it away as soon as he could. Others commented on how quickly he gave money away to anyone who asked for it on the streets or anywhere he happened to be. What flowed in, flowed out just as readily. He took to heart the saying that "shrouds have no pockets." The Church historian Fr. John Tracy Ellis, who served as his secretary, said of Sheen, "I have rarely known a more generous person, for with his increasing income his charities mounted in due proportion."[5] Fulton Sheen was known more than once to take the coat off his back and give it to somebody in need.[6]

For all his perceived wisdom and insight into worldly affairs, Fulton Sheen was not a worldly person. People who knew him best and had the luxury of observing him over time believed Sheen to be a holy man, sincere in his Catholic faith and always close to the Virgin Mary and to her Son, particularly in the Eucharist. Ellis, who lived in the house with Sheen and a few other priests, observed him daily for three years: "I admired his priestliness—I was a witness to his daily Mass and holy hour, to name only two features of his prayer life—and I was impressed as well by his steady work habits, his reading, his love and zeal for the Church, and ... his genuine thoughtfulness for those around him of whatever station in life."[7] An example of Sheen's thoughtfulness was in sending a limousine to pick up his former housekeeper, Fanny Washington, to bring her to Saint Patrick's in New York from Washington, D.C., to receive her into the Church as one of his dearest converts.

At the same time, Sheen also embodied vanity and ambition—the ambition, as Michael Novak would say, of "ecclesiastical lust".[8] Even

---

[4] Joseph Sheen Jr. interview, in Thomas C. Reeves, *America's Bishop: The Life and Times of Fulton J. Sheen* (San Francisco: Encounter Books, 2001), 122.

[5] John Tracy Ellis, *Catholic Bishops: A Memoir* (Wilmington, Del.: Michael Glazier, 1983), 80.

[6] *Positio*, 1.111. This was observed by Joan Sheen Cunningham, his niece.

[7] Ellis, *Catholic Bishops*, 80–81.

[8] Michael Novak, *The Open Church* (Milton Park, Abingdon, U.K.: Taylor & Francis, 2017), quoted in Noonan, *Passion*, 69.

as a young priest in graduate training in Louvain, Sheen prayed to be made a bishop one day. He would say, "What was clearly the motive was the desire to become a successor to the Apostles." On his way to class, he would pass by paintings of the Seven Sorrows of Mary and on each day pray "A Hail Mary at each of the Seven Dolors of the Blessed Mother for that intention and I have continued that prayer", he wrote in his autobiography.[9] In 1934 Fulton Sheen was made a "monsignor", as a papal chamberlain was called. The following year, he was elevated a step higher with the title "Right Reverend Monsignor". With his new monsignor's regalia, his biographer wrote, Sheen was "looking as well as sounding like what he had become: a major spokesman for the Catholic Church in America".[10] He loved his new ferraiolo and sash that hung so well on his 127-pound frame. They made him look bigger and certainly more impressive when he stepped up to the microphone to speak. Sheen would say, "We dress for God.... We are his representatives."[11] Soon Bishop Francis Kelley of the Oklahoma diocese contacted Sheen to ask if he could put his name forward to Rome as a candidate to replace the ailing Kelley as the next bishop of Oklahoma. Sheen turned down the offer, saying he preferred the "vertical elevation which comes directly from God, unsought, unknown, and unexpected" rather than a "horizontal honor due to someone else's pull.... I have already refused on several occasions to accept horizontal honors, for I could never be sure that God wanted me to have them. The Holy Spirit has not seen fit to go further than He has and I suspect it is because He knows how undeserving I am. But if He should call, I care not where, I will accept."[12] The Right Reverend Monsignor Fulton Sheen saw himself, as so many others did, as a man on his way up. He was a national figure on a familiar basis with important people in the hierarchy of the Church, both in the United States and in the Vatican, and when New York's Patrick Cardinal Hayes died unexpectedly in 1938, Sheen's hopes for the promotion he desired most were high when his name was

---

[9] Fulton J. Sheen, *Treasure in Clay: The Autobiography of Fulton J. Sheen* (Garden City, N.Y.: Doubleday Press, 1980), 91.

[10] Reeves, *America's Bishop*, 85.

[11] Ibid., 137.

[12] James P. Gaffey, *Francis Clement Kelley & the American Catholic Dream*, vol. 2 (Bensenville, Ill: Heritage Foundation, 1980), 280–81; Sheen, *Treasure*, 92; Noonan, *Passion*, 20.

bandied about in the press as the cardinal's successor. It was a serious blow to Fulton J. Sheen to learn that Francis J. Spellman was to be the new archbishop of New York. John Tracy Ellis was having lunch with Msgr. Sheen when they heard the announcement of Spellman's elevation. Sheen's reaction is telling: "Leaning his arm on the table with his head in his hand, he exclaimed 'It is incredible. It is incredible. He has nothing.' So deeply dejected was he that he took to his bed and remained there for several days."[13]

Eventually, Sheen and Spellman would work together to do great things for the Catholic Church in America, for the universal Church—especially its missions—and for the war effort, until they had a serious falling-out many years later. In the meantime, Msgr. Sheen would settle into his ever-busy schedule of teaching classes at the university, meeting with convert classes of up to one hundred at a time, and speaking regularly around the country. He also traveled almost annually to Europe to teach, study, and write. From 1939 on, except during the war, he had an annual visit with whoever happened to be the Roman pontiff. Sheen's output of work was prodigious, as was his expanding list of converts, but of course he did not keep count, lest he think that he had something to do with their conversions, when he knew it was the Holy Spirit at work.

Not All Conversions Are Successful

Henry Ford II, a Yale Methodist and heir to the Ford Motor Company, wanted to marry the very Catholic and Irish Anne McDonnell in a big society church wedding befitting his station in life and the desire of his fiancée. To do so, he needed to convert to Catholicism. Sheen gave the groom-to-be instruction in the faith and received him into the Church on the day of his wedding to Anne, July 13, 1940. Kathleen Kennedy, the sister of the future President John F. Kennedy, was one of the bridesmaids, so it was a grand affair, despite the fact that the senior Henry Ford seriously considered disinheriting his son for abandoning the Methodist Church. Later attacked by professional Catholic critic William Ward Ayer, the wedding and Ford's

---

[13] Ellis, *Catholic Bishops*, 81.

conversion gave "the appearance of 'spiritual shot gunnery,' making religion a convenient prerequisite to conjugal love and marital experience".[14] Ayer was attacking Sheen and the Catholic Church for engaging in gimmicks and sham conversions. But in attacking Fulton Sheen, Ayer was attacking the wrong man. The fault was with Henry Ford, not Sheen or the Church. Sheen considered himself a porter, inviting would-be converts to enter the always-open door to the house of the Lord.

But not all who enter God's house choose to remain there. After twenty-four years of marriage to Anne and the birth of three children, Henry Ford let his personal desires delude his intellect into thinking it was the right thing to do to divorce his wife and leave his family to marry the lovely Maria Christina Austin, a divorced Italian socialite. Through an act of what the Church would consider sinful willfulness, Henry Ford entered into a second marriage that would also end in divorce. He was to marry for a third time. At his death, his service was at the Grosse Pointe Christ Episcopal Church, not at a Catholic church. Obviously, not all conversions are successful, and some are, as Ayer said about Ford's, conversions of convenience. At the time of Ford's conversion, Sheen was receiving at least six thousand letters a day, mostly from people seeking information on joining the Church. Losing a convert now and then was surely part of the process. His friend the actress Loretta Young said of him, "Nothing ever got him down." She said, "He was fond of saying 'Everything is God's will.' "[15] Sheen would say of himself with modesty and considerable understatement, "I have had *some* success as a porter."[16]

Winning the War and Winning the Peace

Throughout World War II, Sheen's voice and pen produced a steady drumbeat imploring America to be wary of our Communist Russian allies. He was also concerned about helping keep up the morale of

[14] Reeves, *America's Bishop*, 186.
[15] Ibid., 136.
[16] Hilary C. Franco, *Bishop Fulton J. Sheen: Mentor and Friend* (New Hope, Ky.: New Hope Publications, 2014), 63. Emphasis added.

Americans on the home front and in the trenches. Sheen saw the war primarily as a spiritual and religious conflict that provided an opportunity for the people of the world to turn to God. His other main concern was not that the United States and its allies win the war—he had no doubt they would—but that they win the peace, which was not such a sure thing. He supported the Five-Point Peace Plan of Pope Pius XII as being both Catholic and American:

1. To assure all nations of their right to life and independence;
2. To release nations from the slavery imposed upon them by the race for armaments;
3. To erect some juridical institution which shall guarantee the loyal and faithful fulfillment of treaties;
4. To establish strictly legal right for the real needs and just demands of nations, populations, and racial minorities;
5. To restore deep and keen responsibilities which measure and weigh human statutes according to the sacred and inviolable standards of the laws of God.[17]

Many were asking the question of why there was all this evil in the world. Sheen answered in part that it was because of the apostasy of the world, which had resulted in the "active barbarism of the anti-Christian totalitarian world view [of both the communists and the Nazis]."[18] It was a Christian duty to fight these forms of evil. With the end of the war in mind, if not quite yet in sight, Fulton Sheen's 1944 radio broadcasts focused on "One Lord, One World", urging "One world based on One Lord and One Moral Law".[19] The twin evils besetting society in the West were Communism and secularism, with the latter of the two being the most dangerous in Sheen's mind, because it was secularism that, in diminishing Christianity, paved the way for the acceptance of utopian Communism and pagan Nazism. It was secularism that opened the door to the twentieth century's totalitarian regimes that have wreaked so much havoc on the world.

[17] Kathleen L. Riley, *Fulton J. Sheen: An American Catholic Response to the Twentieth Century* (New York: Alba House, 2004), 119.
[18] Fulton J. Sheen, *Crisis in Christendom*, 3rd ed. (Washington, D.C.: The National Council of Catholic Men, October 15, 1952), 7.
[19] Fulton J. Sheen, *One Lord, One World* (Huntington, Ind.: Our Sunday Visitor, 1944), 12.

More than one hundred million lives have been lost in the names of these persistent ideologies. Sheen believed that "the Church is the only moral authority in the world."[20] In his earliest writing, his doctoral dissertation and the book it produced, he wrote, "The Catholic Church comes forward as the one and only champion of Reason."[21] Once out of school, Sheen continued to use his voice and his pen to shepherd those who would listen and heed his warnings. The Church in its universality was relevant to all times and places and held, he believed, the means to right the upside-down world of the West in the twentieth century. He relied on the Gospels and the social justice principles of the Church, especially as he found them in the papal encyclicals *Rerum novarum* (1891) of Leo XIII and *Quadragesimo anno* (1931) of Pius XI. These encyclicals called for a recognition of the dignity of workers, with just wages and enhanced working and living conditions for everyone, protection of the right to private property, defense of the poor, support for families, solidarity within society, and a recognition of the duty of the individual to promote the common good, making justice a personal responsibility and limiting the scope of government. If society were to follow the principles set forth in these encyclicals, Sheen believed the appeal of the Communist utopia would be undermined. Sheen would even go farther than the encyclicals to suggest that employers should adopt profit sharing and involve their employees in management decisions. If the country did not move forward on the basis of Christian ideals and beliefs, our social edifice will be built, as Pius XI wrote, "not on a rock but on shifting sand".[22] In World War II, Sheen saw the country as fighting not just for victory over the Axis powers, but for salvation. It was an epic battle for the soul of the nation and the West.[23]

Fulton Sheen preached the Gospel and, as the war's end was in sight, especially the Beatitudes. The world would need peacemakers. Sheen always made a distinction between individuals. There were

[20] Franco, *Bishop Fulton J. Sheen*, 153.

[21] Fulton J. Sheen, *God and Intelligence in Modern Philosophy* (Garden City, N.Y.: Image Books, 1958), 7.

[22] Pope Pius XI, encyclical letter *Quadragesimo anno* (The Fortieth Year) (May 15, 1931), no. 127, https://www.vatican.va/content/pius-xi/en/encyclicals/documents/hf_p-xi_enc _19310515_quadragesimo-anno.html.

[23] Riley, *Fulton J. Sheen*, 86.

people who did good things during the war and people who did wicked things during the war. There were good and bad people on both sides. Not all Germans were Nazis, and not all Russians were Communist revolutionaries, here or abroad. When the truth of the death camps became known to the West, the grossest of evils was exposed. Yet, Sheen spoke against hating the Germans or the Japanese (though in truth, Sheen had little to say about the war in the Pacific). The post-war trials and God would dispose of the evildoers. The rest would have to make peace with their own consciences and themselves. It would take Christian love and charity to rebuild a world torn apart by war. The United States and its allies had fought a just war; now was the time to build a just peace.

Because of Sheen's many popular books and pamphlets, not to mention his unnumbered talks and speeches on the radio and in person from pulpits and podiums, his was the face and voice of the American Catholic Church. His thesis was always that Christianity held the keys to personal and national flourishing. During the war, he did what he had been doing all along: He taught his classes at Catholic University, he met converts in weekly classes, and he wrote articles and books, preached, and traveled, although his European travel was curtailed. He railed against secularism, which he warned was like a barnacle on a ship, the ship of democracy— something that must be scraped off and removed lest it multiply and destroy the ship. In November 1947, the American Bishops issued "A Statement on Secularism" in which they identified secularism as "the practical exclusion of God from human thinking and living, [which] is at the root of the world's travails today... In exiling God from life, secularism had cleared the way for the acceptance of godless ideologies." They "begged Americans to be true to their historic Christian culture and to reject secularism, which offered no valid promise of better things for the country or for the world".[24] Sheen identified the barnacles of secularism as the belief in "progress, scientism, and materialism, but they also appeared as the ever-present danger of communism".[25]

[24] American Bishops, "Statement on Secularism", in Hugh Nolan, ed., *Pastoral Letters of the American Hierarchy, 1792–1970*, 2nd ed. (Washington, D.C.: United States Catholic Conference, 1984), 2:74.
[25] Sheen, *Crisis in Christendom*, 6, 16.

Winning the Soul of the Nation One Convert at a Time: Clare Boothe Luce

It was to Sheen that thousands of Americans turned when they considered joining the Catholic Church. He met prospective converts in groups in churches, hotel meeting rooms, and classrooms; these individuals would go, unlike Henry Ford, unnamed in the newspapers or periodicals of the day. He would also privately instruct individuals at a place mutually agreed upon, usually someone's home or Sheen's office or even his home. Sometimes these favored individual converts would become known to the public and sometimes not. The reasons for the private instruction in the faith were as varied as the individuals, but usually it was because the person desiring instruction was a public person, as was Louis Budenz.

One such very public person who sought out Msgr. Fulton J. Sheen for instruction was Clare Boothe Luce. She was a magazine editor, playwright, war correspondent, congresswoman, ambassador, advisor to presidents, and confidante of royalty. She may have thought of herself as self-made, but that cannot be entirely true, as she was wife of one of the richest and most influential men in America, Henry Robinson Luce, the owner of the publishing empire Time Inc. The first Mrs. Luce would say of her, "[Clare] had ... the face of an angel and the morals of a prostitute."[26]

She was indeed beautiful, and if her morals were loose, she learned them at her mother's knee. She and her older brother were the illegitimate children of Billy Boothe, a con man with some charm, little talent, and several aliases—and a mother, Ann Snyder, who believed the way to get ahead was to attach herself to various men, at some points in her life even prostituting herself. Ann Snyder had a series of "benefactors" who would pass through her life and that of her children. Clare recalled, "My childhood had been an unusually unhappy and bitter one."[27] Ann Snyder believed her key to the future was her children, particularly Clare. From an early age, Clare was tutored by her mother in manners and deportment and pushed

---

[26] Ralph G. Martin, *Henry and Clare: An Intimate Portrait of the Luces* (New York: Perigee Books, 1992), 145. Martin interviewed Lila Luce, the first Mrs. Henry Luce.

[27] Clare Boothe Luce, "Under the Fig Tree", in *The Road to Damascus*, ed. John A. O'Brien (Garden City, N.Y.: Doubleday, Image Books, 1949), 206.

onto the stage, first as an understudy to Mary Pickford, then as a little actress in the 1915 twelve-minute Thomas A. Edison film *The Heart of a Waif.* After the editing was done, Clare had exactly thirty seconds of film time. Acting was not to be her forte, but the theater beckoned nonetheless.

Life was about to get much better for Clare and her family when her mother was taken up by Joel Jacobs, a wealthy Jewish bachelor who wanted marriage and a ready-made family. Her mother refused Jacobs' marriage proposal for fear that a Jewish stepfather would dampen the prospects for the social success she had in mind for her children. She had passed herself off as the widow of a musician and ironically believed that a dead musician had a social status that was superior to that of the very respectable bachelor asking for her hand. However, Mr. Jacobs gave Clare's family the stability and security it had sadly lacked for so many years. He purchased a home for them in Sound Beach, Connecticut, and gave them enough money to purchase all the necessities and most of the luxuries they desired. He paid the children's tuition at elite boarding schools, where they mixed with the children of the wealthy.

When Clare graduated in 1919, her classmates wrote in her yearbook that she was their "prodigy and genius".[28] Joel Jacobs gifted her with a new roadster. Their tranquil life in Connecticut was upended by the quite unexpected appearance of Billy Boothe after a seven-year absence. The adults had some explaining to do, and Billy Boothe almost immediately disappeared again, to everyone's relief. Ann Snyder, for her part, forgot Boothe and, it seems, Joel Jacobs, as she was having an affair with a married doctor, Albert Austin, whom she would later marry.

Dr. Austin took mother and daughter to Europe, where the eighteen-year-old Clare had her first affair with a Russian émigré thirty years her senior. She returned home and decided to strike out on her own, with a New York apartment and a twenty-five-dollar-a-week job making paper flowers and frilled cups. Two weeks into the adventure, appendicitis brought her home to Connecticut. After one beau jilted her and another got married, Clare wrote to Ruth

Morton, "I'll marry for money—lots of it. Damned if I'll be a burden to my family much longer and damned if I'll ever love any mere man. Money! I need it and the power it brings, and someday you shall know of me as—famous."[29]

Another trip to Europe in search of a rich husband failed. But on the way home she met Alva Belmont, the wealthy president of the National Women's Party. Mrs. Belmont introduced her to politics and took her to the 1923 NWP convention in Seneca Falls. Clare thought it dull but did adopt Mrs. Belmont's motto, "Failure is Impossible."[30] Fortuitously, Clare Boothe was soon introduced to the forty-three-year-old George Brokaw, one of New York's most eligible and wealthy bachelors. A wedding was brought to pass by Ann Snyder and Brokaw's mother, who wished to see her son settled at long last. The couple lived with his mother in her enormous Loire Valley–inspired mansion with fourteen servants. The newlyweds toured Europe, summered in Newport, and attended all the fancy-dress parties and charitable events Manhattan had to offer. Clare, like Fulton Sheen, hired a clipping service to keep track of her growing public image.

While Clare enjoyed the high life, her marriage was beginning to pall. Brokaw was an alcoholic. His two hobbies were golf and drinking. "He was better known as a first-rate golfer, bon vivant, and clubman", wrote biographer Silvia Jukes Morris,[31] but he was also a mean, abusive drunk. Their only child, Ann Clare, was born on August 22, 1924. There were three miscarriages, possibly due to regular beatings by Brokaw. Clare wanted to leave the marriage, but her mother encouraged her to stay in hopes that Brokaw would die of his degeneracy and leave her a wealthy widow. Of course, Clare was helping to support her mother's extravagances, her grandmother's needs, and her brother's fecklessness. Even Billy Boothe had his hand held out to Clare, only to be rebuffed and die penniless and unlamented. Exhausted by it all, Clare sought help in psychiatry, which she found useless—nothing but quackery. In May of 1929, Clare secured a Reno divorce, which settled on her a personal $425,000 trust fund, an income of $26,000 a year,

---

[29] Morris, *Rage*, 99. Clare Boothe Luce to Ruth B. Morton, November 18, 1921 (Library of Congress Manuscript Division).

[30] Morris, *Rage*, 222.

[31] Ibid., 116.

and the proviso that Brokaw would support their daughter, Ann, and make her his heir. In a letter to a friend Clare said of herself, "I may have married for money, but I certainly didn't divorce for it."[32]

At a dinner party, the newly divorced Clare Brokaw met Condé Nast, the publisher of *Vogue* and *Vanity Fair*, and decided to apply to him for a job. The story of her first job at *Vogue* is legendary. Nast got her an interview with the magazine's editor, who told Clare that she would get back to her. When, after several weeks, she had heard nothing from *Vogue*, Clare took herself up to the office, found an empty desk, and set herself up. When the editor returned from her vacation she assumed Nast had hired [Clare]. He, in turn, thought she had. The new *Vogue* hire had a flair for words and an amazing work ethic unexpected in a society divorcée. She progressed rapidly from writing captions to writing columns. She also attached herself to the society editor, who mentored her and gave her fashion guidance. Clare had money but not yet the taste to dress well. Eventually, she would become a fashion icon.

Down the hall from the *Vogue* offices were the offices of *Vanity Fair*, Condé Nast's flagship magazine since its founding in 1913. *Vanity Fair* boasted the day's best writers and artists. Within a few months of working at *Vogue*, Clare got herself an interview with the editor of *Vanity Fair* and presented him with one hundred suggestions for articles in his magazine. He was impressed and immediately turned her over to his managing editor, Donald Freeman. Freeman became her mentor and lover. He advised her to drop the Brokaw name and introduced her to New York's literati, first via the Algonquin Round Table, where she met Haywood Broun—then ten years away from his conversion to Catholicism—and Dorothy Parker. The acerbic Parker took a dislike to the younger and prettier Clare Boothe, who beat a strategic retreat from the Algonquin. Within a year of joining *Vanity Fair*, she became its assistant editor. Her preferred writing style was satirical, and she churned out copy prodigiously. She enjoyed satirizing the New York–Newport set, and it became a game for readers to try to guess the identity of the "stuffed shirts" she lampooned. *Stuffed Shirts* became the title to her first book, a collection of her *Vanity Fair* articles. The book was largely a financial failure,

---

[32] Quoted in Martin, *Henry and Clare*, 83.

so she decided to break with Freeman to devote her extracurricular activities to writing plays.

Clare met Bernard Baruch, the wealthy, well-connected advisor to presidents and presidential campaigns. He was thirty-three years her senior and completely smitten by her and she by him. Marriage was out of the question, and over their time together, each would engage in affairs with others. Baruch introduced her to party politics as they attended the 1932 Democratic Convention in Chicago that nominated Franklin Roosevelt. Even as Clare continued at *Vogue*, now newly promoted to managing editor, Baruch tutored her in politics, a field to which she found herself drawn for the possibilities it held for improving the common good. After only sixteen months at her new position, which at one time would have been her dream job, she resigned. She published a play, *Abide with Me*, to faint praise and financial failure. Even *Time* magazine panned it, and by then she was engaged to marry its publisher, Henry Luce. She also had rhinoplasty to improve an already-lovely nose.

Henry Luce was born in China to Presbyterian missionary parents, ensuring that he would always be the scholarship boy at his schools, Hotchkiss and Yale, sweeping floors and serving at table. Instead of feeling daunted by the wealth of his fellow students, he determined to join them in their success. He became an outstanding student. Just three years out of Yale, Luce and his friend Briton Hadden launched *Time*: volume I, number 1, was printed in March of 1923. By the time Luce was thirty years old, he was a millionaire. Hadden died at the age of thirty-one, and Luce had the intuition to buy out Hadden's share in Time Inc., putting Luce on the road to becoming one of the wealthiest and most significant men in America. He was married with two sons when he met Clare Boothe at a birthday party given by Elsa Maxwell for the composer Cole Porter. Porter also was celebrating the opening of his smash hit on Broadway, *Anything Goes*. Luce would say that Clare gave him a *"coup de foudre"*, an overwhelming case of love at first sight.[33] He sent his wife home from the party and stayed to talk with Clare Boothe. He then pursued her day and night around New York, down to Florida, across to Cuba, and on to Europe until she agreed to marry him. For Clare, at last here was a man she could admire, who intellectually challenged her, who was extremely rich, and who was a mere three years older than she. They married in Connecticut at a congregational church with only four guests present. His family disapproved of the marriage.

Theirs was a troubled marriage from the beginning, although it was punctuated by many happy moments in their thirty-two years together. They were two strong-willed, independent individuals who maintained very different ideas about society, morality, and even the meaning of life. Together, Henry and Clare were the power couple in the United States. Presidents and senators read *Time* to know what was going on in the world, and so did U.S. allies and enemies abroad. Luce added to Time Inc.'s empire with *Fortune, Sports Illustrated*, and—Clare's brainchild—*Life*. For Clare, the years with Henry Luce were her most successful and prolific as an artist and politician. She wrote several plays, including her most successful Broadway hit, *The Women*.

The Women had an all-female cast. Its twelve stage settings were designed by Jo Mielziner, a Sheen convert who would later design the set for Sheen's television program, *Life Is Worth Living*. *The Women* toured the United States and eighteen other countries and was translated into ten languages. Its first run on Broadway was for a year and a half. The play became a popular film in 1939, starring Norma Shearer, Joan Crawford, and Rosalind Russell. It was named one of the best pictures of the year, later to be remade in 2008 with Meg Ryan, Annette Bening, and Bette Midler.

Despite her successes, Clare was often unsettled, restless, and anxious. Her mother was killed in a car accident, leaving Clare feeling abandoned first by her father and then by her mother. Notwithstanding her mother's manipulation in her life, mother and daughter had been quite close. Her death left Clare at loose ends. She would begin a play only to tear it up. She and Henry moved residences. Their homes were in Manhattan, Connecticut, and South Carolina, where Henry bought her a large plantation near Bernard Baruch's estate. Relaxing, writing, and entertaining did not fulfill her. Henry gave her an opportunity for adventure and value as a war correspondent when he sent her to Europe in the spring of 1940. In Europe, she met Pope Pius XII and then managed to make it to the Maginot Line in France, becoming the first female correspondent to get there. In May she was in the blitzkrieg bombing of the Hague. By then Henry had joined her, and the two rode out on one of the last trains to leave for Paris. Not long after she arrived, with Henry having left Europe to oversee *Time*'s war reporting, the concierge asked Clare Boothe to check out of the Ritz Hotel because the Germans were coming. When asked how he knew, the concierge replied, "Because they have reservations."[34] She left Paris four days ahead of the German entrance into the city. Once home, she published her photo-journalistic book, *Europe in the Spring*, dedicating it to "H.R.L. who understood why I wanted to go".[35] Most of the time the Luces understood one another very well. Each wanted to leave a positive mark on society. Both felt that the United States needed to join the war sooner rather than later, and, to that end, they campaigned for a strong America and American war preparedness. Clare gave most of the speeches, as Harry had a debilitating stutter. The pair traveled to China, with Clare returning by way of the war-torn areas of the Orient and the Pacific, taking pictures and creating copy for *Life*.

Back in the States, Clare was approached to run for the U.S. Senate as a representative from Connecticut. She had name recognition, glamour, and money enough to win two terms in the House of Representatives (1942–1946). She found the work and the people there tedious, pompous, and lazy—and besides, she missed her husband and New York. After Eleanor Roosevelt, Clare Boothe Luce was the most admired woman in America. But she was bored, and the worst was yet to come.

Her daughter, Ann Brokaw, had been largely ignored by her mother, who thought she was protecting Ann from the public gaze by sending her to boarding schools and keeping her well behind the scenes. Certainly they got together for holidays and vacations. Henry particularly enjoyed having a daughter, and the two were quite close. In early January of 1944, mother and daughter met in California for one of their periodic holidays together. Ann was then at Stanford. One afternoon in San Francisco, Ann asked that they step into Old Saint Mary's Catholic Church, where they stayed for Mass before going back to the hotel to eat. The following morning, having said good-bye the night

---

[34] Morris, *Rage*, 383.
[35] Clare Boothe Luce, *Europe in the Spring* (New York: Alfred A. Knopf, 1940), v.

before, Ann left her sleeping mother to drive down to Stanford with a friend. She never arrived. A few blocks from campus, their car was hit by another, and Ann was thrown from the spinning car and pinned against a tree. Ann died at the scene, and Clare woke up to the worst news a mother could ever receive. Clare wanted no one about her and proceeded down the street to Old Saint Mary's once again. The only prayer she could think of was the Our Father. Henry Luce flew to his wife's side, and the Time Inc. people took care of all the details. Clare buried her daughter on the estate in South Carolina, where the family had pleasant memories. According to Wilfrid Sheed, Ann seemed to be her mother's one regret: that she had not spent more time with Ann,[36] that they had never been close, that she had missed so many of Ann's important events, and that she would never see Ann married and a mother. Clare was devastated.

The very public Clare Luce was getting ready to run for her second term at the time of Ann's death. She wanted to withdraw from the race, but, on the other hand, she knew Ann would have expected her to go forward. It was a sacrifice Clare made for her daughter. Clare had written to a friend, "I hate Washington. I don't like being in Congress ... and the way it circumscribes my life. After two short months of it I know that power and office are two things I don't want.... Frankly, my health is wretched. I am abnormally tired and feel like chucking it all and going off to a sandy beach somewhere."[37] She felt like she meant it, but she did not really. She had more to give, but she was incredibly tired, especially after Ann's death. Grief can do that to people.

What gave Clare energy and focus was the coming end to the war. Like Sheen, Clare Luce was concerned about winning the peace to come. Back in Europe on a congressional tour, she observed American GIs kneeling for a Catholic Mass in a snow-covered field. It was a scene that moved her. She said a quick prayer for them and for herself. The 1944 Associated Press' Woman of the Year, Clare Boothe Luce was humbled by what she saw in that field. On a second congressional tour a few months later, Pope Pius XII told her that he believed "American women would be a great influence for world

---

[36] Wilfrid Sheed, *Clare Boothe Luce* (New York: Berkley Books, 1982), 102.

[37] Clare Boothe Luce, letter to Charles Willoughby, March 15, 1943, Clare Boothe Luce Papers, Library of Congress, Manuscript Division.

peace after the war".[38] She was appalled by what she saw with the U.S. Army when it liberated the Buchenwald concentration camp. World peace became one of her passions. She recognized that international Communism posed a great threat to the post-war peace. Anti-Communism and non-nuclear proliferation were causes she shared with Fulton Sheen.

In the autumn of 1945, Clare Boothe Luce was alone in a hotel room in the depths of a great depression. She was crying and trying to pray, but she had no words other than the Our Father. She was distressed to the point of suicide, a definitive act that four of her close friends had taken, all of whom, according to Sylvia Morris, "had sought solace in work and sex", as had Clare.[39] She reflected later, "I tasted at long last the real meaning of meaninglessness."[40] Clare's creative career seemed over. Her mother, her daughter, and Joel Jacobs had all died, and her marriage was a sham. She and Henry had grown apart and gone their separate ways socially and romantically. Henry was having a serious affair and talked of divorce. Of course they were still a powerful couple when they presented a united front to the rest of the world, but it was all a facade. At wits' end and grasping at straws, she called a Catholic priest from Cincinnati who had told her that "God and love are part of the soul."[41] It was two in the morning when she called to say her mind was greatly troubled. His response was startling: "We know. This is the call we have been praying for."[42] Realizing she was an intellectual in spiritual torment, the priest told her he would have Msgr. Fulton J. Sheen call on her.

Msgr. Sheen invited her to dinner at his apartment and set the ground rules: no discussion of religion over dinner, and then he would talk for five minutes, and she could take all the time she needed to ask him questions. Almost immediately, Sheen talked of the goodness of God, upon which she exploded, "If God is good, why did he take my daughter?" Sheen replied, "Perhaps it was in order that you might become a believer. In order that you might discover God's truth.

[38] Sylvia Jukes Morris, *The Price of Fame* (New York: Random House, 2014), 124, audience with Pope Pius XII, March 29, 1944.
[39] Morris, *Price*, 148.
[40] Lorene Hanley Duquin, *A Century of Catholic Converts* (Huntington, Ind.: Our Sunday Visitor, 2003), 148.
[41] Martin, *Henry and Clare*, 258; see also Morris, *Price of Fame*, 146–49.
[42] Martin, *Henry and Clare*, 258.

Maybe your daughter is buying your faith with her life.... Ann's death was the purchase price of your soul."[43] With this exchange, Clare Luce recognized Sheen as the right catechist for her, and he knew she would be a good candidate for conversion. The two would meet frequently for up to four hours at a time. He gave her hundreds of hours. He would not allow an easy leap of faith; he knew that she had to be convicted. Sheen would say of Clare, "No man could go to Clare and argue her into the faith. Heaven had to knock her over."[44]

As a teenager, Clare had had what she believed was a mystical experience. She had felt the sensation of being utterly alone, and then what she described as "Something was." "My soul was cleft clean by it.... My whole nature was adrift in this immense joy."[45] After many hours with Fulton Sheen, Luce came to recognize that the "Something was" was Jesus Christ. Amid her grief over Ann, she envied those whose faith gave them purpose and consolation; she envied those soldiers kneeling for Mass in the snow before their next battle. She felt her own sinfulness and feared for her afterlife. She was also hoping to honor her marriage with Henry. But Henry Luce, his old Presbyterian anti-Catholicism coming to the fore, was having none of Clare's interest in Catholicism and was opposed to her conversion. He would be conspicuously absent at her reception into the Church.

Before her First Communion, she would have to go to confession. Sheen asked Archbishop—soon to be Cardinal—Spellman to be her confessor.[46] Clare Boothe Luce presented a bit of a problem for the Church. She was a divorced woman living with a divorced man.[47] How could the Catholic Church countenance such a scandal? It would be said that there was one standard for the glamourous and wealthy and another for the lowly and poor. Spellman said with characteristic bluster, "To hell with public opinion." The truth of Henry and Clare's relationship was, as her biographer Wilfrid Sheed writes, that they "had not lived together connubially for many

---

[43] Ibid., 259.

[44] Stephen Shadegg, *Clare Boothe Luce: A Biography* (New York: Simon & Schuster, 1970), 211, from his interview with Sheen twenty-one years after Clare's conversion.

[45] Luce, "Fig Tree", 205.

[46] Spellman became a cardinal two days after Clare's reception into the Church.

[47] George Brokaw had died, so the Church viewed Clare as a widow; but because the Church does not recognize divorce, Henry was still considered married to the first Mrs. Luce, making Clare and Henry's relationship an adulterous union.

years before the conversion".[48] The length of time of their marital estrangement is open for debate, but it seems to have occurred early in the marriage.

Quite naturally there was speculation as to why Clare Boothe Luce would embrace the Catholic faith. Some thought it some sort of gimmick on her part to enhance her image—"another chic move by that icy blonde", as Sheed writes.[49] Or perhaps to tie Henry to their marriage. Clare wrote a three-part series for *McCall's* called "The 'Real' Reason" explaining herself. "What Catholics believe is precisely why *I* became a Catholic. . . . It seemed to me to be the objective truth."[50] She found that she believed what the Catholic Church taught about Christ. If one is honest, on finding the truth, one is obliged to assent to it with both intellect and will. Clare may have practiced duplicity with others, but she was honest with herself and became a Catholic. She did not become perfect, but her conversion changed her in ways that were obvious to those who knew her. A friend wrote about her, "Clare always had the capability of being great. There was her wonderful brain, her beauty, and her real desire to serve her country and all the peoples of the world. But there was something lacking. Her conversion to Catholicism had given her the humility, the gentleness, and the warmth to love individual people, as opposed to a sense of duty to humanity. These were the things she needed to make her the really great woman she is."[51] The actress Loretta Young later recalled that Luce completely changed. "She remained strong, but in a positive way. I couldn't believe she was the same woman after her conversion."[52]

Some would ask her if she would have become a Catholic had it not been for Fulton Sheen. To this she answered, "Of course. God intended me to be a Catholic or he would not have sent me to Fr. Sheen. . . . For this brilliant teacher, this good and gifted professor of Catholic philosophy, I thank God."[53] Of Clare, Fulton Sheen would say, "Never in my life have I been privileged to instruct anyone who

[48] Sheed, *Clare Boothe Luce*, 113.

[49] Ibid., 111.

[50] Clare Boothe Luce, "The 'Real' Reason", Part One, *McCall's*, February 1946, 117.

[51] Reeves, *America's Bishop*, 177

[52] Originally from an interview with Loretta Young by Thomas Reeves, quoted in *America's Bishop*, 177.

[53] Clare Boothe Luce, "The 'Real' Reason", Part Three, *McCall's*, April 1947, 85.

was as brilliant and who was so scintillating in conversation as Mrs. Luce. She has a mind like a rapier."[54]

Henry and Clare never divorced. Their happiest time together may have been during her tenure as ambassador to Italy under President Eisenhower—she was the first woman to head a major embassy (1953–56). Henry was ever at her side. When she was exhausted, he would take her on long yacht cruises or tours to the capitals of Europe. She took her assignment seriously and worked long hours. Ambassador Luce managed to bring about a diplomatic coup by helping Italy and Yugoslavia solve a territorial dispute and avoid war.

Conversion to Catholicism did not cure Clare's sense of abandonment, nor did it brush away her bouts of depression. Her literary and political achievements were behind her; her beauty was waning. She and Henry had a complicated relationship. They could not live together and they could not live apart. As they both aged, their marriage settled into a more comfortable pattern. Henry would even accompany her to Mass. He supported her at Catholic events and in various fundraising efforts. She still dabbled in politics as an advisor to every subsequent president during her lifetime except Jimmy Carter. She introduced Henry Kissinger to Richard Nixon. Nonetheless, she was on the periphery of events. Her restlessness never left her, and she and Henry changed homes frequently. They donated their seven-thousand-acre South Carolina estate to the Trappist monks. Her mother and daughter were buried there. Henry was buried on the estate in 1967; Clare would join him in death twenty years later, perpetually prayed for by the monks.

Bigger Pastures, More Sheep

Clare Boothe Luce was perhaps the brightest star in the firmament of Fulton Sheen's converts. At the time of Clare's conversion, Msgr. Fulton Sheen was seeing classes of up to one hundred converts in both New York and Washington, while teaching his Catholic University graduate students and preparing his weekly radio broadcasts. Fulton Sheen was driven to bring people into the Church: "To be

[54] Sheen, *Treasure*, 264.

at peace I must find more sheep for His green pastures."[55] Almost everything Sheen did was to that end. He had been speaking to millions of Americans across the country since 1930 on the radio's *Catholic Hour* and reaping many converts. In 1948 Cardinal Spellman gave Msgr. Sheen the opportunity to broaden his audience by joining the cardinal's entourage on an extensive trip across the Pacific and around Asia, where there were millions more to hear the Gospel and heed the call to conversion.

Cardinal Spellman was the national president of the Society for the Propagation of the Faith and the military vicar for the United States Armed Forces. In those capacities, he was planning to visit military bases and tour the mission territories of the Far East. Despite Sheen's initial reaction to the Cardinal's elevation, they had become friends and worked closely together. Spellman particularly appreciated Sheen's oratorical skills and was "grooming the monsignor 'for higher things'".[56] On the trip, Spellman would do the politicking and Sheen would do the sermonizing and speechmaking, a division of labor that suited the considerable skills of each. It was a trip that would change Fulton Sheen and prepare him for the next stage of his career.

[55] Reeves, *America's Bishop*, 315, quoting a letter from Fulton J. Sheen to Clare Boothe Luce, undated, box 43, Clare Boothe Luce Papers, Library of Congress, Manuscript Division.

[56] Robert J. Gannon, *The Cardinal Spellman Story* (Garden City, N.Y.: Doubleday, 1962), 367–68.

5

Immediately after the War

Sheen Joins the World Stage

Msgr. Fulton Sheen's 1948 trip with Francis Cardinal Spellman took fifty-two days, during which he gave over two hundred speeches, lectures, and sermons. He spoke to tens of thousands at a time, several times a day, with his talks often recorded for later broadcasting, enlarging his audience and influence considerably. After a Holy Hour in Melbourne in which he was joined by the local cardinal, forty bishops, 250 priests, and thousands of people standing outside in the streets, Sheen said he had never seen anything like it. "After the Hour it took me an hour and a half to get through the crowds even with cops and motorcycle policemen. I never heard so many 'God bless yous' in my life."[1] However, some local Protestant clergy were less than enthusiastic about Sheen and thought he was the greatest menace to ever visit Australia. When Spellman's party finally landed in Los Angeles, Sheen wrote "Thank God" in his diary.[2] While the trip must have been exhausting and the homecoming welcome, it was an experience that left Fulton Sheen with a great appreciation for the universality of the Catholic Church and its appeal to those of very different backgrounds than his own American and European perspectives. He recorded in his diary, "A visit like ours ... enlarges a point of view, develops sympathy for others, and makes one mission-minded."[3] Kathleen Riley writes of the impact the Asia trip had on

---

[1] Fulton J., Sheen, Travel Diary, May 4, 1948, quoted in Thomas C. Reeves, *America's Bishop: The Life and Times of Fulton J. Sheen* (San Francisco: Encounter Books, 2001), 189–90.

[2] Reeves, *America's Bishop*, 196.

[3] Kathleen L. Riley, *Fulton J. Sheen: An American Catholic Response to the Twentieth Century* (New York: Alba House, 2004), 242.

94

Fulton Sheen: "In terms of his personal awakening to the realities of life around the world, and the long-lasting effects of the education he gained on these trips, these experiences had a genuine formative influence on his life.... It would forever change his outlook.... It was not the Gospel that changed, but Sheen's broadened understanding of its implications."[4]

Across the Pacific and the Far East, Fulton Sheen was always on the lookout to help an individual in need. In Tasmania a woman wrote to him that her husband had been away from the Church for forty years. So, Sheen telephoned the woman and asked her to send her husband to him at his hotel. As soon as the man arrived, Sheen asked him to kneel down for confession. The man was stunned but complied. "Without further ado he made a very good confession. He was almost dancing when he went out.... When the Holy Spirit stirs a soul there is very often a greater desire to return [to the Faith] than we realize."[5]

In the Philippines, Sheen traveled several hours out of Manila to a leper colony. It was a visit that required a great deal of courage on Sheen's part, because the ravages Hansen's disease wreaked on its victims left them horribly disfigured, and Sheen, who loved beauty, was repulsed by what he initially encountered there and feared its contagion. At first, he found himself dropping rosaries into the often fingerless hands from high above. It then came to him that he was seeing the face of Christ as he looked at the lepers as they came to him for a blessing. It was a graced moment for him, for he then took their hands in his as he blessed them and passed out rosaries. Reeves tells us, that from that time, "all the fear left him."[6] Years later he would all but adopt Paul Scott, a young man who had suffered from leprosy that left him disfigured and crippled. Feeling miserable and friendless, Scott turned to Sheen, who took him into his care, finding and furnishing an apartment for him and inviting him to dinner, sometimes twice a week. Sheen's biographer D.P. Noonan wrote, "Because it was difficult for Paul to use his hands, the Bishop cut the meat for him."[7] Paul Scott would be one of Sheen's many unsung converts. When Sheen

[4] Ibid., 239.

[5] Fulton J. Sheen, *Treasure in Clay: The Autobiography of Fulton J. Sheen* (Garden City, N.Y.: Doubleday Press, 1980), 134.

[6] Reeves, *America's Bishop*, 193.

[7] D.P. Noonan, *The Passion of Fulton Sheen* (New York: Dodd, Mead & Company, 1972), 5.

would give public talks, Paul Scott would sit in the front row. Sheen's friendship with him, and his conversion, might not have been possible if Sheen had not had that experience at the leprosarium on his trip across Asia with Cardinal Spellman.[8]

The trip to Asia was a time of great accord between Cardinal Spellman and Fulton Sheen. Spellman graciously said of Sheen, "I want to say a word about Msgr. Sheen who in America is doing more than any Cardinal, any Archbishop, or any Bishop to make the faith known and loved. He is one of the truly apostolic souls of our time. He has the ear of Catholics and he has the ear of non-Catholics and I rejoice to know that the Australians love him as much as we do. I brought him on this trip to give him some recognition and to pay a debt, but I find that I have only increased the debt, if there be such a thing."[9] Sheen would return the compliments, writing in his diary about Spellman, "He is a wonderful man! God bless him." He saw no "spark of jealousy" in the cardinal.[10] Clearly, though, Sheen was not looking deeply enough. The cardinal occasionally took exception to the clever and charismatic monsignor he had brought along. After one incident when Spellman feared that Sheen had outshone him, Spellman confided to a friend in a letter, "Not wishing to engage in any debates with the redoubtable Monsignor, I decided not to continue the discussion."[11]

In Japan, Spellman's delegation met with the emperor, General Douglas MacArthur, and General Charles Willoughby, a fond friend and former lover of Clare Boothe Luce. Entertaining them at dinner, General MacArthur opined that he wished he had eight hundred Catholic missionaries in Japan for every one then there. MacArthur feared Communism in the post-war world. "The world struggle", MacArthur told the visiting Catholics at his table, "is not economic nor political but religious and Theological. It is either for God or atheism."[12] Sheen was impressed with MacArthur's commanding presence, but was totally unimpressed by the emperor, complaining that

[8] Ibid.

[9] Sheen, *Treasure*, 135–36.

[10] Sheen, Travel Diary, May 14, 1948, quoted in Reeves, *America's Bishop*, 191.

[11] Robert J. Gannon, *The Cardinal Spellman Story* (Garden City, N.Y.: Doubleday, 1962), 369.

[12] Sheen, Travel Diary, June 8, 1948, quoted in Reeves, *America's Bishop*, 194.

the emperor did not sit on a throne, but in a nondescript chair. Of the emperor, Sheen wrote, "If he is a god, I am an atheist."[13] In China they met with the Luces' friends, Madame and Generalissimo Chiang Kai-shek. Madame Chiang Kai-shek, though a Christian, appeared uninterested in Catholicism, much to Sheen's disappointment. What interested Sheen in China was Eastern philosophy, particularly the idea of yin and yang. He was unfamiliar with the terms but felt that they were analogous to the various strains of Western dualism. He could see a way forward in proselytizing in Asia: "It struck me during the trip that it might be shortsightedness on our part to impose the Aristotelian philosophy on the Eastern mind; that it would have been better to have gathered up the good religious aspiration of the Eastern people in the natural religions to bring them to Revelation. God is not proven to them; He is, rather, 'given.' Confucius is relatively just as good for some minds as Aristotle is for others."[14] Sheen's tour of the Pacific and Asia broadened him in ways he might not have realized when he, as a European-trained philosopher of note, could consider Confucius as a starting place for conversion to the Catholic Church.

Sheen and the Furious Psychoanalysts

His extended trip out of the country came at a good time for Sheen, as he had previously stirred up a hornets' nest by taking on Freudian psychoanalysis as anti-God, scientifically unsound, and ultimately unhelpful to suffering individuals. The furor following a sermon, "Psychoanalysis and Confession", he gave at Saint Patrick's Cathedral on March 9, 1947, was predictably immediate. Reeves wrote, "According to a *New York Times* story, Sheen said that psychoanalysis was 'a form of escapism' that failed to relieve 'the unresolved sense of guilt of sin' from which 'most people who consult psychoanalysts are suffering.'"[15] Sheen recommended the Sacrament of Confession, as he believed it was sin that was alienating individuals from their true

---

[13] Sheen Travel Diary, June 9, 1948, quoted in Reeves, *America's Bishop*, 195.
[14] Sheen, *Treasure*, 146.
[15] Reeves, *America's Bishop*, 198.

selves as children of God, from their friends and neighbors because of their unrelieved shame, and from God for the offense against Him. Only the absolution that comes from a sincere sacramental confession could, according to Sheen, restore peace of soul to the repentant sinner. He charged Freudians with "materialism, hedonism, infantilism, and eroticism". He noticed that the idea of transference of affection to the analyst seemed to work well "when the patient is a young and very beautiful woman. It is never found to work among the ugly or the poor", as "most psychoanalysts cater only to the rich."[16] While Sheen was only attacking Freudian psychoanalysis, his remarks were taken to be an attack on all psychology and psychiatry.

Prominent psychiatrists publicly denounced him in letters to the *New York Times* and resigned their positions at various Catholic hospitals. His views were labeled false and foolish, and Sheen was belittled as an enemy of true science. Msgr. Sheen fought back in his own letter to the *Times*, complaining that he was misquoted and words were taken out of context. He reiterated his support of non-Freudian psychiatry as a valid science. He took exception to Freud's atheism and his emphasis on sex, to the denigration of the whole person. A person is more than his emotions; emotions are a symptom, not a cause, of anxiety and distress. Discounting true mental illness that has organic causes and that is treated by psychiatrists and other medical doctors, Freudian psychoanalysis with its atheism denies the reality of sin and the damage that sin can do to the individual. Sheen quoted Freud: "The mask has fallen; it [psychoanalysis] leads to a denial of God and of an ethical ideal."[17] Sheen identified the suffering brought on by the loss of God and of any absolute ethical ideal as spiritual and therefore requiring spiritual remedies. He saw denial of guilt as the root flaw in Freudianism. To deny sin is to deny the consequential guilt attendant to sin. To sin is to act with full knowledge and free consent contrary to God's will, one's conscience, and right reason. It ruptures communion with God. Depending on the gravity of the matter, the rupture with God may be permanent unless remedied appropriately.

[16] "Sheen Denounces Psychoanalysis; He Recommends Confession of Sin as 'Key to Happiness of the Modern World'", *New York Times*, March 10, 2947, quoted in Reeves, *America's Bishop*, 198.
[17] Sigmund Freud, *The Future of an Illusion* (New York: Horace Liveright, 1928), 64.

The repression of sin and guilt can lead to mental distress and even physical impairment or illness. It requires a spiritual resolution found only in the confessional. To prepare for the confessional, one preforms an examination of conscience; in psychoanalysis, it is the subconscious that is examined in an effort to find inner peace. Inner peace, according to Sheen, can only be found in returning to God and following his commandments. God never gives up on the sinner; it is the sinner who gives up on God or who never knew God in the first place. In a thoroughgoing secular and materialistic society, many people do not even recognize what it is they are missing. But, often in recognizing that something is missing in their Thoreauvian lives "of quiet desperation", individuals are drawn to explore religion, as did Clare Boothe Luce.[18]

Luce described her journey to Catholicism as first going through liberalism, where one determines the boundaries of his own moral behavior. When behavior unfettered by any type of external moral authority did not satisfy her, she sought solace in psychoanalysis, thinking she was neurotic. From the perspective of a new convert to Catholicism, she wrote: "My psychoanalyst was a soul-quack. I do not hold it against him now. For he was honestly trying to get along without God. It was our misfortune that we happened for a number of months to get lost together in the godless and atavistic underbrush of Freudianism."[19]

Luce would go on to say that not many people find God on the analyst's couch, but that is whom they are seeking. None of the "isms" answered the questions Luce was asking. It was only in finally finding God in the Catholic Church that Clare Boothe Luce felt she had the answer to questions about the meaning and purpose of life and death. It is not clear how much Luce's experience with psychoanalysis influenced Fulton Sheen, but they were certainly in accord in condemning it.

One of Sheen's most popular books, *Peace of Soul*, came out in 1949. In it he clarified his support for psychiatry and psychology as necessary and useful, while reiterating his disdain for Freudian psychoanalysis.

---

[18] Henry David Thoreau, "Walden", in *A Week on the Concord and Merrimack Rivers; Walden, or Life in the Woods; The Maine Woods; Cape Cod* (New York: Library of America, 1985), 329.

[19] Clare Boothe Luce, "The 'Real Reason'", Part Two, *McCall's*, March 1947, 16.

The opening paragraph is stark: "Unless souls are saved, nothing is saved; there can be no world peace unless there is soul peace. World wars are only projections of the conflicts waged inside the souls of modern men, for nothing happens in the external world that has not first happened within a soul."[20] To start with modern man as he is found in the post-war atomic bomb world, Sheen offers an understanding of sin as alienating man from God, self, and neighbor. Man needs to be integrated back into the proper relationship with Jesus, the crucified and risen Lord who died for each individual in all his sinfulness, and only then will the individual find the peace of soul that was divinely intended to be his. One can know God by never having lost him, or by finding him after losing him. One finds God through repentance, absolution, and self-submission.

It is through the embodied participation in the Sacrament of Reconciliation (Confession) that one hears the priest proclaim the words of absolution, bringing freedom and relief to the penitent: "God, the Father of mercies, through the death and resurrection of his Son has reconciled the world to himself and sent the Holy Spirit among us for the forgiveness of sins; through the ministry of the Church may God give you pardon and peace, and I absolve you from your sins in the name of the Father, and of the Son, and of the Holy Spirit."[21] A sincere confession begins with true contrition for one's sins and a firm commitment to sin no more and even to avoid the near occasion of sin. The priest usually assigns a penance to be performed in recompense for one's sins and in order to be fully reconciled to God. Once reconciled to God, one can begin to establish the proper relationships with others who have been harmed by the sins, and, more importantly, the individual can become known to himself as beloved of God. After the words of absolution have been pronounced, the priest blesses the individual: "The Lord has freed you from your sins. Go in peace."[22] "God give you pardon and peace" and "Go in peace" are not the words a Freudian psychoanalyst could ever say, but they are the exact words the tortured soul needs to hear. He wrote, "A sinner,

[20] Fulton J. Sheen, *Peace of Soul* (New York: Whittlesey House, 1949), 1.

[21] International Commission on English in the Liturgy (ICEL), *The Rites of the Catholic Church as Revised by the Second Vatican Ecumenical Council* (New York: Pueblo Publishing, 1976), 362–63.

[22] Ibid., 363.

unrepentant, cannot love God any more than a man on dry land can swim; but as soon as he takes his errant energies to God and asks for their redirection, he will become happy, as he was never happy before. It is not the wrong things one had already done which keep one from God; it is persistence in that wrong.... The secret of peace of soul is to combine detachment from evil with attachment to God, to abandon egoism as the ruling, determining element in our lives and to substitute Our Divine Lord as the regent of our actions."[23] Sheen's *Peace of Soul* sold thousands of copies. In post-war America, people were hungry for peace in the world and peace for themselves.

Hell's Kitchen and Carnegie Hall: Kitty and Fritz Kreisler

A good confession can change somebody's life in unexpected ways. When Msgr. Sheen was working in a parish in New York City's Hell's Kitchen, he was approached by two little girls who came to him because "Kitty is sick." Kitty was apparently seriously ill, so Sheen rushed out with the Viaticum and holy oils to confer on Kitty what are often called the "last rites". He found Kitty in a filthy, run-down tenement slum apartment. He could see that she was quite sick, so he inquired about her physical condition and also about her spiritual health. Kitty appeared to be near death. She protested that she could not make a confession because "I am the worst girl in the city of New York." Sheen told her, "You are not the worst girl in the city of New York; the worst girl in the city of New York says that she is the best girl in the city of New York." He found that he had confused her with his paradox, so he begged her to give her confession. After he cajoled her for over half an hour, she reluctantly agreed to give him her confession, which she did before falling unconscious. From her mother and a friend who were on hand, Sheen learned that Kitty's husband would beat her if she did not bring home enough money from walking the streets. Her husband was also administering poison to her that was beginning to affect her brain. When Kitty regained consciousness, Sheen told her, "Kitty, you are back in the world." She replied, "Yes, in order to prove that I can be good."

[23] Sheen, *Peace of Soul*, 192–93.

Sheen wrote, "From then on she worked to help the same people she had been with on the streets." At Saturday confessions, many came to him telling him that Kitty had sent them. One time she brought a girl to him who had committed murder so Sheen could hear her confession. Kitty's apostolate was brought about through her confession and reconciliation with God. She could then be the "good girl" she had always wanted to be, and she could help others on their way to their own encounter with the mercy of God.[24] Kitty gained peace of soul and found her Christian vocation in helping others. Other conversions were not as dramatic as Kitty's.

One evening, Msgr. Sheen went to a fancy Manhattan apartment to console a gentleman whose wife had committed suicide, but the man was not home. Not wanting to waste a trip, Sheen asked who lived in the apartment across the hall. When he learned that the apartment belonged to the violinist and composer Fritz Kreisler and his wife, Harriet, Sheen proceeded to knock on their door. After introducing himself and exchanging a few pleasantries, Sheen asked Maestro Kreisler and his wife if they would like to take instruction in Catholic teaching. Astonishingly, the Kreislers both answered in the affirmative. Sheen remembered, "Fritz Kreisler was one of the finest and noblest men I ever met in my entire life. When I would quote a text from the Old Testament, he would read it in Hebrew; when I would quote a text from the New Testament, he would read it in Greek."[25]

Friedrich "Fritz" Kreisler was born in the musical city of Vienna on February 2, 1875.[26] His father was a mild-tempered doctor and amateur violinist, and his volatile mother was the opposite in temperament, perhaps due to her paralysis. Fritz said he never saw his mother walk, yet she seems to have been the backbone and disciplinarian of the family of five children, two of whom died quite young. His father was from Poland and may have been at least partly Jewish, though Fritz and his wife always denied any Jewish heritage.[27]

---

[24] Sheen, Treasure, 268–69. See also Reeves, America's Bishop, 64–65. Reeves puts Kitty in Peoria, which seems unlikely, considering Sheen's extensive memory of her conversion and her subsequent apostolate to other prostitutes. Also, Sheen spent very little time in Peoria, except to visit family.

[25] Sheen, Treasure, 258–59.

[26] The facts of Fritz Kreisler's life come largely from his biography by Amy Biancolli, Fritz Kreisler: Love's Sorrow, Love's Joy (Portland: Amadeus Press, 1998). Used with permission.

[27] Ibid., 25. Kreisler's religion is covered extensively in chapter 8.

Born into a musical city and into an haute bourgeoisie family, Fritz claimed, "I was born with musical feeling. I knew music before I knew my ABCs, so I deserve no credit, no thanks for my art."[28] He began formal violin lessons from his father at the age of four. By the age of seven he had outgrown his father's talents and, after his mother lied about his age, he was admitted to the Vienna Conservatory, the youngest student to that date. Three years later he earned the conservatory's gold prize. He had studied composition with Anton Bruckner, who impressed him more with his religiosity than his music. He recalled, "Religion was very real with him. If near-by bells tolled, he would either fall on his knees in the midst of class lesson and pray, or, more often, would leave and rush over to the church for his devotions."[29] That must have made quite an impression on the young Fritz, as the Kreisler family was apparently thoroughly secular and utterly nonreligious. Young Fritz Kreisler also studied and played with Johannes Brahms, often getting to play Brahms' compositions before they were even published. Many years later in an interview, Kreisler would say of Brahms and his experiences as a student at the conservatory, "To talk to an Olympian like that, to actually be present at the creation of superb music, was priceless.... We knew then a wine of the spirit. We were preoccupied with beauty. And thank God, the spirit did not wear off. How distinctly I remember the circumstances of my early years."[30]

His musical education was not yet complete. From age ten to twelve, Fritz studied at the Paris Conservatoire, where he won the Premier Kreisler's Prix, the school's highest juried award. After winning the coveted award, Fritz left formal music lessons behind. Despite his love of beauty and music, the boy hated to practice his music and preferred to spend time out of doors playing with his chums. He said, "I was ... much more interested in playing in the park."[31] Nonetheless, his experiences at the conservatories gave Fritz Kreisler the opportunity to hear great music performed by some of the most famous artists of his time

[28] Basanta Koomar Roy, "The Personality of Kreisler", *The Mentor*, December 31, 1921.

[29] Louis P. Lochner, *Fritz Kreisler* (New York: Macmillan, 1950; reprinted by St. Claires Shores, MI: Scholarly Press, 1977), 11.

[30] Olin Downes, "Talk with Kreisler: Violinist Discusses His Early Days and Some Contemporary Problems", *New York Times*, November 8, 1942, sec. 8, 7.

[31] Interview with Kreisler, Frederick H. Martens, *Violin Mastery: Talks with Master Violinists and Teachers* (New York: Frederick A. Stokes, 1919), 102.

and that was what stuck with him throughout his life: "I really believe hearing Joachim and Rubinstein play was a greater event in my life and did more for me than five years of study!"[32] His ambition as a musician was to convey only the beautiful and noble. Sheen would later build on Kreisler's dedication and love of beauty and nobility to bring him to God in the Catholic Church.

In October of 1888, at the age of thirteen, Fritz Kreisler was invited to join Moriz Rosenthal on an American tour to perform fifty concerts. It was a great thrill for the young violinist to cross the ocean and come to America. Unfortunately, his playing in New York and Boston gained but tepid praise. A Boston critic commented, "He plays like a nice, studious boy who has a rather musical nature ... but cannot be ranked among prodigies and geniuses."[33] His biographer Amy Biancolli points out, "The *New York Times* critic was more generous: 'He is at present not a phenomenon but a promising youth.' "[34] He was "Charming, if not astonishing."[35] Feeling damned by his faint reception in America, Fritz Kreisler returned to Vienna and told his parents that he had decided to abandon music as a career and go back to the Piaristengymnasium, a Catholic secondary school. With help from his father, he was able to earn his *Abitur*, a diploma equal to the completion of American high school and the first two years of college. At the age of eighteen, he then enrolled in the medical school of the University of Vienna to follow his father into medicine. But medicine was not for him either, so after two years of medical school, he joined the Imperial Army, where he only picked up his violin to amuse his friends. His mandatory service commitment was over in 1896, leaving the twenty-one-year-old Fritz with no specific ambition or direction. He turned back to the violin, this time with more enthusiasm and effort. In a matter of weeks, Fritz Kreisler composed the first of three cadenzas for the Beethoven Violin Concerto in D Major and an arrangement of a Paganini piece.

He was also composing what are referred to as his "fakes". These were pieces Kreisler composed under the names of other composers.

[32] Martens, *Violin Mastery*, 101.

[33] Howard Malcolm Ticknor, *Boston Daily Globe*, quoted in Lochner, *Fritz Kreisler*, 28.

[34] "A Wonderful Pianist", *New York Times*, November 10, 1888, quoted in Biancolli, *Fritz Kreisler*, 41.

[35] "Music", *The Independent*, November 15, 1888, quoted in Biancolli, *Fritz Kreisler*, 43.

He explained, "I resolved to create a repertory of my own. I then began to write music under the composers' names. I took the names of little known composers.... Not for one moment did it enter my head to imitate them.... That wasn't my plan at all. I just wanted some pieces for myself ... and I wrote them.... I wanted to be a violinist, not a composer. I wanted to give recitals and I couldn't put several pieces on the program and sign them all 'Kreisler.' It would have looked arrogant.[36] Kreisler's "fakes" have been praised by many reputable artists, including Efrem Zimbalis and Yehudi Menuhin.[37] When the hoax compositions were made public in the 1930s, Fritz Kreisler was already an established virtuoso, so his audience and most of his fellow musicians were willing to be forgiving of the younger aspiring Kreisler. Olin Downes, the American music critic, summed up the feelings of most musicians on learning about Kreisler's hoaxes, "Let us admit that Mr. Kreisler has hoaxed us rather handsomely. Has not the principal harm, if any, been done to the feelings of the hoaxed? ... Mr. Kreisler has added to the gaiety of nations and the violinist's repertory."[38]

It took time for Kreisler to become appreciated as an extremely talented violinist. He had a unique bowing style that produced an unusual sound with an emotional quality previously unknown. He also made extensive use of vibrato when playing. While his feet were firmly planted in an earlier style of music, loving, as he did, seventeenth- and eighteenth-century music, his playing of that music was modern. In other words, Fritz Kreisler was ahead of his time in the sounds he created and the responses his playing evoked from his audiences. After such a difficult time at the beginning of his career, his ultimate success must have been very sweet. Biancolli wrote, "When the world caught up with him, he succeeded. He was ahead of his time."[39] Richard Strauss counted him among his two favorite violinists.[40] The coloratura soprano Lilli Lehmann believed Fritz Kreisler to be the best violinist of her day: "I prefer Fritz Kreisler because

---

[36] Fritz Kreisler, "The Great Kreisler Hoax", as told to Louis Biancolli, *Etude*, June 1951, 18.
[37] Biancolli, *Fritz Kreisler*, 160–61.
[38] Olin Downes, "Kreisler's 'Classics': The Story of Their Authorship—Some Rumors and Interpretations of His Course", *New York Times*, March 3, 1935.
[39] Biancolli, *Fritz Kreisler*, 75.
[40] Ibid., 65.

he sings on his instrument as does no other living violinist."[41] Carl Flesch wrote, "[Kreisler] was the first who nearly *divined in advance* and satisfied the specific type of emotional expression demanded by our age."[42] His rising popularity came at an especially opportune time because he was one of the first musicians to commit his playing to 78 rpm records, a recording format that had just become available. It allowed his art to be brought into the living rooms of the world. He composed and played catchy short pieces suited to the format produced by Victor and sold around the world, making him into the phenomenon he had failed to be as a thirteen-year-old. He became a star performer. By 1911, he had sold seventy-five thousand copies of his music. People were listening to him at home and buying his scores to play him at home. His concerts were fully subscribed by eager fans.

Perhaps of greatest importance for the rising popularity of Fritz Kreisler was the influence of his strong-willed wife, Harriet Lies. They met in 1901 when they were both passengers on the ship *Prince Bismark*, returning to Europe from America. For Fritz, it was truly love at first sight. She was from New York, a divorced woman, slightly older, and the only child of a wealthy German American in the tobacco business. Mr. Lies was not happy that his daughter wanted to marry a musician, thinking Kreisler beneath her in social standing. However, Mr. Lies had no say in his daughter's attachment to Fritz Kreisler, as the couple had become engaged on the ship. The two were married in New York City the following year. There was a second ceremony officiated by the Austrian Ambassador in London. The delighted Fritz wrote, "To satisfy the national and church requirements—and our double marriage took." According to his biographer, Fritz and Harriet had a third marriage ceremony in Hoboken, New Jersey, perhaps to remedy some slight technicality previously overlooked.[43] Harriet Kreisler was the woman behind the successful man. She managed his career, his contracts, even the programs he would play, and their family finances, giving him a meager allowance. Their union was a mystery to Fritz's friends. Yehudi Menuhin called Harriet a "virago". Others thought her "brash" and "bossy" and believed that Fritz was

[41] Lilli Lehman, quoted in Arthur Abell, birthday letter to Fritz Kreisler, Library of Congress Fritz Kreisler Collection.

[42] Carl Flesch, *The Art of Violin Playing*, trans. Frederick H. Martens (New York: Carl Fisher, 1930), 2:75.

[43] Biancolli, *Fritz Kreisler*, 79.

"henpecked". His friends felt sorry for him. While Fritz obviously adored his wife, he occasionally needed to escape her firm control. She would not allow him to drink or gamble, two things he loved to do, so he would sneak out some nights to meet his friends.[44] On the other hand, his friends also credited Harriet with his astonishing career. One of his accompanists remarked, "Without Harriet Kreisler, there would be no Fritz Kreisler."[45]

Harriet Kreisler inherited nearly a million dollars and some real estate when her father died. Fritz was making good money concertizing, but neither was much taken with money and preferred to lead a simple life. Fritz would say, "I am constantly endeavoring to reduce my needs to a minimum.... In all these years of my so-called public success, we have not built a home for ourselves. Between it and us would stand all the homeless of the world." On another occasion he said, "I get a kick out of feeding poor children.... I get a kick out of bringing home a stray dog and feeding it. I just get my kick in different ways. That is the spirit of my wife and I have absorbed it from her."[46] These sentiments reflect a kind of spiritual poverty, a detachment from the things of this world that is surprising considering the popularity and financial success of Fritz Kreisler. Because Harriet and Fritz never had any children to possibly to fill this void, the Kreislers became known for their philanthropy for children.

In 1914, the Kreislers were in Europe taking the waters at a Swiss spa when war broke out between Austria and Germany with Russia. Even though Fritz had resigned his commission in the Imperial Army two years before, he felt duty bound to report to his regiment. The war had a profound effect on him. He told the *New York Times*, "It [the war] has made me mournful when I have thought how quickly we all threw over everything the centuries have taught us. One day we were all ordinary civilized men. Two or three days later our 'culture' had dropped aside like a cloak and we were brutal and primeval."[47] His war was a short one. When his regiment was overrun by the Russian cavalry, he was wounded in the hip by a Cossack rider,

[44] Ibid., 82–85.

[45] Michael Raucheisen, quoted in Lochner, *Fritz Kreisler*, 80.

[46] "Kreisler, Fritz", in Anna Rothe and Helen Demarest, eds., *Current Biography 1944* (New York: H. W. Wilson, 1945), 359.

[47] "Kreisler, Wounded, Tells of War", *New York Times*, November 29, 1914. See also Fritz Kreisler, *Four Weeks in the Trenches* (Bristol, U.K.: Last Post Press, 2015), 21.

whom Fritz remembered shooting just before he lost consciousness from his wound. He was eventually carried to a field hospital where the physician mistakenly reported him as killed in action. Later, Fritz managed to send Harriet a telegram to let her know he had survived. She reached Fritz and took him to Baden to recover for three weeks. The army surgeons declared him unfit for battle and discharged him with the rank of captain. The war, for Fritz Kreisler, lasted less than three months; his limp would remind him of it for the rest of his life.

Because the United States was not as yet engaged in what would become World War I, Kreisler received an enthusiastic welcome when he returned to American concert stages after his discharge from the Army. Music critic Henry T. Finck called him "the lion of the musical season".[48] His biographer wrote that at this time, "America, it seemed, could not get enough of Fritz Kreisler."[49] But, as soon as the United States joined the war in 1917, Fritz Kreisler was no longer the lionized star of the concert stage; he was the enemy alien. His concerts were canceled. The *Washington Post* published an editorial aimed at Kreisler, "Kreisler might remember that he is in the enemy's land by sufferance.... Lieutenant Kreisler should remember that there are a number of internment camps in this country where enemy aliens are detained, and that among them are a great many men who could present a better argument for their freedom than he has."[50] Kreisler's concertizing career would lie fallow until at least a year after the armistice.

During his time in concert limbo, Kreisler continued to compose; he just did not perform on stage. One project he enjoyed at the time was composing, along with Victor Jacobi, the music for the operetta *Apple Blossoms*, which opened in New York in 1919 and ran for over a year. Kreisler composed more than half of the operetta's songs, many of which were refined and adjusted during the course of the rehearsals he attended. Fritz Kreisler greatly enjoyed the creative process of the production, watching the actors, dancers, and singers, not to mention

---

[48] Henry T. Finck, "Lion of the Musical Season", *The Nation*, March 18, 1915, 313, quoted in Biancolli, *Fritz Kreisler*, 104.

[49] Biancolli, *Fritz Kreisler*, 105.

[50] "Lieut. Kreisler", *Washington Post*, March 10, 1918, quoted in Biancolli, *Fritz Kreisler*, 115.

the money he was making. His canceled tour in 1917–1918 had cost him eighty-five thousand dollars in lost revenue. It was a slow process to worm his way back into the hearts of his patriotic audiences in both America and France. By the end of 1919, his performance on the Metropolitan Opera stage earned him a standing ovation. His popularity and income rose in the post-war years. He and Harriet moved to Germany, where they had a large house outside of Berlin.

As Germany moved toward totalitarian fascism and anti-Semitism, Fritz Kreisler was a vocal public opponent of the Reich's racial policies. He refused to perform in Germany, even though he claimed to be Aryan and gentile, having been baptized a Catholic at the age of twelve. His denials aside, many believed that Fritz Kreisler was Jewish. His brother admitted his Jewish heritage. When Harriet insisted, "Fritz hasn't a drop of Jewish blood in his veins", their friend Leopold Godowsky retorted that Fritz "must be very anemic".[51] Adolph Hitler became chancellor of Germany in 1933 and began pushing anti-Jewish policies and inflaming the population against the Jewish people. Hitler's insanities would eventually lead to World War II and the Holocaust. From 1933 until his departure from Germany for the United States in 1939, Fritz Kreisler continued to believe in the universal nature of art. The German ban on music composed by Jewish composers and on Jewish musicians was bewildering to him. Music is music. It was apolitical as far as Fritz was concerned. He was naïve in the extreme. Harriet, on the other hand, was a supporter of the Reich and even displayed the Nazi flag. The unfortunate truth was that she was an anti-Semite who had fallen in love with a man who was at least partially Jewish on his father's side. She must have thought that if they were united in denying Fritz's heritage, that somehow it would be all right for them. She even hoped that the Nazis would "make her husband an 'honorary Aryan'".[52] They were both foolish. Fortunately, Fritz Kreisler had a long-standing invitation from the French government to become a French citizen, which he finally accepted in May of 1939, renouncing his Austrian citizenship. Later that autumn, after the fall of France to Germany, Fritz and Harriet moved to the United States, where they made their home in New York City. He

[51] Biancolli, *Fritz Kreisler*, 184.

[52] Dennis Rooney, "Instinctive Partnership: Franz Rupp Reminisces about Playing with Fritz Kreisler", *The Strand*, January 1987.

became an American citizen on May 8, 1943. "Fritz Kreisler never publicly revealed his Jewishness. Nor did he ever formally renounce it", wrote his biographer, Amy Biancolli, who characterized him as "secular, but saintly, a known philanthropist whose deep but vague monotheism effectively camouflaged the complex religious and ethnic identity at his core".[53]

When Msgr. Fulton Sheen knocked on the Kreislers' door in 1947 and offered them instruction in the Catholic faith, Harriet must have seen it as an opportunity to put the questions of Fritz's religious heritage behind them. But, in fact, Sheen was offering them much more than that. Catholicism is more than a label. It is a life centered on the person of Jesus Christ. Fritz Kreisler was always a good and decent man. What he lacked was an understanding of God's love and man's true response to that love. In loving and caring for war orphans, Fritz could understand himself as acting as the face and hands of Jesus. In composing and playing beautiful music, Fritz could see himself as participating in the divine beauty of God. On March 30, 1947, after only two months of instruction from Sheen, Fritz and Harriet Kreisler received Holy Communion at the Blessed Sacrament Church in New Rochelle, New York. Sheen married the couple in the Church a short time later, their fourth marriage ceremony. The *New York Times* reported their conversion to the Catholic Church. Louis Lochner, a journalist, wrote a correction to the *Times* insisting that the Kreislers' was a "reversion" not a "conversion", as both had been raised Catholic. Fritz's mother was Catholic and had raised her children as Catholics. His father, or perhaps his grandfather, may have converted to Catholicism, but with his Jewish background, that would not have mattered to the Nazis. It is likely that he had been baptized at twelve, but in post-war Germany there was no record of Fritz's Baptism. Harriet's previous marriage had been to a Protestant, and the fact that her first husband had died allowed the Kreislers to be sacramentally married in the Catholic Church by Sheen.

It seems that interest in the possibility of Fritz Kreisler's Jewishness does not go away. His great-nephew, Kurt Kreisler, said in a 1995 interview that he does not know of any Jewish blood in the family,

---

[53] Biancolli, *Fritz Kreisler*, 204–5.

and that he remembers his famous uncle only as a devout Catholic who thought of his entrance into the Catholic Church as a return rather than a conversion.[54]

The Fritz Kreisler that Fulton Sheen met in 1947 had had a terrible accident six years earlier when the absent-minded maestro stepped off a curb in Manhattan into the path of an oncoming egg truck. The impact of the truck fractured his skull, broke several bones, and left him in a coma for a month. When he regained consciousness, he had lost his sight and his hearing. While he would partially regain his senses and be able to once again take up his violin, life would never be the same for the sixty-six-year-old Fritz Kreisler. Newspaper accounts of the accident referred to him as "Beloved Kreisler", a far cry from the "enemy alien" of twenty-some years before.[55] He was at the top of his career when a momentary lapse of mind put him in the path of a truck. His public was praying for his recovery. A letter of disputed origin signed with the name of Charles Foley states, "The entire Catholic public took care of these prayers. One prayer actually took place through priests and nuns in the hospital ... and his wife ... Harriet, immediately expressed her absolute faith in the deliverance of her husband through an immense Catholic miracle."[56] If this letter is factual, it would point to a deep-seated faith on the part of Harriet, and that might explain why the couple so immediately acquiesced to Fulton Sheen's invitation six years later to join—or rejoin—the Catholic Church.

It took almost two years for Fritz to recover enough to play for his adoring public. His first venture was not before an audience, but in a recording studio. When he again played for audiences, only the most astute critics would have noticed that while he played beautifully, the programs he put on were not nearly as demanding as what he had previously played. But for Fritz Kreisler, beauty was all. The concertmaster of the Detroit Symphony spoke of Kreisler's magic: "Well, he played the Beethoven concerto at the rehearsal and concert. It was God's given gift. During the G-minor episode in the first movement, I had to stop playing because I was so choked up. Oh, it

[54] Ibid., 207.
[55] Ibid., 211.
[56] "Charles Foley", letter to Harold Holt and Laurence Mackie, undated, Library of Congress Fritz Kreisler Collection, quoted in Biancolli, *Fritz Kreisler*, 212.

was something out of this world."[57] To audiences and fellow musicians, Fritz Kreisler "captivated everyone". To fellow violinists, "He was our God."[58] At Kreisler's first post-accident recital in Carnegie Hall, the audience gave him a standing ovation for just walking onto the stage.

When Fritz Kreisler met Msgr. Fulton Sheen, Fritz was in his seventies, still playing to audiences, but certainly in the twilight of his career. He was the grand old man of the musical world but clearly belonged to the pre-war generation. His concerts were becoming fewer. The monsignor came into Fritz's life at just the right moment. Msgr. Sheen wrote: "I was a very close friend of the Kreislers from the time of their reception into the Church, and it was tragic to see Fritz in his last days, blind and deaf from an automobile accident, but radiating gentleness and refinement not unlike his music. I visited them every week for some years, until the Lord called them from the Church Militant to the Church Triumphant, where I am sure the music of Fritz Kreisler is in the repertoire of Heaven."[59] Sheen was present at the maestro's seventy-fifth and eightieth birthday dinners when the praises of presidents and celebrities rained down. His seventy-fifth birthday party was also a fundraiser for the Musicians Emergency Fund, underscoring the Kreislers' ongoing philanthropy. Fritz received greetings from President Harry Truman, Pope Pius XII, and dozens of other luminaries. Sheen toasted him with "When God decides that He wants you, you will be met by nine angels with violins. And they will say to you. 'Maestro, teach us how to play the violin as divinely as you do!' "[60] So fond of Kreisler's music was Sheen that he asked Fritz to compose the theme music for Sheen's television program, *Life Is Worth Living*. When presented with a piece set in march time, Sheen said that he simply could not march onto the set and asked if Fritz could please rewrite the piece to waltz time, which he did.

Fritz Kreisler died on January 29, 1962. He was buried from Saint John the Evangelist Church in Manhattan. Bishop Fulton Sheen gave the eulogy at his funeral, comparing Fritz Kreisler's soul and body

[57] Josef Gingold, interview by Amy Biancolli, July 13, 1992, quoted in Biancolli, *Fritz Kreisler*, 227.

[58] David Sackson, interview by Amy Biancolli, September 16, 1992, quoted in Biancolli, *Fritz Kreisler*, 262.

[59] Sheen, *Treasure*, 259–60.

[60] Biancolli, *Fritz Kreisler*, 313–14.

to a violin and bow. When the two are separated, music cannot be played, but "One wonders if the violin does not retain every melody, every tune, every concert played upon it. Whether this be true of ... violins, we are certain it is true of the soul." Kreisler had told Sheen sometime in the past that he did not practice before concerts because in playing he was returning God's gift to him. Sheen recalled in his eulogy that he had gone to give Fritz the last rites and as he was anointing him "to prepare him for the afterlife", he said, "I was to cleanse his mouth, eyes, ears, hands. But when it came to cleansing his hands, I didn't want to erase the magic and beauty of what those hands had given us." He recalled in his remarks that he and Fritz would recite the Lord's Prayer together in Hebrew. Sheen prayed that Fritz Kreisler would be greeted in heaven by angels singing Vieuxtemp's "Fantaisie Caprice", the piece with which the thirteen-year-old Fritz had made his American debut in 1888.[61] William Stidger quoted Fritz Kreisler: "I want to share my thoughts of God and truth. I want to share my music. I want to share my worldly goods. ... I want to give of myself, all my music and of my possessions to others. That is supreme happiness."[62]

Fulton Sheen's great friend Fritz Kreisler could rest in peace, knowing he had done all he could with the gifts that God had given him and that he had so generously given to others. It was a life well lived. It was a life largely removed from politics and the real condition of man in the world. Fritz Kreisler, apolitical himself, believed that music was apolitical, above the mundane world of nations and wars, of ideologies and political parties. Music was something divine, appealing in its beauty to all peoples in all places across the ages. Fritz Kreisler lived for music and for love.

Sheen and the Coming Cold War

Msgr. Fulton Sheen, as a priest, was keenly aware of the proclivities of man to be unlovely, to oppress the weak, and, if given enough power, to wage wars of conquest, aggression, and terror. The horrors of the

---

[61] "Bishop Sheen Gives Eulogy at Mass for Violinist", *New York Times*, February 2, 1962, 4.

[62] William L. Stidger, *The Human Side of Greatness* (New York: Harper and Brothers, 1940), 76–77.

Holocaust and the destructive power of nuclear weapons had proven to Sheen the absolute necessity of avoiding war, but also of combating a totalitarian regime intent upon subduing the entire world to its perverse system of government. With his March 5, 1946, Iron Curtain speech, Winston Churchill created the image of the Cold War against the Communist Soviet Union and the great divide between the competing ideologies. The contrast was stark: freedom or submission. Sheen was a willing warrior in the Cold War against Communism, using all his rhetorical powers against the pernicious ideology.

Msgr. Sheen first attacked Communism as a substitute for religion. Despite its atheism, Communism maintained all the attributes of a religion with its pantheon of gods and saints such as Marx and Lenin, its complete worldview with an appealing utopian end, an exacting dogma, and a magisterium, its public rites such as its May Day parades, and its bible in *Das Kapital*, all combined with an absolute assurance in its inevitability. Sheen wrote that Communism was "like Christianity in all things save one; it is inspired not by the spirit of Christ but by the spirit of the serpent ... the Mystical Body of the Anti-Christ."[63] He always maintained his belief in the dignity and goodness of the Russian people, whom he knew suffered under their dictatorship. Especially from the Virgin Mary's apparition in Fatima in 1917, the Catholic Church prayed for the conversion to Catholic Christianity for the Russian people and those subject to Russia. In the suffering of those under the thumb of the Soviets, Sheen emphasized social justice reforms here and abroad because it was the right thing for the people, but also to lessen the appeal of Communism, which tried to speak to the downtrodden to stir up jealously, greed, and class warfare. One did not have to be a Communist to believe in social justice; in this, Jesus and the Beatitudes were Sheen's guides. His ultimate appeal was to the goodness and beauty of the democratic way of life in the United States. The country did not always live up to its ideals, but it recognized its ideals as superior. The post-war period saw Fulton Sheen as preoccupied with the need to right the wrongs in American society and the imperative to conquer Communism.

[63] Riley, *Fulton J. Sheen*, 139.

6

Rome or Moscow?

The Communists Come for Sheen

Msgr. Fulton Sheen viewed the post-war world with his characteristic optimism, colored with a certain caution brought about by what had gone before and what the future might hold in a bifurcated world of free countries, led by the United States and its allies, and those under expanding international Communism inspired by the Soviet Union. His weapons were his pen and his microphone, soon to be enlarged with the new medium of television. Sheen's anti-Communism began in the early days of his priesthood, in accordance with the request at Fatima from the Virgin Mary to pray for the conversion of Russia, and only intensified in the post–World War II years. Sheen's anti-Communism was consistent with that of the wider Catholic Church's hierarchy, from the Vatican on down. In his day, the entire Catholic Church in America was focused on combating Communism. There were widely divergent approaches to that opposition within the Church. There were those on the Right, like Fr. Charles Coughlin, whose approach was alarmist. Others fought Communism more from the perspective of the need for reform of institutions and social justice among people. These anti-Communists on the Left did not see Communism as evil, just as misguided in its approach to problems; its ideals were laudatory. Sheen saw the conflict as one between contending ideologies or philosophies of life, and he was adamant that Communism, with its atheism, was inherently evil. Sheen was probably the best-informed American Catholic churchman of his day when it came to Communism. He made a life studying Communism from its roots. He read its documents and manifestos and delved deeply into understanding its beliefs. Sheen spent five decades fighting Communism; he was zealous, but not fanatical. He was following the direction given him in 1935 by Pope Pius XI to speak out against Communism.

How he spoke was often dictated by to whom he spoke. Like any good speaker, he would tailor his remarks to his audience, but the intent was always the same: to unmask the evil and insidious ideology embraced by the Kremlin. Sheen's attack was spiritual because he saw Communism as a kind of religion. Its errors were to be combatted with prayers and the elevation of ideas in opposition to it. It was either "Rome or Moscow; Christianity or Chaos; Christ or Communism; the Cross or Double-Cross."[1] It was a battle between "brotherhood in Christ and comradeship in Anti-Christ ... love vs. hate ... the Five Year vs. the Eternal Plan ... the red flag of Communism vs. the red sentinel of the Altar; the Internationale vs. Panis Angelicus".[2] It may sound simplistic, but Sheen drew these distinctions to show clearly what surrender to Communism would mean: man could serve the state as his god, or he could serve the state by serving God first. In a 1934 book *Moods and Truths*, Sheen allowed that the premise of Communism is the brotherhood of man, a tenet of Christianity, but he averred it was so exaggerated as to preclude the sovereignty of God. God and Communism are mutually exclusive, he insisted. "The communion rail", he would write, "is the most democratic institution on the face of the Earth ... The modern world tries to unite men on the basis of economic equality ... as in Communism.... The Eucharist unites men on the basis of brotherhood."[3] For Sheen, the choice was stark: it was the Body of Christ against the body of the antichrist.

It was not just Fulton Sheen who saw the dichotomy so clearly. Msgr. Sheen quoted Anatoly Lunarcharski, the Soviet Commissar of Education: "We hate Christianity and Christians. They preach the love of neighbor and mercy, which is contrary to our principles.

---

[1] Kathleen L. Riley, *Fulton J. Sheen: An American Catholic Response to the Twentieth Century* (New York: Alba House, 2004), 135. Sheen was not above using polarizing language in his fight against Communism. For other examples, see Fulton J. Sheen, *Communism Answers Questions of a Communist* (New York: Paulist Press, 1937) and *Crisis in Christendom*, 3rd ed. (Washington, D.C., The National Council of Catholic Men, October 15, 1952).

[2] Fulton Sheen, "The Mystical Body of Christ, or The Church and Communism", lecture, Sheen Archives, 16.

[3] Fulton Sheen, *The Mystical Body of Christ* (New York: Sheed and Ward, 1935), 373, 367.

Christian love is an obstacle to the development of the Revolution."[4] Whittaker Chambers, an ex-Communist turned government witness against Alger Hiss, wrote a letter to his children trying to explain Communism, which he included in his book *Witness*. He said that Communism posited the most revolutionary of questions in all history: God or Man? The Communists came down on the side of man: "Man's mind is the decisive force in the world.... Man's mind is man's fate."[5] There is no need for God if man can control his destiny. The Communists' tools were science and technology, and their vision one of progress toward brotherhood by the control of the all-powerful state.

According to Kathleen Riley, there are five points to Sheen's anti-Communism:

- Communism is essentially religious in its seeking for an absolute.
- Sheen loved the Russian people and all others under Communism; he was attacking the "sin" of Communism and its leaders, not the common people.
- He had faith that Communism would be defeated, and its captive peoples converted back to Christianity.
- He continued to preach the need for social reforms and social justice here and abroad.
- Communism not only threatened Christianity, but also American democracy.[6]

In the 1930s, Msgr. Fulton Sheen was in a public debate with Louis Budenz, then the editor of the *Daily Worker*, over the means and ends of Communism. Under the guidance of Sheen, Budenz would eventually recant his Communist beliefs and almost ten years later rejoin the Catholic Church of his youth. But their initial battle was played out on the pages of the *New York Times* and the *Daily Worker*. Later, Budenz admitted that he had been bested by Sheen, who gave

---

[4] Sheen, "Mystical Body", 27. See also W. Cleon Skousen, *The Naked Communist* (Salt Lake City: Ensign Publication Company, 1960), 308. Also quoted by David O. McKay in a talk at Brigham Young University, "Karl Marx", May 18, 1960, printed by the Joseph Smith Foundation.

[5] Whittaker Chambers, *Witness* (New York: Random House, 1953), 10.

[6] Riley, *Fulton J. Sheen*, 137.

a "definite and devastating rebuttal to my queries ... replete with damaging admissions of Soviet crimes and crudities taken from the official Soviet Press."[7]

After World War II and the fall of the Iron Curtain, Sheen's anti-Communism was popular with almost the entirety of the Catholic Church and most Americans. With Poland and Hungary behind the Iron Curtain, American Catholics learned of the persecution of their coreligionists in those countries and called out for justice.[8] In mid-1948, Stalin blockaded the western sector of Berlin, cutting off its people from the West and denying them the benefits of the Marshall Plan's aid to the devastated post-war European countries, which had resulted in the Berlin Airlift. The airlift produced photographs and moving pictures of desperate people behind the Iron Curtain rushing out onto the fields to secure the food and supplies, including Christmas toys for children, delivered by air, courtesy of the United States of America. Those images and those of the Berlin Wall became familiar to Americans and helped them to form their opinions on the efficacy of Communism and the danger posed by the Soviet Union to free peoples everywhere. The Chinese Communist Party was founded in 1921, and in 1949 it succeeded in founding the Peoples Republic of China under the Party's dictatorial rule of Mao Zedong. The Christian Chiang Kai-shek, with his Nationalists, fled to Taiwan, leaving China completely under the control of the Communist Party. In 1949, the Soviet Union detonated its first atomic bomb. Americans and American Catholics, in particular, had good reason to fear the spread of Communism.

The Soviets understood that it was the United States of America that stood between it and world dominion. To that end, it supported and directed the Communist Party in the United States to gain members to its cause and to undermine the American way of life and its society, economy, and politics. Communists in the United States had been active since at least the 1920s, but at that time they were mainly European immigrants who brought with them from Europe various strains of Communism and anarchism. As the economy faltered

[7] Louis Francis Budenz, *This Is My Story* (New York: McGraw-Hill, 1947), 158–59.

[8] "Iron Curtain" denotes the division that cut off the part of Eastern Europe in the Soviet sphere of influence and control from the West after World War II. Winston Churchill first used the term in a speech on March 5, 1946, at Westminster College in Fulton, Missouri.

during the Great Depression, many native-born citizens were lured by the wiles of a classless society based on the brotherhood of man and a system that tied their economic woes to the greed and avarice of the wealthy. Communists were particularly active in trade unionism and other front organizations. Front organizations were nurtured by the Communist Party, which stayed hidden deep within the shadows. The front organizations were largely philanthropic and reformist, usually quite innocuous sounding, with no overt ties to Communism as a discrete entity; nonetheless, the ties were there. People joined such organizations as the American League Against War and Fascism, Committee for the Protection of the Bill of Rights, Industrial Workers of the World, the Jewish Cultural Society, and the American Student Union without knowledge of the organizations' real intent and lineage. Such people would be labeled "fellow travelers" of the Communist Party. Surely some knew of the Party's involvement, but many did not. Many Americans who became members of the Communist Party in the United States were unaware of the instrumentality of the Soviet Union in directing and guiding the Party in America. They thought it was an American version of Communism, somehow distinct and different from Soviet Communism.

This was the initial experience of Louis Boudenz, and it took several years for him to finally see the truth of the Soviet control of the Party in America and its decidedly anti-Christian intent. Budenz so thoroughly believed in the social ends of Communism that he was blinded to its insidious realities of atheism and anti-Christian insistence. Budenz's public battle with Fulton Sheen helped him to finally begin to see Communism for what it is: an ideology intent on world dominion cast in the light of the Soviet experience. As the ex-Communist Whittaker Chambers testified before Congress, "The Communist Party (in the U.S.) exists for the specific purpose of overthrowing the (U.S.) Government, at the opportune time, by any and all means; and each of its members, by the fact that he is a member, is dedicated to this purpose."[9]

Sheen's many loud and public comments on Communism naturally brought him personally to the attention of the Communists. One afternoon after his Catholic University class in Washington,

---

[9] Chambers, *Witness*, 542.

D.C., Sheen was approached by a man who had just audited his lecture who told him that he was a former Communist. He gave Sheen a pamphlet entitled *The Story of My Escape from Communism*. The man asked Sheen to read the pamphlet carefully and then to give him a call—he wanted to travel around the country with the monsignor as he gave his anti-Communist talks and then recount his personal story of escape from the clutches of Communism. Sheen was dubious, to say the least. He called the Federal Bureau of Investigation and gave the agent the man's name. The response from the F.B.I. was startling: "Oh, he is a very well-known spy; we didn't know that he was in the United States. Last we heard, he was in the Philippines. He's very dangerous; your life is in danger."[10]

Sheen was also approached by another individual claiming to be close to the high offices in the Communist Party in the United States. Sheen questioned the man's authenticity, so he asked the man to show him his membership card. He again called the F.B.I., who agreed to check out the man's claims. They asked Sheen to meet him in a hotel, where the F.B.I. agents could listen from the room next door. This time, it turned out that the contact was indeed a high official in the local Party, and he continued to be a source of information for Sheen for years to come. Sheen considered the individual to be one of his three sources of information on the Communist Party in the United States; the other two were a daily reading of *Pravda* and other publications (a Russian-speaking secretary read the Russian newspapers for him) and the combing of scholarly works on Communism by reputable scholars. The F.B.I. opened a file on Fulton Sheen in 1943 and filled it with newspaper clippings of his speeches. Soon Sheen became a personal friend of F.B.I. Director J. Edgar Hoover. Hoover was obsessed with Communists and saw in Sheen an effective fellow combatant in the war against Communism.

Sheen's Prescience and Communist Espionage Efforts

In 1948, Sheen came out with one of his best books, *Communism and the Conscience of the West*. In it he pointed out that most civilizations

---

[10] Fulton J. Sheen, *Treasure in Clay: The Autobiography of Fulton J. Sheen* (Garden City, N.Y.: Doubleday Press, 1980), 85.

that fail, fail from the inside; they decay from within. "As Western civilization loses its Christianity it loses its superiority. The ideology of Communism rose out of the secular remnants of a Western civilization that was once Christian."[11] He also wrote that the idea of progress is incorrect and misleading. Society tends to equate progress with technological and medical advances and material abundance. While the West may have labor-saving devices, lifesaving medicines, and enough material benefits to provide all man's necessities, he is still not happy. Happiness is an elusive quality that cannot be attained by material gains, Sheen thought, but only by spiritual gains. The fight against Communism was "moral and spiritual and involves above all else whether man shall exist for the state, or the state for man, and whether freedom is of the spirit or a concession of a materialized society."[12]

Sheen would speak to a crowd of thirty thousand people at an anti-Soviet rally called by Cardinal Spellman, who also spoke that day. The goal of the rally was "to pledge the loyalty of all Catholics, to pray for the persecutors of Christians in the Soviet-ruled countries, and to identify with their victims".[13] It was the kind of setting and rhetoric at which Fulton Sheen excelled. As Msgr. Sheen spoke around the country, he had an ex-Communist bodyguard, since there had been credible threats against his life. Besides offering physical protection for the monsignor, the guard's duty was to survey the crowd and to mark with an X on the seating chart the presence of Communists in attendance. When one evening almost every seat on the chart was marked with an X, Sheen announced that he was not going to give his prepared remarks but would instead spend the time quoting from various Communist sources to allow Communism to speak for itself. It was an opportunity not only to show off his prodigious memory, but to condemn the means and ends of Communism using Communism's own words.

The Soviet Union not only supported various front organizations and kept tabs on the outspoken Msgr. Fulton Sheen, but it also

[11] Fulton J. Sheen, *Communism and the Conscience of the West* (Indianapolis: Bobbs-Merrill, 1948), 8. See also Sheen's 1947 radio address of the same name, https://www.youtube.com/watch?v=9awHSzqTWoU.

[12] See Sheen, *Communism and the Conscience of the West*, 17–23.

[13] *New York Times*, May 2, 1949, quoted in Thomas C. Reeves, *America's Bishop: The Life and Times of Fulton J. Sheen* (San Francisco: Encounter Books, 2001), 209.

actively sought influence within and engaged in espionage of the federal government. While Senator Joseph McCarthy tainted anti-Communism with his extremism and excesses as he hunted for Communists in government posts, there were in fact many Communists who had managed to gain access to high positions in the government and many more who had low-to-middling positions that nonetheless allowed them to pass classified documents and secrets to Soviet agents. Many were Party members, but most were merely "fellow travelers" sympathetic to the Communist cause.

The federal government was not completely naïve about Communists and fellow travelers in the government. In 1939, Congress passed the Hatch Act, making membership in any organization that advocated for the overthrow of the Constitutional form of government of the United States cause for termination from a federal position. In 1940, Congress passed the Smith Act, making it a crime to print, publish, edit, issue, circulate, sell, distribute, or publicly display any written or private matter advocating the overthrow of the government. President Truman promulgated his Executive Order 9806 on November 25, 1946, which established the President's Temporary Commission on Employee Loyalty. A few months later the commission issued a report recommending the establishment of a Loyalty Review Board. Established on March 2, 1947, the Loyalty Review Board was charged with vetting all federal employees, taking their fingerprints, and submitting a questionnaire to each one about personal political affiliations and opinions. The F.B.I. would do background checks on each new employee.

All this security and surveillance apparatus sounds impressive, but most would agree that none of it would have stopped the individuals who were fingered by Elizabeth Bentley, a former director of two Soviet spy rings active in the federal government, a Communist defector, and a government informer. On January 25, 1954, R. W. Scott McLeod, a State Department security officer, was asked about the effectiveness of the government's security procedures. He replied, "They would not have [caught the communists in the government]... No security program, however stringent, will succeed in uncovering an espionage agent as deeply buried and entrenched as Hiss. Only the effective work of counter-intelligence or a defector like Whittaker Chambers or Elizabeth Bentley is likely to accomplish this."[14] Bentley's testimony before the F.B.I. and various congressional committees implicated dozens of individuals in a Communist conspiracy to infiltrate the U.S. government, steal its secrets, and undermine America. Her testimony was key to the convictions in the later trials of William Remington, Alger Hiss, and Julius Rosenberg. Remington had worked for the Tennessee Valley Authority and later for the War Production Board, where he had access to production schedules and data on airplane designs. Hiss had been in various important positions in the Agriculture, Justice, and State Departments; he was even at the Yalta Conference with President Roosevelt. He was the temporary secretary general of the nascent United Nations and the chair of the Dumbarton Oaks Conference. Julius Rosenberg was an electrical engineer working on the top-secret Manhattan Project to develop the atom bomb. All passed secrets to the Soviet Union. The revelations of Elizabeth Bentley shocked the country.

How a New England Girl Became a Communist Operative[15]

Elizabeth Bentley was the perfect spy—a Connecticut Yankee of Puritan stock from one of New England's most picturesque towns, New Milford, Vassar educated, intelligent, and willing. Her code name was "Clever Girl". To her underground contacts she was Myrna, Helen, or Jane, sometimes with the last name Johns, Johnson, or Grant. Elizabeth was the only child of parents who had married in their thirties: a schoolteacher and the son of an unbelieving Baptist minister who had sworn off religion. Because of her father's unstable employment, Elizabeth and her parents moved from town to town throughout her school years, making for a bookish, shy, awkward girl with few friends. As an avid reader, she was an excellent student and won a scholarship to Vassar.

Vassar was and remains an elite institution, populated largely by the wealthy and privileged. Bentley did not fit in—her grades toppled,

---

[14] James Rorty and Moshe Decter, *McCarthy and the Communists* (Boston: Beacon Press, 1954), 134, n. 4.

[15] Many of the details in this section come from Bentley's autobiography, *Out of Bondage* (Auckland: Muriwai Books, 2018).

she briefly joined one club, played on no teams, and went to no proms. Mostly friendless, she fell in with the progressives on campus. Their motto was "production for use, not for profit". But the group was all talk and no action as far as Elizabeth Bentley was concerned. She came under the influence of Professor Hallie Flanagan, "a one-woman political movement at Vassar", who had been to Russia and preached its virtues.[16] Elizabeth took three classes from Flanagan and admired Russia until it was almost too late.

After college, she taught Italian and French at a girls' school and enrolled in a master's degree program at Columbia. Summers took her to Italy, where she observed the excesses of Mussolini's fascism and threw off whatever New England prudishness she might have had. "She was wild and promiscuous", writes her biographer, Lauren Kessler;[17] there was always something about her "that was restless, reckless, and needy".[18] Back in Columbia, she was invited to join a Columbia University Communist cell, where she learned that greed was at the heart of social inequity. She wrote, "Greed isn't essentially a part of human nature. It is a by-product of the profit motive.... If, however, we could eliminate the profit motive ... we would have the beginnings of a good social set up."[19] She envied the purpose and direction Communism gave those in the cell—she desperately wanted to have faith in something. Embracing Communism also appealed to Bentley's taste for the risky and disreputable. She liked to think of herself as a good girl gone bad. She joined the Communist Party in 1935.

The Communist Party of the United States of America (CPUSA) was a legal entity in the 1930s. It publicly supported Roosevelt and the New Deal. It stood for full employment and unionization of labor. During the Depression the membership in the CPUSA tripled. Nobody knew of the Kremlin's planned starvation in the Ukraine or of the purge trials to come. To most Americans, the CPUSA was another reformist movement that stood for social justice.

As a newcomer, Bentley attended the Communist Worker School at the Party headquarters in New York. According to Kessler, the school taught Bentley that "drinking, profane talk, and 'loose morals'

---

[16] Lauren Kessler, *Clever Girl* (New York: Harper Colins, 2003), 21–22.

[17] Ibid., 27–28.

[18] Ibid., 32.

[19] Elizabeth Bentley, *Out of Bondage* (Auckland: Muriwai Books, Kindle edition), loc. 182.

were seen as positive steps toward breaking the bourgeois code of behavior, making for a social life that was simultaneously salacious and politically correct."[20] A fellow student at the Worker's school told her, "I am convinced that communism is the Christianity of the future."[21] Msgr. Fulton Sheen had long been saying that Communism is not a political movement, but a religion. Before the House Committee on Un-American Activities, Bentley would testify, "I think the mistake you make when you look at Communism is that you take it for an intellectual process. It is not. It is almost a religion, and it gets you so strongly that you take orders blindly."[22] The Party's upper echelon had recognized Elizabeth Bentley's intelligence and zeal and had her assessed for espionage by Juliet Poyntz, a Barnard, Oxford, and Moscow–trained member of the Soviet secret police. Poyntz introduced her to another Party member who told Bentley that she was a member of an organization like the Catholic Church, except, he told her pointedly, "if you leave the Catholic Church, all you lost was your soul."[23]

After finishing her degree at Columbia, Elizabeth got a job as a secretary and researcher at the Italian Library of Information on Madison Avenue. What she found there appalled her. The library was full of anti-Semitic and anti-Communist fascist propaganda. At first she thought to quit the place, then decided to take advantage of her position to supply information to the Communist headquarters— her career as a spy began on her own initiative. It was October of 1938, and she was about to meet the man who would change her life. He was Jacob Golos, her third contact to receive the materials she spirited out of the Italian Library. He was introduced as "Timmy", but his real name was Jacob Raisin, a Ukrainian Bolshevik who had escaped czarist Russia as a teenager and made his way across Asia and to the United States. Elizabeth called him Yasha, and he would be her controller and lover until his death five years later. He took her deeply underground into Soviet espionage; he taught her spycraft.

[20] Kessler, *Clever Girl*, 46.

[21] Ibid., 47.

[22] Alistair Cooke, *A Generation on Trial: U.S.A. v. Alger Hiss* (New York: Alfred A. Knopf, 1950), 53.

[23] Kessler, *Clever Girl*, 51. The man who said this to Bentley was Michael Endeman, known to her as Marcel, a KGB agent. She repeated this statement in her signed F.B.I. declaration, November 30, 1945, 6.

Step by step he involved her more and more in espionage. At first he only received her materials from the library. Then he used her address as a letter drop for himself; later she became a courier, bringing him documents from his contacts. One of Bentley's first contacts for Golos was Abe Brothman, a New York engineer, who would ultimately be a link to Julius Rosenberg.[24] She did not know and would not have cared that at the time she met him that Jacob Golos had a mistress in New York and a wife and child he had sent back to the Soviet Union. They shared their commitment to the Communist cause and love for one another. If undercover Communists were not supposed to have friends, they certainly were not supposed to have lovers; it made them vulnerable to manipulation and blackmail. They did not care. "They were living ... in bourgeois sin and Leninist bliss", writes Kessler.[25] Life with Golos was exciting. She helped him wine and dine visiting Communists from Canada and Mexico, including those involved in the murder of Lev Davidovich Bronstein, better known as Leon Trotsky.

Golos set Bentley up in a Communist front business that ran a legitimate shipping company but on the side provided false documents to Party members traveling between Russia and the United States. When in 1939 the Justice Department was investigating Earl Browder, the head of the CPUSA, it found that Browder had traveled to Russia on a false passport supplied by the company for whom Bentley worked. Golos, but not Bentley, was caught up in the investigation, pleading guilty to a charge of not registering as an agent of a foreign power. He was fined and given a suspended sentence.

When the Justice Department started looking into Gaik Ovakimyan, the chief of scientific intelligence for the KGB in America, Golos was again worried. He carried documents from his office to Bentley's apartment to burn in her fireplace. Golos had Bentley take over his Washington, D.C., contacts. Kathryn S. Olmsted wrote in *Red Spy Queen* that she was "responsible for far more than collecting gossip; she would be controlling an entire ring of agents in Washington, some of whom had access to the White House itself. Bentley would be moving from the margins of Soviet espionage in America

[24] Kathryn S. Olmsted, *Red Spy Queen* (Chapel Hill, N.C.: University of North Carolina Press, 2002), 36.

[25] Kessler, *Clever Girl*, 65.

to its strategic center."[26] She collected information from Duncan Lee, a distant relative of Robert E. Lee, who worked for William Donovan, the head of the Office of Strategic Services (OSS), later to be called the CIA. Kessler writes that Duncan provided her with diplomatic insights into activities "in Turkey and Romania, operations in China and France, secret negotiations with the Balkan bloc. He told her about the location of OSS personnel in foreign countries and the nature of their activities."[27]

Maurice Helperin collected daily summaries of the intelligence compiled by the State Department to pass on to Bentley. Nathan Gregory Silvermaster worked first in the Department of Agriculture and then at the Treasury. It was Silvermaster who suggested that material be photographed to make it easier to transport in Elizabeth's bag back to Golos. Soon Elizabeth Bentley was carrying forty rolls of filmed documents every other week from Washington to New York. Perhaps the most prominent individuals who would be accused of espionage by Bentley were Harry Dexter White and Lauchlin Currie, who never saw themselves as spies or traitors. As economists, they were friends of Silvermaster, but neither was a Party member. Bentley never met White and only knew him through the oral reports he gave Silvermaster. White's source of information came from his position as the chief monetary expert and assistant to Henry Morgenthau, the secretary of the Treasury. Currie was a special assistant to President Roosevelt and instrumental in helping place Communists in sensitive positions of influence within the government.

In the meantime, Jacob Golos was being eased out of his position by his handlers in Moscow. The Communist espionage in the United States had been under the direction of the CPUSA before the war. By the mid-1940s, Moscow wanted to control espionage in the States. Golos was told to turn over all control to Bentley, and she would be controlled by a Moscow man. Golos would receive the Order of the Red Star and retire to Russia as a hero. He was given three days to make up his mind. He never made it to the third day. On Thanksgiving night, 1943, Jacob Golos died of a heart attack in Elizabeth Bentley's apartment. He was dead before the ambulance arrived. She blamed the Soviets for the death of her lover.

[26] Olmsted, Red Spy Queen, 43.
[27] Kessler, Clever Girl, 83.

It was awkward in the extreme to have a dead Soviet spy in your apartment, but Elizabeth was up to the task. She emptied his pockets and called Party men to remove the body. Early the next morning, she went to Golos' office and cleaned out his safe of $2,000 and any incriminating documents, which she turned over to Earl Browder. Browder was concerned about Golos' apparatuses and contacts and asked Elizabeth to carry on with his help. She agreed, but only out of loyalty to her Yasha. Her controller would be Ikshak Akhmerov, who went by several aliases. Olmsted explained, "Elizabeth just knew him as 'Bill.' He was the leading NKGB 'illegal,' or spy without diplomatic cover, in the United States."[28] She would be, in effect, reporting directly to Moscow.

Under Bill, Bentley took over another Washington apparatus, the Perlo Group, and several unaffiliated sources of information. Bill demanded to meet with her Washington sources and interfered with the procedures she had learned from Golos. She was lonely without Yasha, frustrated and upset by Bill, and under a great deal of stress. She began to drink heavily. To smooth her feelings, Bill offered Bentley a salary and other emoluments she refused. She was insulted. She had never taken money for her services to the Communist Party. She was an ideologue, driven to espionage out of conviction, not gain. Bill too was frustrated; he suggested Moscow find her a husband. Bill eventually just took over the Silvermaster group.

She would have another controller, Joseph Katz, known to her as Jack, who seemed to her like a nice enough young man. In November of 1947, Katz would agree to kill Bentley on orders from Moscow. Perhaps, he suggested, he would poison her food. In the meantime, Bentley was demanding to meet with someone of importance, the real "boss". Anatoly Gorsky, known to her as "Al", met her in Washington. Olmsted wrote, "Gorsky was not only the chief of the NKGB operations in America, but also the First Secretary at the Soviet Embassy."[29] He was to be her last controller. He told her that Moscow had awarded her the Red Star and that if she would go to Moscow she would be treated like royalty. In fact, Moscow wanted her out of Washington and New York, and out of American

[28] Olmsted, *Red Spy Queen*, 63.
[29] Ibid., 74.

espionage altogether—all for her own good, of course. But Bentley recalled that Golos had also been awarded the Red Star as he was being eased out of his position—she was not buying any of Al's blandishments and could clearly see the handwriting on the wall. No longer employed by a Communist front corporation and no longer wanted in demand for espionage activities, Elizabeth Bentley decided to leave the Communists and defect to the United States. She was afraid for her life, remembering that Juliet Poyntz had disappeared and was presumed dead. Bentley was afraid, yet she dithered.

Bentley Turns State's Evidence

On August 22, 1945, she approached the F.B.I. office in Connecticut. She played coy with the agent, refusing to tell him anything specific, so he filed a bland report and showed her the door. A few weeks later, a Canadian Embassy employee defected, publishing his story of espionage in the newspaper. Also, Louis Budenz, a contact of both Golos and Bentley, publicly announced his conversion to the Catholic Church and his repudiation of Communism. Inspired by the convergence of circumstances, Bentley wrote a letter to the F.B.I. office in New York City, which contacted her for an interview. Again, she equivocated with the agent. She hinted at her involvement with the Communists, but was not forthcoming. She did appear to the agent to honestly fear for her safety. However, this more astute agent got in touch with somebody at the Bureau in Washington whose specialty was Soviet espionage. Suddenly the F.B.I. became very interested in Elizabeth Bentley. On November 7, she again sat down with two F.B.I. agents and this time told her story. Kessler wrote, "Her own immunity from prosecution was not discussed. It was assumed."[30]

The agents sat with Bentley for over eight hours and as she gave them names and dates; they took copious notes. They cabled J. Edgar Hoover at 1:30 in the morning to let him know what they had learned. The next day Hoover received the agents' seventy-page summary of Bentley's testimony. She was interviewed fourteen times that month. Agents would surveil Bentley and Gorsky meeting in Washington.

[30] Kessler, *Clever Girl*, 128.

She gave them an envelope of money Gorsky had given her. Even if she could not provide documentary evidence in support of her claims, there was plenty of circumstantial evidence for her assertion that there were Communists in high places in the U.S. government. In her 107-page signed statement, Elizabeth Bentley named eighty individuals who were known to her personally or by association and who, through her, had provided the Soviet Union with important and sometimes top-secret information.

More than two hundred federal agents would work on the Bentley case. Every named individual in her statement would have to be surveilled and investigated. It would be one of the Bureau's longest and most expensive operations. During its entirety, the Soviet Union was made aware of Bentley's accusations and the Bureau's every move through a leak in the London office of the British Secret Service. Kim Philby, a senior agent in MI6 and a British double agent working for the Soviets, read the cables from Washington and passed them on to Moscow.[31] Kessler wrote, "Bentley had delivered what the head of the KGB intelligence called 'the most tangible blow to our work.'"[32] The Soviet espionage apparatuses set up over several years had to be disbanded and reestablished. Gorsky was recalled to Moscow. The Soviet spying efforts in the United States were inoperative for over two years.

Of the twenty-seven individuals named by Bentley who still worked for the government, most resigned. Eventually, because of what was called the Red Scare, more than twenty-five thousand individuals were brought before loyalty boards, although most were cleared of any taint of disloyalty. Yet some could manage to slip through the cracks. Brought twice before loyalty boards and twice exonerated, William Remington was later convicted of perjury concerning his espionage activities and jailed. He sued Bentley for libel and lost.

In 1946, the Army succeeded in decrypting Russian diplomatic cables in what was called the Venona Project. The decryption allowed the F.B.I. to identify 150 people from the cables, including many named by Bentley, such as Perlo, Silvermaster, Lee, and Currie. But because the Venona Project was top secret, the decoded cables could not be entered into evidence against the defendants.

---

[31] Philby escaped to the Soviet Union in 1963, dying there in 1988.
[32] Kessler, *Clever Girl*, 142.

Without documentary evidence of their guilt, none of the defendants accused by Bentley were successfully prosecuted for spying. The statute of limitations on espionage having run out by the times of their indictments, several of those accused by Bentley were found guilty of perjury. The Venona Project remained secret and unknown to the public until 1995.

During the multiyear investigations and trials, Elizabeth Bentley found herself alone and afraid. She had no income and no friends. She turned to Louis Budenz, the one person in a similar circumstance. When he denounced the Communists he, too, lost his income and his friends. But he also had his wife and daughters, and he had his faith in the Catholic Church—Bentley had nobody and nothing. If his faith had given him strength and courage, she could have that too. Budenz introduced her to Msgr. Fulton Sheen. She was baptized almost three years to the day from when she first walked into that Connecticut F.B.I. office. Louis and Margaret Budenz were her sponsors. Olmsted wrote of her, "The woman who had sought community and acceptance in ... communism had found a new 'ism' to give her meaning. Elizabeth was taking refuge in Catholicism."[33] Budenz had landed on his feet after his conversion; he taught at a Catholic university and was widely praised as an anti-Communist speaker. He was her link to her old way of life and could become her help toward a more promising future. She described her conversion as "sort of like coming home.... You'd be surprised how all sorts of things that have bothered you before just disappear, once you have faith in something."[34]

One suspects that Elizabeth's conversion to Catholicism was convenient and part of her attempt to remake herself for the public. If she had enjoyed her reputation as a "good girl gone bad", now she wanted to be the "reformed bad girl". In her various testimonies, she emphasized her New England upbringing, which she claimed was undone by the progressives and Communists at Vassar. It had been the brotherhood of man that had drawn her to the Communists. Her motives were always pure. It had ultimately been her love for Jacob Golos that had enthralled her and brought her into the Communist

---

[33] Olmsted, *Red Spy Queen*, 146.

[34] "Elizabeth Bentley Is Happy to Be Herself Once Again", *New York World-Telegram*, December 6, 1948.

underground. She was an idealistic young woman who had fallen for the wrong man: a sad but common tale. She would tell her story in four installments in *McCall's* in 1951. The same year, she published an autobiography, *Out of Bondage*, based on her *McCall's* series. She was in financial trouble, depressed, and drinking regularly and excessively. Constantly called on to testify, she could not hold down a job. She made unwise liaisons with men, including a bodyguard/handyman who beat her and tried to blackmail her. She relied on her F.B.I. contacts to scare him off. She made constant demands on the F.B.I. agents assigned to her. She needed money, transportation, or even just someone to talk with her. Hoover realized that he needed to protect Bentley's reputation, as a stain on her could easily bleed over onto the Bureau. He finally consented to pay her a small amount, and later, a small stipend for when she was actually testifying. She leaned on Msgr. Sheen to help her find a job in a Catholic school. He had helped Budenz get a job at a Catholic university; he could help her, too.

Sheen found her a position at Mundelein College, a women's college outside of Chicago, where she was to teach political science. But Elizabeth Bentley could not accommodate herself to life at Mundelein. Her drinking and her cohabitation with a "man not her husband" caused the college community shock and scandal. It was bad enough to have a confessed Communist, albeit reformed, on the faculty, but her immoral behavior was not to be countenanced. The college president, in the time-honored way of Catholic nuns, parted with Bentley on good terms and told Bentley she would pray for her. The college's official explanation was that Professor Elizabeth Bentley needed to devote more time to testifying.

Indeed, Bentley was about to be very busy testifying. There would be the trials of William Remington, Abraham Brothman, and Julius and Ethel Rosenberg. In the fall of 1948, British scientist Klaus Fuchs admitted to having given the Soviets top secret details about the Manhattan Project, the building of the atom bomb. He said he had received his information from an American engineer (or chemist) by the name of Abraham Brothman. After checking their files on Bentley, the bureau found that she had mentioned one of her first sources as being Brothman. Brothman gave them Harry Gold. When confronted, Gold gave them the name of David Glassman, a soldier at

Los Alamos, whose brother-in-law was Julius Rosenberg. It was to be a sensational trial that would result in the conviction of Brothman and the executions of Julius Rosenberg and his wife. It was Elizabeth Bentley who provided the key to opening the prosecutions of the Rosenbergs. It was a straight line from Bentley to Brothman, to Gold, to Glassman, and to the Rosenbergs. Elizabeth Bentley should have felt vindicated. Instead she was reduced to manipulating the F.B.I. for money to keep her afloat. Her only "friends" were the F.B.I. agents who only put up with her because they had to. By the end of 1952 she was contemplating suicide. Her newfound Catholic faith was not giving her peace of mind—neither were the liquor bottles piling up in her wastebaskets.

Despite her problems, when Elizabeth Bentley was in the witness chair, she always managed to control herself and her facts, which she was able to present with coherence and conviction. She had amazing recall of distant events and persons. Her next big trial was the spy case against Alger Hiss brought by the ex-Communist Whittaker Chambers. Chambers was unknown to Bentley because he had left the Party long before she had joined. When Chambers left the Party, he was perspicacious enough to secrete away incriminating documentary evidence. He kept the papers in a pumpkin on his farm, so they were characterized by the media as the "Pumpkin Papers". Chambers had brought Alger Hiss to the F.B.I.'s attention as early as 1939. Bentley did not know Hiss personally and had only heard his name, which she remembered as "Eugene Hiss". Hiss now stood accused of spying by two ex-Communists, so the Bureau investigated Hiss, his family, and his associates for two years. Chambers had been brought into another trial to corroborate Bentley's testimony, which he did, but then he mentioned Hiss' name. It was an electrifying moment in court. Hiss became a cause célèbre for the Left; his case became the watershed that divided Right and Left for decades to come. The Left claimed the evidence against Hiss was false and manufactured. The Right maintained that evidence in Hiss's own handwriting was impeccable. He was convicted of perjury and sentenced to five years in jail. Elizabeth Bentley was all but forgotten in the fray between the supporters of Hiss and those of Chambers. She had to have been grateful for Whittaker Chambers' corroboration of her testimony, but, at the same time, he was stealing her place in the limelight.

Elizabeth Bentley had been called the Red Spy Queen, a neurotic spinster and liar, and, worse, was largely forgotten once the Hiss case took off without her. In 1953, she turned again to Bishop Fulton Sheen for help. He found her a teaching job far from the glare of the press. She taught government and romance languages at the College of the Sacred Heart in Grand Coteau, Louisiana, 130 miles from any town of size. Out of boredom and a great need of money, she again published her life story in a six-part special in the *St. Louis Dispatch*. It came out just before Thanksgiving. She recapitulated her former stories, concluding that she was "rehabilitated ... and restored to the society of decent men".[35] She went on to appear on *Meet the Press*. The Bureau men were afraid for her and for the Bureau; they knew how she had deteriorated. But they need not have worried. Kessler wrote, "Bentley emerged unscathed.... Those who might have read ... that she was hysterical, neurotic, a liar, and a Red-baiter saw only a mild mannered, unflappable schoolteacher who spoke carefully and appeared to know what she was talking about."[36]

A Sad End for One of Sheen's Lost Sheep

In 1956, Sacred Heart closed its collegiate level and did not renew Bentley's contract. When she left Sacred Heart, Elizabeth added one more "ex" to her résumé and abandoned the Catholic Church. Over the next few years, she bounced around from one school to another. Her Communist reputation and her immoral behavior always got the best of her. In 1958 Elizabeth Bentley was worn out after ten years of testifying for the government, friendless, and broke. She lived in a rooming house. She asked J. Edgar Hoover for a recommendation in hopes that his name would open a door somewhere for her. He wrote a tepid letter saying that her testimonies had been accurate and that her cooperation with the Bureau "is a matter of public record".[37]

---

[35] In an attempt to rehabilitate herself as a good girl led astray by loving the wrong man, Elizabeth Bentley wrote a six-part series, based on her *Out of Bondage* book, printed by the *St. Louis Dispatch*, November 30 and December 1, 2, 3, 4, 5, and 6, 1953. She also needed the money.

[36] Kessler, *Clever Girl*, 257.

[37] Ibid.

His letter was enough to get her a job at the Long Lane School in Middletown, Connecticut. It was a residential school for troubled girls remanded there by the courts. It was a place where Bentley could at last feel at home, "a misfit among misfits".[38] Even when she was at Long Lane, F.B.I. agents would show up on her doorstep with photographs and questions. She was uncooperative and noncommittal. The school administration asked her to look for another position, but she stayed on at Long Lane until she died. In November of 1963 Bentley complained of a virus and checked into the Grace New Haven Community Hospital. The doctors who operated on her discovered that her abdomen was full of cancer.

Elizabeth Bentley died on December 3, 1963, at the age of fifty-five, a sad, lonely woman who had loved being the center of the 1940s Communist infiltration of the federal government and then at the center of the government's quest to rid itself of those same subversive elements. Both had given her a role to play and a purpose in life. Outside of those two roles, Bentley was adrift with few social or emotional resources on which to draw. In her conversion to Catholicism, which might have given her a sense of personal dignity, she did not find the solace she needed, so she left the faith behind, as she had other commitments. She had no friends and little family. Her funeral was definitely not in a Catholic Church—a small funeral with a few cousins and two F.B.I. agents. Elizabeth Bentley was not inconsequential to the political tenor of mid-century America; in many ways, she opened the door for others to rush in. She was the one to push the first domino to fall against the Communists in the government. It is difficult to recall at this distance in time what the early Cold War years were like, but undeniably, Elizabeth Bentley was an important part in America's response to the real and perceived threats from the Soviet Union and the world Communism it represented.

Bishop Fulton Sheen did what he could for Elizabeth Bentley, but she had too many demons of her own to have stayed long in the Catholic Church. She was a confused and manipulating woman who reached out to whatever seemed best to her at the moment. Were her motives opportunistic? Her morals too flawed? Her intellect dimmed and her will weakened? Sheen would not have asked

[38] Ibid., 288.

her these questions, but he would have prayed fervently for her soul and mourned her loss.

Msgr. Fulton Sheen was not a political man. He was neither a Democrat nor a Republican; he was a priest. As Riley wrote, "He continued to speak out forcefully on the subject of communism, from an ideological and religious point of view. Remaining removed from the political conflicts and tensions generated by McCarthyism, Sheen never offered an opinion on Senator McCarthy in public, and he steered clear of the political controversy surrounding him."[39] In an interview years later, Sheen would say, "I have no interest in politics ... there is no reason that I should have discussed him [Senator McCarthy], and he was not an authority on communism in any case."[40] Sheen's efforts were to save souls. He would not pass judgment on Elizabeth Bentley—that was up to God. As the decade of the 1950s made its debut, Fulton Sheen was about to be given much larger pulpits than he had ever had. First, in 1950, he would be appointed the national director of the Society for the Propagation of the Faith, and then, in 1952, he would take the television world by storm with his popular series *Life Is Worth Living*. He would also earn his coveted bishop's miter. The 1950s were good to Fulton Sheen.

[39] Riley, *Fulton J. Sheen*, 172.

[40] Ibid., 175, n. 202. From an interview of Sheen by Sr. Mary Jude Yablonsky, "A Rhetorical Analysis of Selected Television Speeches of Archbishop Fulton Sheen on Communism, 1952–1956" (Ph.D. diss., Ohio State University, 1974).

7

The Golden 1950s

Sheen Propagates the Faith Worldwide

In the 1950s Msgr. Fulton Sheen would become a preeminent cleric in the American Catholic Church. With his new position as the national director of the Society for the Propagation of the Faith, he would even have considerable standing in the Vatican as the most celebrated fundraiser for the Church's worldwide missions. With the coming of the television age and his part in it, Fulton Sheen's would be one of the most recognized faces in the country. His influence was about to be tremendous.

Francis Cardinal Spellman, as a chair of the Episcopal Committee for the Society for the Propagation of the Faith, had Msgr. Fulton Sheen named its national director in the United States. Moreover, Sheen would soon be given his miter as an auxiliary bishop in the Archdiocese of New York. The announcement of his appointment to the directorship of the Society came in the summer of 1950, when Sheen was fifty-five years old. After a quarter of a century teaching at the Catholic University of America, Fulton Sheen resigned his professorship, sold his stunning home in Washington, and moved into an apartment on the fourth floor of the Society's national headquarters in a New York City brownstone at 109 East 38th Street. He was thrilled to have his talents and resourcefulness recognized. He wrote, "It was very consoling to have a universal mission and to consider the world as my parish."[1] Here was a man who had been a priest for over thirty years, had spent less than a year living in a rectory and never as

---

[1] Fulton J. Sheen, *Treasure in Clay: The Autobiography of Fulton J. Sheen* (Garden City, N.Y.: Doubleday Press, 1980), 106.

the pastor of his own parish, who now considered the world his parish. His was a most unusual career path for a priest. He would continue his convert classes and his *Catholic Hour* radio broadcasts, but his "entire energies [would] be dedicated to this work (promoting the world-wide missions of the Church and raising money) which has the unique value of contributing to the peace of the world through peace of soul."[2] Fulton Sheen was not a person with a limited supply of energy to be divided among his various apostolates; rather, he multiplied his energy, especially when world peace and peace of soul were two of his enduring concerns, now brought together in a single entity under his care. The missions have both a vertical and a horizontal aspect. It is always about more than just feeding the hungry and clothing the naked; the goal is to bring men and women to the Lord by feeding their souls as well as their bodies. Here was an opportunity on a global scale for Fulton J. Sheen to bring converts to the faith both directly and indirectly. He would say, "I always contended in talking to missionaries that we are not so much to bring Christ to peoples as we are to bring Christ out of them.... Because His person was divine, every single human nature in the world was potentially in that human nature of Christ."[3]

He indeed threw his prodigious energy into his new position. Under the directorship of Sheen, 130 dioceses had an office for the Society for the Propagation of the Faith.[4] He would get to know the diocesan leaders and visit with each one. Missionaries from around the world would make trips to his New York offices, and often his dinner table. They would tell the director about their missions and the problems and troubles they were having, and, of course, ask for funds. He was vitally interested in their plight—kind, patient, encouraging, and openhanded with the Society's checkbook.

The Society had thirty employees who came and went from the New York headquarters every day. One of the first things Msgr. Sheen did on taking over the reins of the Society was institute daily prayer for the entire staff. He wrote, "Every day at two forty-five our whole staff would recite the Rosary together.... Later on we used

---

[2] "Msgr. Sheen Appointed to New Post", *The Tower* (newspaper of Catholic University of America), vol. 28, issue 1, September 27, 1950.

[3] Sheen, *Treasure*, 148.

[4] D. P. Noonan, *The Passion of Fulton Sheen* (New York: Dodd, Mead & Company, 1972), 36.

the fifteen minutes to give a spiritual commentary on certain passages from the Bible."[5] He had no experience as an administrator and found the day-to-day running of an organization less than stimulating; therefore, he left the administrative running of the Society to his staff. His admitted lack of interest and talent for administration would resurface when he later became bishop of the Diocese of Rochester, New York. He was gifted in many areas, but administration was not one of them.

Sheen was always good to those who worked for him, though. James C. G. Conniff wrote, "Morale among his (Sheen's) staff can challenge any in New York."[6] Sheen's administrative assistants were staunch supporters. Gloria Dixon, who mostly dealt with his convert classes and others seeking his advice and counsel, joined the Society staff in New York and remained with him until she died in 1965. Edythe Brownett was his personal secretary from 1950 and would stay with "the Boss" until he died. Both women remained unmarried and devoted to him. Sheen had met the Brownett family when they regularly attended his radio broadcasts. Both Edythe and her sister Marlene were young teenagers when they first encountered Sheen. It was to become a lifelong friendship with their whole family. As his personal assistant, Edythe was charged with keeping his calendar and making his travel arrangements. She also scheduled the director's time with visiting missionaries and various dignitaries. Edythe guarded her boss fiercely and served him loyally.[7]

When Fulton Sheen took over the national directorship of the American Society for the Propagation of the Faith, the workload for the staff increased tremendously. He preached about the importance of the missions on *The Catholic Hour*. At times he would ask his audience to send money for the missions. The letters would cascade into his office. School children would send him their allowances, usually in dimes and pennies taped to a paper. He remembered, "One day, thirty thousand letters arrived, and the staff coped as best they could."

[5] Sheen, *Treasure*, 110.

[6] James C. G. Conniff, *The Bishop Sheen Story* (New York: Fawcett Publications, 1953), 30.

[7] Sheen was friends with the entire Brownett family for many years. He helped the girls through college. He gave Marlene her veil when she became a nun, and she traveled with Sheen to Europe on more than one occasion. The never-married Edythe was his secretary at the Society for the Propagation of the Faith, as well as in his later years when he retired from the Rochester diocese.

Reeves estimates that about one-third of the letters would be from non-Catholic listeners of *The Catholic Hour*.[8] Sheen wanted every letter writer to receive a personal response, a challenge to his staff when up to twenty-five thousand letters would arrive in the daily mail. He looked upon his entire staff as participants in his mission: "Everyone in our office was a missionary.... The good and faithful friends in our office are, therefore, considered sharers in the heavenly triumphs as much as those who left home for foreign missions and those who made sacrifices for the missions every week."[9]

Sheen's main job as the national director of the Society for the Propagation of the Faith was to raise money for the Church's vast missionary vocation: "Go therefore and make disciples of all nations" was the command of the risen Lord before his ascension (Mt 28:19). From its very beginning and by its nature, the Church is missionary. The missions, mostly serving non-Catholic and non-Christian peoples in Asia, Africa, Latin America, and the Pacific—the two-thirds of the world's population that went to bed hungry every night—were largely funded by the generosity of American Catholics under the leadership of Fulton J. Sheen.[10] He estimated that only about 10 percent of the beneficiaries of the world Catholic missions were actually Catholic[11] and that "Americans were contributing almost two-thirds of the collections made by the Society across the world."[12] Sheen would call the Society for the Propagation of the Faith

> the greatest philanthropic charitable organization in the world. Not one of our 135,000 missionaries, doctors, nurses, teachers, or social workers receives a cent of salary. They all labor for the glory of God. Our aid is not to Catholics alone. We help maintain 55,000 schools in Asia, Oceania, and part of Latin America. We have 6,000 hospitals and dispensaries, more than 300 leper colonies, with almost 50,000 living in those colonies, and 10,000,000 outpatients. We have 1,300 orphanages and 700 homes for the aged.[13]

---

[8] Thomas C. Reeves, *America's Bishop: The Life and Times of Fulton J. Sheen* (San Francisco: Encounter Books, 2001), 215. Gregory Ladd testified that "a third of his audience was Jewish, a third was Protestant, and a third was Catholic." *Positio*, 1.15.

[9] Sheen, *Treasure*, 110–11.

[10] Noonan, *Passion*, 37.

[11] Robert Considine, "God Love You", *Cosmopolitan*, July 1952, 97.

[12] Ibid.

[13] Noonan, *Passion*, 39.

Besides using *The Catholic Hour* airwaves, Sheen kept the needs of the missions before American Catholics through the Society's twice-monthly magazine. He renamed the magazine *Mission* and reduced its dimensions to pocket size. Under Sheen's direction, every Catholic became a missionary, if only by listening to him, reading his magazine, praying for the success of the missions, and, of course, donating whatever he could. Sheen personally wrote a monthly column for the magazine and added appealing photographs and touching articles from the missionary fields. He was such an effective promoter of the magazine that in a single year after he took over its editing, the magazine went from losing $200,000 a year to earning $200,000 a year, money he sent to Rome for the benefit of the missions.[14] *Mission* soon had a multimillion circulation.[15] Sheen designed a world mission rosary, with colored beads representing the five continents of the missions, that would be given to those who donated. His signature call-off on every *Catholic Hour* broadcast was "God love you." He had a medal designed by noted jeweler Harry Winston with the image of the Virgin Mary on one side, the seal of the Society on the other, and "God Love You" in raised letters around its edge. The ten raised letters could be used as a decade of the Rosary. To those who donated $5 for the missions, a silver medal was sent; to those who gave $10, a gold-plated medal was sent. Donations poured in.

Soon Sheen began another, more intellectual, magazine, *Worldmission*, for the Society. It was another vehicle to publicize the plight of the world's poor and ask for donations. He was a prolific writer, and words flowed freely from his pen. In addition to the two mission magazines, Sheen had a syndicated column in secular newspapers called *Bishop Sheen Writes*. He began the column in 1949 and continued it for thirty years (the column started out with the name *Monsignor Sheen Writes*). A second syndicated column, *God Love You*, was aimed at Catholic newspapers. In all his endeavors, he publicized the missions and solicited funds to help the world's poor, those who were called "Sheen's poor".[16] His was a public relations job to bring the plight of the poor to the relatively prosperous and materially comfortable American Catholics, and he was amply suited to the

---

[14] Reeves, *America's Bishop*, 216.
[15] Noonan, *Passion*, 39.
[16] Ibid., 40.

job. The director of the Indiana diocesan Society, Msgr. Clarence Schlachter, said, "He just sold you, and you were convinced that what you were doing was the most important job, the only job, really in the world."[17]

Within a year of Sheen's advancement to national director of the Society for the Propaganda of the Faith, the officials of the National Council of Catholic Men, which sponsored *The Catholic Hour*, began to criticize Sheen for his overemphasis of the missions on their weekly radio broadcasts. The audience was beginning to send in funds to the Council asking that the monies be directed to the missions. The Council's most prominent and popular speaker was losing money for the Council. Sheen would have to demand from the Council that donations for the missions be forwarded to the Society, costing the Council staff extra time and effort. The Council complained, once again, that Sheen was not submitting his scripts to it one month in advance of each broadcast as he had agreed to do. In the 1940s, the Council had complained he spoke too much about politics; now the problem was with the missions as a constant topic of his talks. They complained, "Our listeners are not able to distinguish between Monsignor Sheen, the Missions and the *Catholic Hour*."[18] If they wanted to have a popular weekly broadcast, they were stuck with Fulton J. Sheen. However, the National Council of Catholic Men would not be stuck with him for much longer, as television would shortly beckon their star performer.

Sheen's Elevation to the Episcopacy

At about the same time as the National Council of Catholic Men was complaining to Cardinal Spellman that Msgr. Sheen was too enthusiastic about the missions, the monsignor received notice that he was being elevated to the episcopacy. Sheen wrote to the Most Reverend Amleto Giovanni Cicognani, the apostolic delegate to the United States who had informed him of his coming promotion, "The Bishopric shall be to me, not an honor, but a responsibility, not a reward,

---

[17] Reeves, *America's Bishop*, 216.
[18] Ibid., 218.

but as a summons to sacrifice."[19] Cicognani announced on behalf of the Vatican that Sheen had been appointed titular bishop of Caesariana and one of four auxiliary bishops to Cardinal Spellman of New York.

On June 11, 1951, Fulton J. Sheen was consecrated a bishop in Rome in the Basilica of Saints John and Paul, whose titular head was Cardinal Spellman. Spellman was unable to attend the consecration of his new bishop, which was carried out by Adeodato Giovanni Cardinal Piazza. Sheen's advancement came about not only because of his manifest skills and outstanding service to the Church, but in part due to the patronage of Francis Spellman. Also, it was the fruition of a near lifetime of prayers petitioning the Virgin to be made a bishop, beginning with his days as a student in Louvain. Immediately after the three-hour episcopal consecration service, Bishop Sheen and his nephew, Fulton Sheen II, met privately with Pope Pius XII. Bishop Sheen had a close relationship with the pope, who called him by his first name. The Holy Father invited the new bishop to remain in Rome for a vacation, but Sheen demurred: "I thought Your Holiness had me made a bishop because there was a job to be done."[20] But before getting back to his job, he went to Lourdes to thank the Virgin for his new title and to ensure her continued support for his priesthood. He was back at his office at the Society on Monday morning ready to go to work.

Of course, his elevation to the episcopacy brought him a rush of pleasure, as it would any new bishop. He wrote, "The ring on the finger, the zucchetto on the head and the title 'Bishop'—all these things have a ring about them and all contribute to a sense of false euphoria, which I confess having had.... I also confess to the joy at the privileges that are given to a bishop—his place at table, the extra soft prie-dieu and the reverence born of faith."[21] Such feelings could not last long, however, for one as dedicated as Sheen was to his priesthood and to his particular job at the time of overseeing the fundraising for the missions to the benefit of the poorest of the world's poor. He wrote, "In a very short time I discovered that I was no different than before, that the clay was just as weak as ever, that the esteem people paid me was

[19] From Sheen's May 15, 1951, letter to Cardinal Cicognani, quoted by Reeves, *America's Bishop*, 218, and found in the Sheen Collection in the St. John's University Archives.

[20] Sheen, *Treasure*, 220.

[21] Ibid., 93.

not necessarily the way the Lord looked at me. It took some time to discover that the jewel in the ring does not necessarily become a jewel in a crown of Heaven."[22]

The realization that his lifelong goal of becoming a bishop was but another step and personal sacrifice in his service to God and fellow men began to change Fulton Sheen. His position at the Society brought the plight of the world's poor constantly to his mind. While his apartment was a four-story walk-up in New York City, he was a radio personality, well-dressed and well-fed in a world where millions lived in dire poverty and died of hunger. As bad as the Great Depression had been in America, those living through it did not even come close to the poverty of those in Africa and Asia. Once he received a telegram while traveling in Italy: "Send $200,000 immediately for the starving children who are eating sand in Pakistan."[23] In his autobiography years later, he wrote that he came slowly to recognize that

> soul-winning and society-saving are the concave and convex side of the love of God and love of neighbor; that in addition to begetting children of God through evangelization, we have to give witness of fraternal love in a sensitiveness toward humanity's desire for freedom and justice; that as Christ is both divine and human, so the mission of every Christian is to be transcendent in lifting eyes to Heaven but also immanent in the care of the way he lives on Earth; that earthly liberation is an integral part of evangelization and that they are united as Creation and Redemption.[24]

Sheen perceived that he was far from being the person the Lord was calling him to be. He had become too worldly. To remind himself of his true stature in the eyes of the Lord, he eventually changed his episcopal ring for a small silver ring with a carved mother of pearl image of the Virgin Mary, and on the chain around his neck, he wore a crucifix with the attached corpus of the crucified Jesus to recall to himself his true calling to be another Christ, another victim, crucified for his brothers and sisters. The crucifix would replace the large gold

[22] Ibid., 93.
[23] Ibid., 109.
[24] Ibid., 108.

pectoral cross he had received from Pope Pius XII at his episcopal ordination. His motto as a bishop was "To Jesus through Mary".

His new title and even more colorful regalia did not alter his commitment to the missions or his work schedule. In 1951, he personally donated $42,980 to the missions out of his royalties and speaking fees. His nineteen-hour days continued to be filled with meetings, writing his columns, preparing for his weekly broadcasts for *The Catholic Hour*, meeting with converts, and, of course, fundraising. If the bishop thought he was a busy man in the fall of 1951, his life was to become even more hectic in 1952, when he was tapped to present a weekly television program—for the better part of the year, he did both a weekly radio broadcast and a weekly television program.[25]

A Man Made for Television

If radio had helped to unite the country during the two world wars and the Depression, post-war America would be shaped by the advent of television and its explosion into the homes of its citizens. By the mid-1950s, the vast majority of households could boast at least one television set, and many had two or more; there were more TV sets than bathtubs in American homes.[26] Television was the medium of the future, conveying sights, sounds, and ideas to entertain, reassure, or challenge the audiences. There were news programs, serious dramas, comedy programs, variety shows, game shows, sporting events, singing, and dancing to be viewed from the comfort of one's living room. In 1954, TV dinners were introduced so that families did not have to interrupt their viewing pleasure to take time out for dinner. Dinner hot from the oven would be served on TV trays in the living room or den before the television set. Sheen had begun his radio broadcasting back in 1928 for the Paulist Fathers. Through 1951, he had been the most popular speaker on

[25] Kathleen L. Riley, *Fulton J. Sheen: An American Catholic Response to the Twentieth Century* (New York: Alba House, 2004), 311–15; Francis Cardinal Spellman letter thanking Fulton Sheen for his generosity, February 8, 1952, Spellman Papers, New York Archdiocesan Archives.

[26] Christopher Owen Lynch, *Selling Catholicism: Bishop Sheen and the Power of Television* (Lexington, Ky.: University Press of Kentucky, 1998), 9.

the weekly *Catholic Hour*, almost since its inception in March of 1930, so he was a practiced and comfortable public speaker. Indeed, he was a gifted orator with a message to impart. When the American Catholic Church started to look around for an individual to go on a television network to present its message, Bishop Fulton J. Sheen came immediately to mind.

He was initially approached by Monsignor Edwin Broderick, who had been tasked by Cardinal Spellman to develop a Catholic presence on television. Spellman had appointed Broderick as the director of the Catholic Apostolate for Radio, Television, and Advertising. Creating a Catholic presence on television was Broderick's first goal. Most religious programing on both radio and television was scheduled for the very early or very late hours of the day. Spellman wanted something different. Sheen was immediately interested in Broderick's idea. What Sheen proposed was to do programs that resembled the format of his convert classes with a twenty-minute presentation followed by ten minutes of questions Sheen would answer. He thought it could be televised from various churches around the New York diocese. Msgr. Broderick took the idea to the Du Mont Network, a decidedly minor network, but one that had several Catholics on its executive board. Du Mont liked the proposal, but thought it more economical and practical to film from a single location. It chose the one-thousand-seat Adelphi Theater off Broadway on Forty-fourth Street. The network proposed the title *Is Life Worth Living?* which Sheen changed right away to *Life Is Worth Living.* The program was to be filmed in front of a live audience, yet it was the camera and the audience at home that held Sheen's attention. Sheen intuitively knew that while the audience in the Adelphi Theater was important, it was the millions of viewers at home who were his main audience; they were coming into his "study", and he was being welcomed into their living rooms.

The first show debuted on February 12, 1952. *Life Is Worth Living* would be seen by home audiences at 8:00 on Tuesday evenings, originally only on three channels: in New York City, Chicago, and Washington, D.C. Msgr. Broderick was its producer, and Frank Bunetta, who directed the Jackie Gleason show, was the director. *Life Is Worth Living* played opposite Milton Berle's *Texaco Star Theater* on NBC and Frank Sinatra's CBS show, placing the newcomer in an almost impossible position in the "obituary slot".[27] Berle and Sinatra were two of the biggest stars in the country, and Sheen was largely unknown outside of New York and the audience of *The Catholic Hour*. Most television people thought Sheen's program was doomed to failure. Broderick had to pass out free tickets just to get an audience to the Adelphi Theater for the first production.[28] What did Sheen have to offer but a guy in a skirt alone on a stage, talking into the camera and occasionally writing on a blackboard, his only prop? They had no idea.

But Sheen was made for television. Despite his short stature, his was a commanding presence on the screen. Most Americans, even most Catholics, had probably never seen a Catholic bishop in full regalia before. In planning his program, Sheen asked for advice on how he should dress. The majority of those he asked advised Sheen to appear before the camera in a black clerical suit with the Roman collar. But he had always worn his cassock and formal clerical attire before live audiences, and he insisted on doing the same for television. Many who saw him in person or on television remember his eyes especially; they were considered hypnotic. His voice was well modulated and controlled, and his gestures never seemed rehearsed or overly dramatic, even when he would throw his hands up in the air to make a point or approach the camera to give it his full face; it all seemed natural. He came to his audience from what looked like a learned rector's study with books on shelves, a statue of the Virgin Mary on a pedestal, and a blackboard, on which always he wrote at the top, "J.M.J.", for Jesus, Mary, and Joseph. Against the wall was a fireplace and, above the fireplace, a cross. The cross was without a corpus, the kind of cross used by Protestants. Catholic crosses are most often crucifixes with the body of Christ attached. This was the study of a nondenominational clergyman. It was a set for all Christians designed by Broadway set designer and Sheen convert Jo Mielziner, who had worked the sets for convert Clare Boothe Luce's hit *The Women*. The theme music for the program was written by another Sheen convert, Fritz Kreisler, set in waltz time so Sheen could glide

---

[27] Reeves, *America's Bishop*, 224. See also Timothy H. Sherwood, *The Preaching of Archbishop Fulton J. Sheen* (New York: Lexington Books, 2019), 37.

[28] Reeves, *America's Bishop*, 224, from an interview with Edwin Broderick.

onto the stage. He only wore a touch of makeup to lighten the beard on his cheeks and to highlight and dramatize his eyes. Bishop Sheen would take five minutes before each show opening to pray and only then would he greet his audience.[29]

On his first show there were three guests to ask canned questions of him: journalist and convert Gretta Palmer; Herbert Trigger, a Jewish friend; and Marlene Brownett, the eighteen-year-old sister of Sheen's secretary. His topic for the evening was in a question form, "Is Life Worth Living?" The bishop addressed what all people seek in life: happiness. Yet although they pursue it, some people spend their lives directionless or at loose ends. They find their lives empty, without worth, and not much worth living. Happiness eludes them. Other people look for their happiness in achieving goals, such as position, wealth, or power. These proximate goals, once gained, never truly satisfy. What man really wants is "pure life, pure truth, pure love". Bishop Sheen concluded that life produces peace and happiness only if one is properly oriented to his ultimate end: God. All other goals are merely near ends and are thus not lastingly fulfilling. Only a life oriented to God makes life worth living, gives meaning to one's life, and brings true happiness.[30]

As a format, the guests with questions did not last, but one can look at the first list of guests to determine who Sheen thought his audience would be. It would be a diverse audience the program sought. The letters proved that the home audience was made up of all ages, races, and religions—or no religion at all. Both Protestants and Jews sent him letters, usually polite and inquiring. Sheen claimed that there were more letters from Jewish viewers than from Catholic readers.[31] They were all responding to Sheen personally and to his material. The manager of the Adelphi Theater, Saul Abraham, said, "Most Tuesday nights I just stand backstage and let the guy hypnotize me. He's got everything. In more than 50 years of show business I've

---

[29] Lynch, *Selling Catholicism*, 124–25. Lynch gives a detailed description of the stage setting for *Life Is Worth Living*.

[30] Fulton J. Sheen, *Life Is Worth Living* (New York: McGraw Hill, 1954), 15–20 (an edited transcription of his talk). Unfortunately, the video for this episode has been lost or destroyed. Sets of *Life Is Worth Living* that are advertised as "complete" do not include the first episode.

[31] Sheen, *Treasure*, 73.

never seen such respectful, intelligent audiences as this man draws."[32] The audience was respectful of Fulton Sheen because he was respectful of them. He never talked down to his audience. "They listened to him because he spoke the truth with sincerity," the writer Patricia Kossman remembered, "and they deeply respected him for it."[33]

He would always find a common level where all could understand his points, even when what he was talking about was quite complex or technical. He could even make atomic fusion and atomic fission understandable to his audience. He would say, "I am on television for the same reason I enter a pulpit or a classroom. Namely, to communicate and diffuse Divine Truth. I am not the Author, but only an heir and trustee."[34]

Very quickly, *Life Is Worth Living* took on the format it would keep for as long as Bishop Sheen would do the program (1952–1957). It would be a twenty-seven minute and twenty second talk without commercial interruptions, without notes, and without a teleprompter.[35] Commercials would air in the beginning and at the end, but never cut into the bishop's talk. The show's opening logo would be the same as that of the Society for the Propagation of the Faith, a corpus-less cross, and at the end of each program, the society's mailing address would be displayed across the bottom of the screen. The program for Sheen was an opportunity to raise more money for the missions. In the early Du Mont years, there were no commercials at all, as the program was considered a public service that fulfilled an F.C.C. requirement for broadcasters. Eventually the Admiral Corporation would become Sheen's sponsor, making him "the first religious communicator to have a sponsor for a program in prime time".[36] It was also the only religious program of its day to compete for ratings with commercial programming.[37] Albert Cutié wrote, "Billy Graham often referred to Bishop Fulton Sheen as 'the greatest communicator of the

---

[32] Reeves, *America's Bishop*, 227. See also James C. G. Conniff, *The Bishop Sheen Story* (New York: Fawcett Publications, 1953), 15.

[33] Patricia Kossmann, "Remembering Fulton Sheen", *America*, December 6, 2004, America magazine.org/issue/521/article/remembering-fulton-sheen.

[34] Reeves, *America's Bishop*, 227. See also Tim Taylor, "Fulton Sheen: Verities on TV", *CUE*, November 22, 1952, 20.

[35] Sheen, *Treasure*, 69–70.

[36] Lynch, *Selling Catholicism*, 27.

[37] Ibid., 7.

twentieth century.' *Time Magazine* called him 'God's microphone.'"[38] There would be approximately 125 episodes of *Life Is Worth Living* over the five years of the show. For his last two years in television, his program ran on the American Broadcasting Corporation (ABC) on Thursday nights. His competition was always stiff. The shows that played opposite his in the same timeslot were some of the most popular shows on television, but he bested all of them. After Milton Berle and Frank Sinatra, his competitors for viewing ratings were *The Bob Cummings Show* and *You Bet Your Life* with Groucho Marx, the top-rated *I Love Lucy*, and *Medic*. By 1956 he was appearing on 123 television stations, and 300 radio stations carried the audio portion of his program.[39] Sheen mused that he had probably managed to address more people in one of his half-hour television programs than the Apostle Paul reached in the entirety of his preaching career.[40]

Sheen knew well how to put together a compelling talk. Archbishop Timothy Dolan reminisced, "Fulton Sheen used to say that the three essentials of an effective talk were a good beginning, a good end, and keeping the two as close together as possible."[41] He would not be giving a speech to his audience, but rather a "talk"—with the word's connotation of intimacy, friendship, and mutual respect. A speechmaker addresses an audience from on high, but a talk is between equals. It was a challenging duality Sheen had to maintain. He needed to be both the expert and the friend, to be at the same time superior in knowledge to his audience and socially equal to it. If he was not the expert, then why listen to him at all? But if he came across as condescending to his audience, he would lose them altogether. It was a delicate balance that Bishop Fulton Sheen maintained beautifully year after year.

Sheen always ended his talk on time with a thirty-second cue from the director. He was able to adhere to the time limitations of his program because of the enormous preparation he put into each episode. He wrote:

[38] Albert Cutié, *God Talk: Preaching to Contemporary Congregations* (New York: Church Publishing, 2012), 20.

[39] Lynch, *Selling Catholicism*, 27. Many of the YouTube videos of Sheen that call themselves *Life Is Worth Living* are later programs that have appropriated the title of Sheen's original *Life Is Worth Living* series. If the program is in color, it is not part of the 1952–1957 series.

[40] Sheen, *Treasure*, 128.

[41] Archbishop Timothy Dolan, quoted in the *Positio* 1.1058.

I would spend about thirty hours preparing every telecast, which meant that enough material was gathered to talk for about an hour or more.... Though I would forget this or that point which I intended to deliver, I could draw on the store of accumulated information to take its place.... A day or two before the actual broadcast I would "try out" my comprehension of the subject by giving the talk in Italian to an Italian professor who was a friend of mine and also in French to a member of the staff who spoke French fluently. I did this not because of great expertise in either language but because I was forced the think out the ideas in another tongue and I knew that would help clarify the subject in my mind.[42]

Sheen did not memorize his material; he mastered it by his meticulous preparation. He would make outline after outline and then toss them out. The only fixed part of the program was its conclusion. He always ended with "God love you!"

Sheen's Unique Style of Presentation

Going on prime time television was very different from being on *The Catholic Hour*. The first obvious difference was that the audience would be much more diverse and much less Catholic. Therefore, the approach needed to be different—more ecumenical. While his talks were almost always explicitly Christian, they generally were not overtly Catholic. Marvin Epstein, an anti-Catholic Jewish viewer, wondered, "How could he be making pronouncements which no person could reject, regardless of faith—because they simply made such maximal common sense?"[43] While Sheen's talks were God-centered, they were largely not sectarian in nature. Sheen wrote:

The new method had to be more ecumenical and directed to Catholics, Protestants, Jews, and men of good will. It was no longer a direct presentation of Christian doctrine but rather a reasoned approach to it beginning with something that was common to the audience. Hence during those television years, the subjects ranged from communism, to art, to science, to humor, to aviation, war, etc. Starting

[42] Sheen, *Treasure*, 70.
[43] Mary Ann Watson, "And They Said 'Uncle Fultie' Didn't Have a Prayer ...", *Television Quarterly*, no. 26 (1992), 3.

with something that was common to the audience and to me, I would gradually proceed from the known to the unknown or to the moral and Christian philosophy. It was the same method our Lord used.... This was the same method used by St. Paul.[44]

Although Sheen denied proselytizing on television, he received many letters requesting instruction in the Catholic faith. He would say of his more indirect approach to winning souls on television, "I depended more on the grace of God and less on myself.... The illumination that fell on any soul was more of the Spirit and less of Sheen."[45] To those who asked for materials on the Catholic Church, he sent books and pamphlets. Those who wanted instructions in the faith would meet Sheen in large church halls or Catholic school auditoriums. As he had always maintained, he would meet converts wherever he found them.

Bishop Sheen tended to open his programs with a joke of some sort, sometimes a very corny one, often at his own expense. He told one audience about a baby who cried in the church as he was giving a homily. The mother got up to take the baby out, when Sheen stopped her saying, "Madam, it's quite all right. The child is not bothering me." She said, "I know, but you are bothering the child!"[46] He worked humor into every program. It was part of his tightrope trick of keeping the audience informed as well as entertained. Both were required for a successful prime time talk show on American television. Often his anecdote would begin with "this week" or "the other day". In this way he let the audience in on his day-to-day life and created an intimacy with them. In one episode, he said:

> The other day I was on an elevator in a department store. I was shopping on the fifth floor and wanted to go to the sixth. I went into the elevator, and several passengers went in with me. Just as the elevator was about to start and the operator said, "Going up." Some woman came rushing in and said, "I don't want to go up. I want to go down!"

[44] Sheen, Treasure, 72.
[45] Ibid., 73.
[46] Fulton J. Sheen, "How to Talk", Life Is Worth Living (television show). See also "How To Talk" in Fulton J. Sheen's text, Life Is Worth Living (New York: McGraw Hill, 1954), 191–97, hereafter, LIWL.

Then turning to me—I don't know why she picked on me [*applause and laughter*]—but turning to me she said, "I didn't think I'd go wrong following you!" I said, "Madam, I only take people up!"[47]

He also liked to mention children as being in his audience. "I bumped into a little boy in the street this week who said, 'I always listen to you on Tuesday night. My father makes me.' [*laughter*] I told him to have his father watch *Howdy Doody*."[48] This kind of anecdote accomplished two things for Bishop Sheen. It showed the bishop as self-deprecating and, therefore, almost equal to his audience, and at the same time let them know that whole families were watching his program, making him the celebrity above the audience. In one brief instant he is both humble and superior. His was an ironic humor that furthered the purpose of his program. Once he told his audience, "I was retarded. I was in school until I was twenty-nine. I'll never forget those six years in the third grade." But then he went on to make some off-handed remark about his graduate education in Belgium at Louvain University.[49] Another time he recounted how he prepared to give his talks by research, meditation, and giving his talk in both French and Italian before giving it to the audience in English. He followed up with "or is it English?" It was a joke on himself that invited the audience to critique him, but of course they found the talk to be in perfect English.

One of his running jokes was that he had an angel named Skippy who would erase the blackboard for him. Everyone realized that it was a stagehand and not a heavenly assistant who did the erasing, but he kept up the fiction. In telling a corny tale, he made himself "just one of the folks", but at the same time, the story was not funny in itself; because it was Sheen who was telling it, and he and the audience knew it was not inherently funny, Sheen somehow became all the more elevated in status. Everyone was in on the humor: it was the attempt at humor that was funny, and not the joke itself. The home audience was invited to join the laughter and applause of the live audience in the

[47] Sheen, "Something Higher", episode 58, *Life Is Worth Living*, https://www.youtube .com/watch?v=WiEKgzYcybQ. See also Sheen, "Something Higher", in *LIWL*, 112–18.
[48] Lynch, *Selling Catholicism*, 136.
[49] Ibid., 126.

Adelphi Theater and feel a part of it,[50] becoming just as much part of the show. Sheen even told the anecdote of a woman who was disappointed in his show, who told him to go off television or refund her hundred-dollar donation. He told the audience that he sent the woman back her money because "I felt it was worth the one hundred dollars to be with you [*applause*]."[51]

Bishop Sheen could be very funny, but he did not consider himself in any way a comedian. He said, "By nature I am a rather serious person. But in a paradoxical kind of way, I am very fond of humor and laughter." He went on to explain, "There may be incidental flashes of it here and there, but it is not one of God's gifts to me. However there is a close relationship between faith and humor.... He who possesses faith knows that this world is not the only one, and therefore it can be regarded rather lightly. To an atheist gold is gold, water is water and money is money. To a believer everything in this world is a telltale of something else."[52] Sheen also believed that an audience enjoyed a good retort. He was reminded of a lecture he once gave in Minnesota when, during the question-and-answer period, he was asked by a student, "'How was Jonah in the belly of the whale for three days?' I answered: 'I have not the vaguest idea, but when I get to Heaven I'll ask Jonah.'" Then someone called out, "'Suppose Jonah isn't there?' I said: 'Then you ask him.'"[53] The comedians Milton Berle, Bob Hope, and Jackie Gleason adored Fulton Sheen. Gleason, who appreciated humor when he saw it, would often sit in the production booth during Sheen's show just to watch him. In admiration of Sheen's technique, Gleason would say, "What a pause!" In humor, timing is important, and, according to Gleason, Sheen had it down pat.[54]

Sheen connived to make the entire audience feel as if they were not only part of the show but also somewhat in control of the evening. He might open by thanking them for allowing him into their homes that night or by asking, "Would it please you if tonight we talked about ...?"[55] He called them "friends". He would flatter them

[50] Ibid., 134.
[51] Quoted in ibid., 120.
[52] Sheen, *Treasure*, 297. For examples of Sheen's favorite jokes, see pages 297–308.
[53] Ibid., 301. Sheen, "How to Talk", *LIWL*, 191–97.
[54] Reeves, *America's Bishop*, 228.
[55] Lynch, *Selling Catholicism*, 126.

by using a Latin phrase, then say, "For the three of you in this vast audience who have forgotten their Latin, I will translate", or "Everybody in the audience who knows philosophy will recall ..."[56] At the same time that he flattered them, he reminded them how well educated he was—but then made up for this superiority with his recognition of his incredibly bad drawing skills. His figures on the blackboard were stick figures that most five-year-olds could draw better. He also remarked that the audience would never see him dance; it was another skill he lacked.[57] He would emphasize his high station as a bishop and then modestly refer to his zucchetto as a "beanie".[58] He told the story of the Jewish boy who wrote to him to complain that his father would not let him wear a yarmulka because he was too young. " 'Bishop Sheen wears one, why can't I?' In secret he wrote to me asking for my zucchetto, which I sent him. Later on the Pittsburgh newspaper carried his picture with his episcopal yarmulka."[59] In this tale he let the audience know that his show was watched by Jewish families as well as Christian.

If Bishop Sheen came across on television as such an imposing figure despite his five-foot-seven or -eight-inch frame, it was due partially to his elevator shoes—but mostly to the medium of television. To begin with, the barrier of the proscenium arch of the theater stage was removed from the camera's view, bringing Sheen's figure closer to the audience—at times with a full-face shot in the camera. The camera angles forced the audience at home to look up to the bishop, making him appear taller. The lighting gave a slight halo effect around his head. The voluminous ferraiolo (bishop's cape) gave him more space and made him look larger. The cameras (there were two and sometimes three) would follow him nonstop the entire half hour of the program. One camera's shot would blend into the next camera's shot. He generally maintained constant eye contact with his audience unless he was at the blackboard, and even then, he would look over his shoulder at them. Christopher Lynch thought even the blinking of his eyes was controlled.[60] With a great deal of understatement, Sheen would say of himself and television, "I have a certain talent for

---

[56] Ibid., 128.
[57] Ibid., 36.
[58] Ibid., 142.
[59] Sheen, Treasure, 68.
[60] Lynch, Selling Catholicism, 137.

it",[61] and he wrote in his autobiography, "I was born in the electronic age."[62] He could have said he was born *for* the electronic age. One television director noted, "His whole technique was the magnetic effect of the way he looked into the camera. I hate to use a cliché, but the word is 'telegenic.' He was made for the medium."[63] *Time* magazine wrote, "The gestures, the timing, the voice. If he came out in a barrel and read the telephone book, they'd love him."[64]

Life Is Worth Living was a popular television program. However good its ratings were, though, Bishop Sheen and the Catholic Church in America had a goal beyond mere entertainment. For Sheen it was a pulpit without being a pulpit; the audience was not there to be preached to. He had a complex message to impart to his audience. When he began in radio broadcasting, the National Council of Catholic Men, which sponsored *The Catholic Hour*, intended the program to "promote a better understanding of the Catholic Church and its doctrines and to contribute to the growth of friendly relations among the several religious groups in the United States".[65] In the late 1920s Catholics were still suspect as unreliable citizens of the country. The Protestant majority looked down upon the mostly immigrant Catholics with their seemingly strange religious rituals and many festivals and saw a foreign people who, they feared, were more committed to the pope in Rome than to the president in Washington. In many ways it was the enthusiastic patriotism of Catholics during World War II, their anti-Communism, and the general move from the inner cities to the suburbs after the war that moved American Catholics into the mainstream of American life. There were pockets of anti-Catholicism that erupted from time to time, but most Americans by the 1950s no longer looked upon Catholics as subversive or dangerous. Indeed, for a hundred years before the debut of *Life Is Worth Living* in 1952, Catholics represented the single largest Christian denomination in America. But their numerical superiority did not assuage the Protestant bias against the Catholics; Catholics had

---

[61] Ibid., 36.

[62] Sheen, *Treasure*, 63.

[63] Quoted in Mary Ann Watson, "And They Said Uncle Fultie Didn't Have a Prayer ...", *Television Quarterly*, no. 26 (1992).

[64] "Fulton J. Sheen: The First Televangelist", *Time*, April 14, 1952.

[65] Reeves, *America's Bishop*, 79.

to earn their acceptance slowly from their Protestant neighbors by their constituting one-third of America's fighting forces in World War II, their assimilation into civic organizations, their climb up the economic ladder, their attendance at universities and colleges after the war, their march into the suburbs, and their joining hands with Protestant anti-Communists.

Sheen's job on *Life Is Worth Living* was to bring contemporary Americans to a greater awareness of right and wrong, of the reality of the sacred dimension of life, of the destructive danger of sin, and of the dangers of modern ideologies that threaten lives and souls. His presentations were always Christ-centered, but never dogmatically Catholic. He only rarely talked of specific Catholic beliefs that distanced Catholics from Protestants. Not that he downplayed the Virgin Mary or the authority of the pope; rather, he spoke of timeless values common to the Judeo-Christian world, while at the same time addressing serious problems in everyday modern life: alienation, teenagers, science, the Cold War, and Communism. Sheen urged his audiences to turn to God and follow the teachings of Jesus in all cases, such as with his admonition, "Nature bids us to be mindful of others; Christ bids us to put love where we do not find it, and thus will we find everyone lovable."[66]

Examples from *Life Is Worth Living*[67]

In his *Life Is Worth Living* episode entitled "Nice People", Bishop Sheen noted that "nice people think they are good; awful people *know* they are not." Nice people do not think they are ever guilty of transgressing a moral law. Nice people always have a good reason for what they have done. "Goodness is always their own, but badness is due to something outside themselves." Nice people are quick to blame their transgressions on psychological problems or someone else. When they sin, they are quick to say, "Oops!" and quickly move on. They judge themselves on their virtues and ignore their

---

[66] Fulton J. Sheen, "Nice People", season 2, episode 8, *Life Is Worth Living*. See also Sheen, *LIWL*, 111–18.

[67] These episodes of *Life Is Worth Living* can be streamed at https://www.bishopsheen.com/pages/stream.

vices. Bad people are aware of the virtues they do not possess and have learned to expect their vices. Nice people follow the "ethics of social orthodoxy, or convention. They lose less sleep over falsifying an income-tax return than over wearing a white tie instead of a black one at a banquet or are more scandalized at a preacher's grammatical errors than at his false doctrine. Refinement and respectability form a large concept of his goodness, and social convention is given the force of a Divine Command; what is respectable or usual is not wrong."[68]

Sheen then used the Gospel tale of the woman caught in adultery to make his point about nice or good people and those thought to be bad.[69] In Christ's day, the scribes and the Pharisees were considered among the nicest of "nice people". An adulterous woman was clearly in the "not nice" camp. But the men who brought the guilty woman before Jesus were less concerned with her sin than with the possibility of calling out Jesus for breaking a law. They proclaimed the Mosaic penalty for adultery, which was death by stoning, and then said to Jesus, "What say you?" If Jesus then told them to kill her, he could have been accused of breaking the Roman law, which only allowed the Roman authorities to condemn someone to death; but if he denied the Mosaic law, he could have been accused of breaking divine law. The scribes and Pharisees thought they had caught Jesus between mercy and justice—but he outwitted them by telling them to let whoever is without sin cast the first stone. In this way he broke neither the Roman law nor the Mosaic law, and the chagrined accusers slunk away. The nice people were not so nice after all. To the woman, he said, "Go, and do not sin again" (Jn 8:11). Sheen concluded:

> The nice people do not find God, because, denying personal guilt, they have no need of a redeemer. The awful people, the adulterous woman in this story, who are passionate, sensual, warped, lonely, weak, but who, nevertheless make an attempt at goodness, are quick to realize that they need another help than their own; that they cannot lift themselves by their bootstraps. Their sins create an emptiness. From that point on, like the woman in sin, it is "Christ or nothing."[70]

---

[68] Sheen, "Nice People". See also Sheen, *LIWL*, 217–18.
[69] See John 8:1–11.
[70] Sheen, "Nice People". See also Sheen, *LIWL*, 221.

After he has made his point about nice people, Sheen brings the audience into the dialogue to reassure them. When we enter the Kingdom of Heaven, he tells them, "The surprises will be threefold: first, we are going to see a number of people there whom we never expected to see.... The second surprise will be not seeing a number of the nice people whom we expected to see. But these surprises will be mild compared to the third and greatest surprise of all, and that surprise will be that we are there."[71]

In his introduction to the volume *Life Is Worth Living*, a collection of transcripts from his programs from his first year on television, Bishop Sheen wrote, "Man wants three things: life, knowledge, and love."[72] In the episode "Teenagers", he elaborates on the kind of life a teenager seeks, the object of his desired knowledge, and the specific type of love he wants. He begins by saying there is no good definition of a teenager, but he goes on to identify three dominant characteristics of the American teenager: "self-consciousness, imitativeness, and restlessness".[73]

As the teenager comes to recognize his own personality and ego as separate from his family, he wants to spend almost all his time with those of his own kind, other teenagers. He believes it is only other teens who can understand him. They speak his language and listen to his music—his parents decidedly do not. He is conscious of being his true self only in the company of other teenagers. The rising teenager begins to imitate what others of his age group are doing, thinking, and saying. They all dress alike. They all belong to what was identified by Harold Rosenberg in a different context as "a herd of independent minds".[74] Teenagers think they are being independent when they are actually melding into the vast and undifferentiated teenage milieu. They are becoming independent from their families, but most are utterly conforming to teen society. Sheen said, "The teenager in such a case never really becomes himself or herself, but *like others*." He feels that his family cannot know him as he truly is, and, not knowing him, cannot love him. Only his fellow teens can understand and love him as he is. He feels loved and accepted by his peers and he loves them in return. The problem for the teenage

---

[71] Sheen, "Nice People". See also Sheen, *LIWL*, 222.

[72] *LIWL*, 19.

[73] Fulton J. Sheen, "Teenagers", season 1, episode 5, *Life Is Worth Living*. See also Sheen, *LIWL*, 81.

[74] Harold Rosenberg, *Discovering the Present* (Chicago: University of Chicago Press, 1973), 23.

individual, however, is that "Imitation without moral standards is loss of personality or the spoiling of character."[75]

The third characteristic of teens is that they are physically restless. They cannot sit still unless by their own choosing. They are enervated by home chores but have boundless energy for playing games, dancing, or hanging out with friends until all hours. It is also a time in life when crushes on another are common, if mercurial: "There are no friendships that seem closer than the friendships of teenagers, and yet there are hardly any friendships that are quite as volatile. Adults must remember, however, that this urge for affection, for love, for friendship, for society, is good and right. God put it in them, and it is not to be crushed but developed along right lines."[76] The teenager in his restlessness often goes from one thing to another, allowing him to try out many possible career paths or vocations. This is one good effect of his restlessness.

To help him develop himself along the right lines, Bishop Sheen recommends helping the teen to develop the virtue of purity. It seems almost laughable today to recommend purity for teenagers, but Sheen was correct then as well as now. He defines purity as reverence for mystery—the mystery of sex. Understanding the mystery of sex begins with being aware of the physical and emotional attributes of femaleness and maleness. Moreover, it has a spiritual dimension in that the creativity of sex belongs to men and women: "Almighty God has prolonged his great creative power in man and woman."[77] He goes on to say, "So sacred has been the consciousness of the power of creativity that all people, Jewish, Christian, and pagan, have always surrounded marriage with religious, sacred, liturgical rites in order to indicate that here is the communication of a great God-given power. Purity is *reverence* for the mystery of creation."[78]

Youth must not be wasted on the young, says Sheen. "Youth has only one arrow in its quiver; it may be shot but once—that is the arrow of youth. Be sure that it hits the target—the Divinely appointed target—love of God, love of country, love of neighbor."[79] These three loves are common themes in Sheen's television programs.

[75] Sheen, "Teenagers". See also Sheen, *LIWL*, 82.
[76] Sheen, "Teenagers". See also Sheen, *LIWL*, 83.
[77] Sheen, "Teenagers". See also Sheen, *LIWL*, 84.
[78] Sheen, "Teenagers". See also Sheen, *LIWL*, 84–85.
[79] Sheen, "Teenagers". See also Sheen, *LIWL*, 86.

Fulton J. Sheen as an infant had been dedicated by his mother to the care of the Virgin Mary. At his ordination, he dedicated his priesthood to the service of the Blessed Mother. He would visit Lourdes and Fatima—places where the Virgin is known to have appeared to children and where pilgrims go to seek her intercession, to be close to her, to thank her—to ask for her ongoing support for his vocation. But rarely would he talk about her on his television program. Many Protestants incorrectly think Catholics worship the Virgin, not understanding the difference between veneration and worship. To be clear, Catholics only worship God, but hold in high esteem the saints, with Mary being the first Christian and premier saint. In his second season of his television show, Bishop Sheen gave a single talk on the Virgin at Fatima, the village in Portugal where, in 1917, the Virgin appeared several times to three young children. He began by noting three occurrences that all happened on the same day, October 13, 1917, when the world was in the midst of World War I.[80]

In Russia on that day, the Bolshevik revolution was launched by revolutionaries who broke into a school room and killed a number of children and teachers in the middle of a catechism class inside the Church of the Iberian Virgin, after having already destroyed the altar and statuary. It was a deliberate and calculated act of violence against the Church and against innocent children. When the noble woman who was in charge of the class ran to the leader of the revolutionaries to protest, he told her he already knew about the massacre and desecration because he had ordered it.

On the same day in Rome, Eugenio Pacelli was consecrated a bishop in the Roman Catholic Church. Communist revolutionaries would break into his home in Munich and threaten to kill him. Staring at the intruders and holding on to his pectoral cross, he responded, "All right—kill me! But you will gain nothing! I am only trying to save Germany." The Communist revolutionaries stole away into the night, leaving Pacelli unharmed. "They were never able to explain why a pair of eyes, a lean figure holding a cross, and a soft voice should be more powerful than their guns, grenades, and orders. There was only one thing that was certain. From that day on that man was

[80] Fulton J. Sheen, "Our Lady of Fatima", season 2, episode 5, *Life Is Worth Living*. See also Sheen, *LIWL*, 202–7.

afraid of absolutely nothing in all the world."[81] Pacelli would go on
to become Pope Pius XII, who stood up to Nazis and Communists.
Looking into the camera, Bishop Sheen then touched the pectoral
cross he was wearing that night and told the audience that it was
the same pectoral cross Pacelli had worn when he stared down his
would-be assassins: Sheen had borrowed it from Cardinal Spellman,
who had received it as a gift from Pope Pius XII, for the evening.

It was also on October 13, 1917, that the Virgin Mary appeared
again in Fatima, Portugal, to Lucia, Jacinta, and Francisco, the child-
shepherds. She had appeared to them on April 13, May 13, June 13,
July 13, August 13, and September 13. Bishop Sheen emphasized
Mary's role as mother—the mother of Jesus, the Second person of the
trinitarian Godhead, and therefore the Mother of God, but also our
mother, given to us from the Cross of Golgotha when Jesus exclaimed
to his disciple, "Behold, your mother!" (Jn 19:27). The Lady who
appeared to the children correctly foretold the early deaths of two of
the children and the end of World War I within a year. The war ended
on November 11, 1918. She also told them: "If people do not stop
offending God, another and worse World War will have its remote
beginning during the reign of the next Pontiff." This, it was disclosed,
was the Civil War in Spain. World War II could have been prevented
by penance and prayer and a return again to God. For the failure of
the world to return to God, the Virgin foretold another World War.[82]

In order that people would believe her prophecies, the Virgin told
the children she would provide a sign, a miracle, to take place on
October 13, 1917. On the appointed day, seventy thousand people stood in the drenching rain and mud to witness a miracle. The
Virgin appeared to the children but was invisible to the gathered
crowd. Portugal, like much of Europe in 1917, was largely Communist, atheistic or agnostic, and anticlerical. The crowd did not really
expect a miracle, but an assurance that the children were not telling
the truth about the Lady who visited them and gave them prognosti-
cations of events to come. Those in the crowd were less faithful and
more curious. What they saw and experienced that day was beyond
description and certainly beyond their experience or expectations.

[81] Sheen, "Fatima", *Life Is Worth Living*. See also Sheen, *LIWL*, 203–4.
[82] Sheen, "Fatima". See also Sheen, *LIWL*, 204.

Toddler Peter John "PJ" Sheen with his grandfather, circa 1898

Graduation from St. Viator College, circa 1917

Young Sheen (left) as a seminarian at St. Paul's Seminary, circa 1910

Fr. Fulton J. Sheen at his ordination to the priesthood, September 20, 1919

Sheen with students and professors at the University of Louvain,
Belgium, circa 1921

A very youthful Monsignor Fulton J.
Sheen, circa 1934

Installation of Fulton Sheen as the
bishop of Rochester, New York,
December 15, 1966

Bishop Sheen gives his first espiscopal blessing,
Rome, June 11, 1951

Fulton Sheen is brought into the homes of millions on
his weekly television show *Life Is Worth Living*,
originally broadcast over the Dumont airwaves

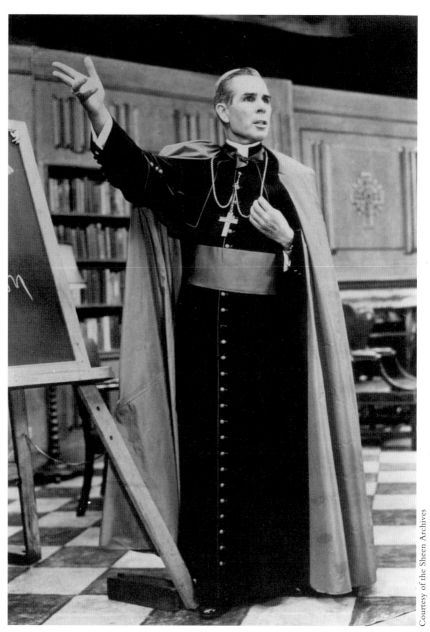

Fulton Sheen in full regalia on the set of *Life Is Worth Living*,
1952–1957

Courtesy of the Sheen Archives

Archbishop Sheen giving out communion in Lourdes,
France, circa 1970. He had a special devotion
to Our Lady of Lourdes.

Courtesy of the Sheen Archives

Archbishop Sheen (front) finding his seat
in St. Peter's in Rome during the
Second Vatican Council, 1962–1965

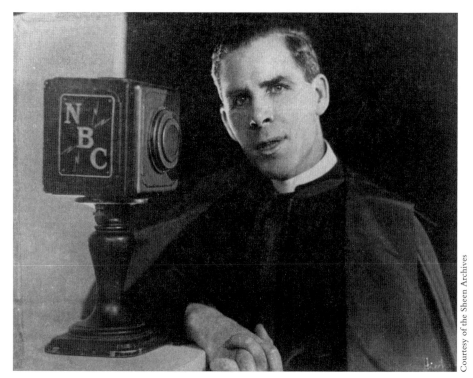

Speaking into the radio microphone, 1930

A *Catholic Hour* broadcast

Street evangelization in Alabama, 1930s

Corpus Christi Church, Chicago,
on Good Friday, April 16, 1954

Francis Cardinal Spellman awards Fulton Sheen a medal for his service as
the national director for the Society for the Propagation of the Faith, 1952

Trip to Asia with Cardinal Spellman in 1948,
in Singapore. Sheen was very interested in
Eastern religion and philosophy.

Sheen at the cathedral in
Nanking (Nanjing) in 1948.
Children followed him
wherever he went.

Archbishop Sheen inspects the
Catholid missions in Africa.
Here he is in Tipperary,
South Africa, 1960.

Sheen had a special care for those with leprosy (Hanson's disease). Here (left) he presents a rosary to a Ugandan leper.

Below, the new bishop of Rochester, New York, greets the children of the diocese, 1966

Sheen preaches to a Holy Year crowd of 75,000 in the New Orleans Superdome, 1975

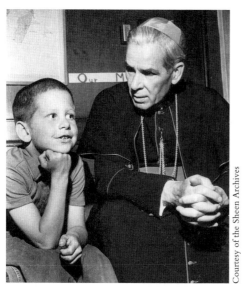

Sheen, seen here circa 1960, had great respect for the dignity of children. He never talked down to them.

A formal portrait by famed photographer, Yousuf Karsh

Fulton Sheen speaks to an assembly at a Jewish Temple in New York

After his retirement from the Rochester diocese, Bishop Sheen focused
much of his energy to giving retreats to clergy—1970s

Sheen began his National Prayer Breakfast talk in 1975 by saying,
"Mr. President, you are a sinner!"

Pope John Paul II embraces his good friend
Fulton J. Sheen, October 2, 1979

Archbishop Sheen lies in state in St. Patrick's Cathedral, December 1979.
In a letter to Mary Baker on June 3, 1979, Sheen wrote,
"As long as I live Christ is with me. When I die I will be with Him."

Sheen, the finder of lost lambs

Below, some notable converts whom Sheen helped bring into the Church

Clare Boothe Luce
Writer, congresswoman, ambassador,
convert

Bella Dodd
Teacher, lawyer,
Communist organizer,
convert

Louis Budenz
Journalist, Communist organizer,
convert

Heywood Broun
Journalist, writer, convert

Elizabeth Bentley
Communist agent, spy, convert

Ada "Bricktop" Smith
Entertainer, saloonkeeper,
convert

Fritz Kreisler
Violinist, composer, conductor, convert

Virginia Mayo
Hollywood actress, convert

It is called the "Miracle of the Sun".[83] At noon, the rain suddenly stopped and the sun came out and seemed to detach itself from its accustomed place in the sky; it suddenly began to dance above the people, swirling, dipping, rising, and falling close to the earth. It shot out beacons of light from itself, and multicolored lights emanated from the silvery sun. Most people there that day fell to the ground on their knees in prayer and supplication to be spared from the swirling mass of the sun. The astounding event lasted for about ten minutes, with the sun seemingly coming perilously close to the earth three times, after which it receded and returned to its normal place in the sky. The people found that their previously rain-soaked clothing had become dry. Most proclaimed the dancing of the sun a miracle that verified the witness of the children and the prophecies of the Virgin. Henceforth, Fatima became a popular pilgrimage site, drawing millions of people a year. The children told the people what the Virgin had told them: "The Heavenly Lady had told them that peace was conditioned on prayer, expiation, and sacrifice."[84]

The bishop went on to tell his audience about his own visit to Fatima on October 13, 1951, the forty-fourth anniversary of the Miracle of the Sun. He joined a crowd of a million pilgrims who prayed through the night for world peace. He said that as a statue of the Virgin Mary was carried through the gathered throngs, the people spontaneously waved white handkerchiefs "as white flags of purity, in tribute to the Lady of Peace". The white squares of the waving handkerchiefs led the bishop to think of the red flag above the Kremlin with its hammer and sickle. The red flag was a symbol under which so many millions had suffered. Sheen predicted that with the intervention of God in a world that had turned back to him, the hammer would become a cross, and the sickle would resemble "the moon under the Lady's feet". He said, "World War II would not have happened if men had returned to God. World War III need not happen, and it will not happen if we as a nation return to God. If there is a cold war in the world, it is because our hearts and our souls are not on fire with the love of God."[85]

---

[83] See Paul Senz, *Fatima: 100 Questions and Answers* (San Francisco: Ignatius Press, 2020), 74–82.
[84] Sheen, "Fatima". See also Sheen, *LIWL*, 205.
[85] Sheen, "Fatima". See also Sheen, *LIWL*, 206.

He then posed the rhetorical question of why God would use revelations by the Virgin Mary to bring about a conversion of the world. One reason, he suggested, was:

> Since the world has lost Christ, it may be through Mary it will recover Him. When Our Blessed Lord was lost at the age of twelve, it was the Blessed Mother who found Him. Now that He is lost again, it may be through Mary that the world will recover Christ their Savior. Another reason is that Divine Providence has committed to a woman the power of overcoming evil. In that first dread day when evil was introduced into the world, God spoke to the serpent in the Garden of Eden and said, "I shall put enmity between thee and the woman; between thy seed and her seed, and thou shalt lie in wait for her heel" (Genesis 3:15). In other words, evil shall have a progeny and a seed. Goodness, too, shall have a progeny and a seed. It will be through the power of the woman that evil will be overcome. We now live in an evil hour, for though goodness has its day, evil does have its hour.... If then we live in an evil hour, how shall we overcome the spirit of Satan except through the power of that Woman to whom Almighty God has given a mandate to crush the head of the serpent?[86]

In this episode of *Life Is Worth Living*, Bishop Sheen was calling on Americans to heed the advice of the Blessed Virgin to turn to God in prayer and repentance in order to bring about the peace all would have. He talked of the Virgin not as Immaculate Mary, the Queen of Heaven, the Queen of Angels, or Ever-Virgin—titles Catholics would commonly employ when speaking of Mary; he instead referred to her role as mother. She found her son in the Temple when he was twelve. She addressed herself to the young children at Fatima as a concerned mother, providing them with the requested sign to let the adults know the children were telling the truth. The Lady at Fatima asked the crowds, through the children, to return to God. She did not put herself forth as intercessor, but rather pointed to God directly.

Protestants were leery of Catholic devotions to Mary and her intercessory role, but they could be comfortable with an exhortation to turn to God in prayer, penance, and sacrifice to bring about world

---

[86] Sheen, "Fatima". See also Sheen, *LIWL*, 207.

peace, something all Americans desired. Sheen grounded his comments about the Virgin Mary in Scripture as a way to assuage Protestant concerns about the role of the Virgin. On other programs, he even referred to the statue of the Madonna and Child on his stage set as the statue of "Our Lady of Television". It is perhaps a flippant title to use, but it is noteworthy that Bishop Sheen almost always began and ended his programs standing in front of this statue. The Virgin Mary was always his lodestar, his "Lovely Lady Dressed in Blue".[87]

[87] One of Bishop Sheen's favorite poems, which he frequently recited, was "Lovely Lady Dressed in Blue", by Mary Dixon Thayer.

8

Two Very Different Converts

Bella Dodd: Educator and Communist Organizer[1]

Another woman who came into the life of Fulton Sheen, one who was red rather than blue, was Bella Visano Dodd. An ex-Communist, she came to Sheen, the most noted converter of ex-Communists, for instruction and reception into the Catholic Church. Born in 1904 in southern Italy, she was reared on a sixty-four-acre farm in New York that boasted a large house without electricity or indoor plumbing. The family had little money, yet did not consider themselves poor. Feeling that they did not fit in at the local Catholic parishes, one German and one Irish, the Italian Visanos did not attend services, but kept a largely culturally Catholic home with crucifixes over the beds and nightly prayers before a statue of the Virgin Mary. The Visano children thought these customs "old world", and they wanted to be modern Americans. Bella wrote in her autobiography, "Willingly, and yet not knowing what we did, we cut ourselves off from the culture of our own people and set out to find something new."[2] Bella turned to books and to the public school for her Americanization. She became an excellent student, curious and open-minded.

Just before she entered high school, a serious accident put her under the wheels of the trolly, resulting in the amputation of her left foot, a missed year of school, and constant pain. She spent the year reading books and writing poetry. When she returned to school the following year, she was determined to do everything her peers could

---

[1] The details of Bella Dodd's life are based on her autobiography, Bella V. Dodd, *School of Darkness* (New York: Devin-Adair, 1963).

[2] Ibid., 15.

do, including bird-watching field trips on unwieldy crutches. She was eventually fitted with a prosthetic foot, which, while not perfect, was better than the crutches. A high school friend lent her a copy of the socialist newspaper, *The Call*, where she learned about the plight of the poor and the inequalities in American life. She found herself drawn to politics and began to think of social justice as her vocation. She wrote, "A stubborn pride developed in my own ability to make judgments."[3] Her pride did not stand in the way of her making friends, though; at graduation she was voted the "most popular girl", something that pleased her even more than her scholarship to Hunter College in New York City.

She commuted from farm to college in one of her two dresses with her one black skirt, along with her mother's hand-knit sweaters. Her favorite teacher was Sarah Parks, who taught English and espoused Communists ideals. She flitted from one group to another searching for someplace to belong. She wrote of her classmates, "Since we had no common basis of belief, we drifted into laissez faire thinking with agnosticism for our religion and pragmatism for our philosophy." She became fascinated by Communism's aim to eradicate inequalities in life, but she wrote, "We had no foundation for solid thinking or effective action. We had no real goals because we had no sound view of man's nature and destiny. We had feelings and emotions, but no standards by which to chart the future." In the progressives, she found her place at college, and she was president of her junior class and president of the student council her senior year. It was in the student council she learned the value of a tightly organized group with a specific aim. Upon graduation, after more surgeries on her left leg, she accepted a job teaching political science at Hunter.

She entered a master's degree program at Columbia. Many of her professors there were politically active leftists and required their students to be the same. So Bella Dodd turned her Hunter students into political activists as well. She was not yet a Communist; that would come later. Her guiding thought was the love of mankind and the need to remake the world as a better place. Looking back, she wrote, "I tried to wreck [my students'] former ways of thought and I had given them no new paths to follow. The reason was simple:

[3] Ibid., 20.

I had none myself because I really didn't know where I was going."[4] She met many foreign students at Columbia and began to think of herself as a citizen of the world. Communism, with its international emphasis, appealed to her. On finishing her degree, she enrolled in law school, and the course of her study brought her to the conclusion that the law was the instrument of society's status quo, the very thing she wanted to change. She therefore decided to remain a teacher, because, she thought, a properly educated populace would, in fact, change the status quo for the better.

With her law degree in hand, Bella took a vacation to Europe, where she came into contact with fascists, who horrified her with their thuggery and theories of racial purity. Coming home onboard the ship, she met several school teachers who convinced her to join the teachers' union. At first she demurred, thinking that a college teacher should not join the teachers' union, but her new friends told her that it was college professors who had first established the American Federation of Teachers (AFT). She would join their union and marry John Dodd, and engineer ten years her senior, whom she had met in Europe.

Bella Dodd's first whiff of political power and success came when, back at Hunter, she confronted the administration with inequities imposed upon the nonteaching staff. Organizing the faculty in support of the staff, she was able to bring about positive financial adjustments for the staff. In this way, she learned that political organization could benefit the poorest people. At a meeting of the teachers' union, Bella met Harriet Silverman, an openly professed Communist who was, unknown to Bella, an international operative for the Soviet Union. Silverman invited Bella Dodd to throw in her lot with the Communists to fight the fascists as a public person with no apparent ties to the Party. Silverman took Dodd to meet with Earl Browder, then head of the CPUSA in New York. Dodd agreed to start the Anti-Fascist Literature Committee, to be made up of teachers who would write and sell pamphlets of Communist ideals. Dodd joined the Class Room Teachers Association (CRTA), a Communist front organization ostensibly for teachers to learn techniques of mass action and the basis of class-struggle philosophy. The CRTA brought teachers a revolutionary approach to problems and served as a

---

[4] Ibid., 41.

recruiting tool for the Party. It brought the plight of unemployed and untenured teachers to public awareness. At the time, the members of the CRTA leadership also belonged to the Teachers Union Local 5 of the AFT, ensuring that the union would be ultimately controlled by the Communists because of their discipline and tight coordination at meetings. Dodd wanted to be an open member of the CPUSA, but the organization would not allow her to; she would be one of many secretly working for the Party.

A friend of hers from her school days, Christopher McGrath, was then a state representative and the chairman of the Education Committee of the New York Assembly. Dodd met with him to craft a bill on college teacher tenure, which passed the Assembly. She became a hero to her Hunter colleagues and to the members of the Teachers Union Local 5. The union named her their legislative representative, which made her a member of the American Federation of Labor. With Communists in charge of the union, membership exploded in the 1930s to include unemployed teachers, substitute teachers, and WPA teachers, making it an impressive political bloc. Dodd's importance in the Party increased accordingly. She proudly marched in the 1936 Labor Day parade at the head of five hundred teachers. "This was my gesture of defiance against greed and corruption", she wrote. "It was also an affirmation of my belief that a better world could be created."[5]

The Communists had made inroads during the Depression by assuring people that their reduced circumstances were the result of a corrupt economic system and the greedy plutocrats at the top of the economic heap—creating class hatred among the dispossessed. Those who opposed the "people" were labeled fascists. Bella Dodd became so caught up by Communist propaganda and her involvement in the union movement that she decided in 1938 to leave her tenured position and pension plan from Hunter College to take up a full-time job with the teachers' union at sixty dollars a week. Hunter's president tried to dissuade her: "These people will take you and use you, Bella, and then they will throw you away."[6] But the teachers' union needed Bella Dodd. The New York Assembly decided to investigate not only the cost of public education and administrative procedures, but

[5] Ibid., 85.
[6] Ibid., 108.

also the subversive activities of New York City teachers. The Communists, realizing that the teachers were the backbone of the Party, gave Bella and the union its full support. Dodd explained, "The strategy decided on was to defend the teachers by defending the Party."[7] After a list of members from among elementary and secondary teachers was turned over to the investigative committee, Dodd burned the list of college teachers belonging to the union. She had been given a Communist Party liaison to teach her delaying tactics, and she instructed Communist teachers under subpoena to refuse to answer questions, and, if they could, to disappear for a while. Non-Communist teachers she told to tell the truth to the committee. Dodd and the teachers' union organized a "Save Our Schools" campaign to paint the real purpose of the investigation as being to shut down schools or drastically reduce funding. At the suggestion of the Communists, Dodd and her teachers engaged in "smearing, name calling, frameup, careful combing of each investigator's history", looking for tidbits to undermine the investigation. "We steadfastly kept before the public the idea that the investigation was intended to rob the public schools ... and to promote religious and racial bigotry."[8] In the end, the Assembly was able to fire forty to fifty teachers out of a membership of four thousand.

While the 1939 Hitler-Stalin Non-Aggression Pact was in force, the official Communist line was to keep America out of the war. Several "peace" committees were set up to that end. Bella Dodd headed the Women's Trade Union Committee for Peace. Her husband was pro-British and believed that America belonged in the war to aid Britain. For this and other reasons, he moved to Florida and divorced Dodd. Now she could put all of her efforts into the teachers' union, the American Labor Party, and the work of the Communist Party. Once the Non-Aggression Pact was dissolved by the German attack on the Soviet Union in 1941, there was a general pivot among the Communists; for instance, the Committee for Peace and Democracy became the American Mobilization Committee pushing for America to join the Allies. After Pearl Harbor, nearly the entire country rallied to the war effort. For Dodd, "it was bitter for me to realize that

[7] Ibid., 120.
[8] Ibid., 124.

the Communist Party leaders looked upon this united front as only a tactic to disrupt this country.... Each Party member was used as a part of the conspiracy, but the majority ... were unaware of it. Only those who knew the pattern knew how each fitted in the picture."[9]

With her parents long dead and herself divorced, Bella Dodd found herself completely alone in the world. But the union and Party members were her associates and friends, creating for her a strange family, many of whom were completely devoid of personal or political morality in their efforts to bring about the Communists' utopian world. She thought of herself as good and moral and projected those virtues onto those in the movement with her. Alexander Trachtenberg, the founder of the Communist Party in America, told her, "When communism came [sic] to America it would come under the label of 'progressive democracy.' It will come in labels acceptable to the American people."[10] Because she understood American capitalism to be decadent, greedy, immoral, and corrupt, no action was too extreme to overthrow it. Capitalism could not be reformed; it had to be overthrown by any and all means. In March of 1943, Bella Dodd agreed to become a card-carrying, public member of the Party. The Party became her all in all. She wrote, "I was rising in importance in this strange world. I had joined as an idealist. Now I was beginning to stay because of the sense of power it gave me and the chance to participate in significant events."[11]

Dodd became enmeshed in Party affairs. What she found at Party headquarters, where she spent the better part of each day, was at the same time attractive and repulsive. She understood her Party job as organizing people around issues of housing and welfare, but when she complained of the lack of files and materials, she was told by a Politburo member, "Bella, we are a revolutionary party, not a reform group. We aren't trying to patch up this bourgeois structure."[12] She saw herself as a reformer, not a revolutionary. She opened a law office to deal with labor law cases, a legal area where business was booming. She also set up a legislative committee for the Party and supervised the Communist-run unions for local, state, and federal

[9] Ibid., 138.
[10] Ibid., 150.
[11] Ibid., 140.
[12] Ibid., 163.

employees, along with various organizations for women and youths. Within a year of beginning to carry her card, Dodd was elected a top member of the National Committee for the Communist Political Association, the short-lived successor to the Communist Party. The rebranding of the Party was an effort by Earl Browder to "Americanize" the Communist organization in America. Browder had called for all the national groups in America to simply be "American". The rebranding effort failed and would lead to Browder being cast out of the Party.

Two Italian Communists spoke at the United States Communist Convention of 1945 emphasizing "the importance of . . . encouraging the foreign-born to use their languages and of circulating foreign language newspapers. They encouraged the organizing of different national groups almost as if these were foreign colonies. It would strengthen the nationalism among them, they asserted, a necessary thing for the building of world communism."[13] At first Dodd thought the Italians were out of step in their promotion of multiculturalism. It was the opposite of what Browder was recommending. An article in the *World-Telegram*, the international Communist newspaper, mocked Browder as a revisionist and called for his removal from the Party. Bella Dodd had been a Browder supporter. She was asked to renounce him in an article she was to write in the *Daily Worker*, something she could not do. While the Party was heaping abuse on Browder, Dodd served on a select committee of thirteen to interview members of the Party's National Board and National Committee to assess any reversionistic errors and to recommend their expulsion from or retention in the Party. "It was the nearest thing to a purge trial I have ever seen",[14] she would write. The 1945 convention went on to dissolve the Communist Political Association and to reestablish the Communist Party. The Party was to "re-dedicate itself to its revolutionary task of establishing a Soviet America."[15] It also expelled Earl Browder from the Party. He was to be the first in what would become a widespread purge of the Party membership. From 1945 to 1947, several thousands were

[13] Ibid., 180–81.
[14] Ibid., 187.
[15] Ibid., 190.

expelled for two main reasons: "one was guilty of either leftism or rightism."[16]

It was not long before accusations were flying at Bella Dodd. She was accused of racism, of white chauvinism, and of not supporting the Party's pick for a union leadership position. She could not support a man she knew to have embezzled union funds. She was so angry over the Party's willingness to overlook the embezzlement that she ran from the room shouting, "You think like pigs!"[17] She decided that the party was corrupt and immoral, and she wanted out. The next day she was called to a meeting to explain herself. When she said she wanted to leave the Party, she was told in no uncertain terms, "Dodd, no one gets out of the Party. You die or you are thrown out. But no one gets out."[18] These words brought to mind what she had been told about Paddy Whalen, who was useful to the Party, but not a committed Communist: "He is a wonderful comrade to help make a revolution but after it is successful, we are going to have to kill him because he would immediately proceed to unmake it."[19] She knew several comrades who had simply vanished or who had died in suspicious circumstances. Now she was terrified for her life.

She became the object of a smear campaign, accused of representing a landlord in a dispute with a tenant and thereby upholding the capitalist right to private property. She was also accused of being anti-Negro, anti-Semitic, and anti–working class. It was the usual compendium of slurs, character defamation, and harassment she had effectively used against the Assembly committee members investigating the teachers' union. There was a sham trial where every one of her requests was denied. On June 17, 1949, she received a call from the Associated Press telling her of the announcement of her expulsion from the Communist Party. Did she have a comment to make? She did not.

As the Party kept up its character assassination on Dodd, her law clients fell away; her friends turned their backs on her. She said of that time, "What I failed to understand was the security I felt in the Party was that of a group and that affection in the strange communist

[16] Ibid., 195.
[17] Ibid., 196.
[18] Ibid., 197.
[19] Ibid., 70.

world is never personal emotion. You are loved or hated on the basis of group acceptance."[20] She was utterly alone in an unforgiving world of ex-Communists. With no work to occupy her, few friends to relieve her solitude, and no energy to even read, she managed to pick up the New Testament. She writes of that time, "I had begun the process of 'unbecoming' a Communist. It was a long and painful process."[21]

It was not long before Bella Dodd was called to testify before the Tydings Committee in the U.S. Senate. Her testimony brought many things into focus for her. "I had regarded the Communist Party as a poor man's party and thought the presence of certain men of wealth within it accidental.... Now I saw this was only a façade placed there by the movement to create the illusion of the poor man's party; it was in reality a device to control the 'common man' they so raucously championed."[22]

In the autumn of 1950 while in Washington, D.C., on a court case, Dodd ran into her old friend, Christopher McGrath, then a congressman. He noted her fatigued and worried look and offered her protection from the F.B.I., which she declined. He offered to pray for her and then made another suggestion: "Bella, would you like to see a priest?"[23] She surprised herself by saying yes. McGrath drove her to the Chevy Chase home of Msgr. Fulton Sheen. When she arrived, the warm welcome she received from him brought her to uncontrollable tears. He took her into his chapel to pray. She did not recall praying, but she remembered the feeling of "stillness and peace".[24] The monsignor gave her a rosary and asked her to call on him in New York, as he was moving to her city in a few weeks.

Back in New York on Christmas Eve, Dodd dined with good friends in their one-room apartment, where after dinner they took turns reading psalms. On her way home that night, she found herself in the Church of Saint Francis of Assisi for midnight Mass, her first in years: "It came to me as I stood there that here about me were the masses I had sought through the years, the people I loved and wanted

[20] Ibid., 222.
[21] Ibid., 224.
[22] Ibid., 228.
[23] Ibid., 231.
[24] Ibid., 234.

to serve. Here was what I sought so vainly in the Communist Party, the true brotherhood of man. Here were men and women of all races and ages and social conditions cemented by their love of God. Here was a brotherhood of man with meaning."[25] She prayed that night for God to help her, and he did help her in various ways. She ran into a caring old friend who introduced her to a Maryknoll priest, Fr. James Keller, who had written a book called *You Can Change the World*. His thesis was that changing the world required personal regeneration first. This was something that Bella Dodd found comforting. Fr. Keller taught her that she was an irreplaceable child of God, and she also learned how little she knew of the faith of her Italian past. Another friend took her to the offices of the newly promoted Bishop Fulton Sheen at the Society for the Propagation of the Faith. In April of 1952, after many weeks of instruction and study, Bishop Sheen received Bella Dodd back into the Church at Saint Patrick's Cathedral with conditional Baptism, confession, and Communion. She would say afterward, "It as if I had been ill for a long time and had awakened refreshed after the fever had gone."[26] Bella Dodd was like Rip Van Winkle waking up after a long sleep to find a new world where the brotherhood of man was only possible under the Fatherhood of God.

Like other ex-Communist Catholics before her, Bella Dodd became active in the anti-Communist Catholic circuit of speakers. In the 1950s she testified seven times before U.S. government committees on her activities in the Communist Party. She testified before the House Un-American Activities Committee on June 17, 1953, about how she had been slowly drawn into the Party's activities and about her eventual success in the top echelon of the Party's leadership. She explained to the congressmen that a small number of Communists could undermine and control a union because at conventions they operated as a unit, having decided in advance what their specific goals and tactics were going to be; and all along the way they would be coached by the Party and obedient to its discipline. She told the committee, "I knew practically everyone in New York City who appeared before the various [congressional] committees. I know of no one who has appeared

---

[25] Ibid., 236.
[26] Ibid., 245.

and claimed the fifth amendment, in New York City, who was not a member of the Communist Party."[27] Part of her testimony told the congressmen how the Party uses and abused minorities. "There is no more depressing problem than the way the Party uses the minority groups for the purpose of creating chaos and division among the people, creating fear and hatred among themselves in order that the many Communist organizations may promote the things in which they are interested."[28] The Communist Party in America received its orders from Russia, though most members were unaware of the extent of Russia's control. In discussing why teachers were so important to the Party, Dodd noted that Communist or Communist-leaning teachers and professors have influence well beyond themselves on those who come under their tutelage, even setting the proscribed curricula. "From the period of 1925 to 1948 or 1949 ... most colleges ... dropped their courses on ethics or religion ... even law schools dropped their courses—on constitutional law."[29] Teachers control the youth of the nation and therefore the future of the nation. The Party advocated for universal nursery school to mold America's youngest citizens into little materialists. "If you are going to seize the minds of children, you seize them as young as possible."[30] Preschool teachers were taught to change nursery rhymes to follow the Party line, to eliminate anything religious from stories and holidays, and to emphasize materialist values and the value of the collective over the individual.

Accusations of Communists in the Church

Bella Dodd made many horrifying statements in her talks around the country, but none would be as horrifying to her Catholic audiences as her assertion that the Communist Party, under direction from Stalin himself, had infiltrated the clergy of the Catholic Church with radical and immoral men intent upon undermining the Church from

---

[27] "Testimony of Bella V. Dodd", in *Hearing before the Committee on Un-American Activities, 83rd Congress (First Session)* (Washington, D.C.: United States Government Printing Office, 1953), 1750–51.

[28] Ibid., 1756–57.

[29] Ibid., 1768–69.

[30] Ibid., 1770–71.

within. The Party offered stipends and encouraged men to enter the Protestant ministry and the Jewish rabbinate, but it was the Catholic Church it most hated and feared. Though it is oddly not contained in her autobiography or in Sheen's, Bella Dodd claimed before several audiences that she and the Communists put over one thousand men into Catholic seminaries.[31] It is not known which seminaries or even if they are all in the United States. It is not known how many of the young men actually ordained and became active priests, and there are serious doubts about the veracity of her claim—it could all have been a great exaggeration on Dodd's part. But Catholic philosophers Dietrich and Alice von Hildebrand, who met her in the mid-1960s, believed Dodd. They heard her accusations as a confirmation of their own fears for the Church. Once, when Dodd was visiting the von Hildebrands' home in New Rochelle, New York, Dr. Dietrich von Hildebrand said he feared that the Catholic Church had been infiltrated by Communist agents. Dodd agreed.

In an interview in the *Latin Mass Magazine*, Dr. Alice von Hildebrand was quoted as saying, "I can only tell you what I know. It is a matter of public record, for instance, that Bella Dodd, the ex-Communist who reconverted to the Church, openly spoke of the Communist Party's deliberate infiltration of agents into the seminaries. She told my husband and me that when she was an active Party member, she dealt with no fewer than four cardinals within the Vatican 'who were working for us.'"[32] When the von Hildebrands asked for the names of the cardinals, Bella Dodd demurred, saying that Bishop Sheen, her spiritual director, had asked her not to name names. What his motives were or what he did with her information is unknown. If true, in all likelihood, Sheen probably reported it to

---

[31] Kevin Symonds presents a good analysis of the veracity and the lack thereof in "Rethinking Bella Dodd and Infiltration of the Catholic Priesthood", *Homiletic & Pastoral Review*, December 24, 2021, https://www.hprweb.com/2021/12/rethinking-bella-dodd-and-infiltration-of-the-catholic-priesthood/. Several individuals, including Alice von Hildebrand, professed to have heard Bella Dodd make this claim. Alice von Hildebrand entertained Dodd in her home and recalled Dodd saying that she knew of Communist infiltration of the Church. Others purported to have heard Dodd at talks at Fordham University, Detroit, Chicago, and Orange, California.

[32] "Present at the Demolition", Interview with Dr. Alice von Hildebrand, *The Latin Mass Magazine*, Summer 2001, http://www.latinmassmagazine.com/articles/articles_2001_su_hilde bran.html.

his superior, Cardinal Spellman. The co-postulator for Sheen's cause for sainthood, Fr. Andrew Apostoli, C.F.R., who was ordained by Sheen, said of Sheen and his association with Bella Dodd:

> The Lord also brought individuals to him who told of experiences which he probably wished he didn't have to know. For example, the one time ardent Communist Bella Dodd was a convert of Archbishop Sheen. She told him that while she was a Communist Joseph Stalin told her and other Communists that the Catholic Church was the greatest enemy of Communism. He wanted to undermine the Church by recruiting men into the priesthood who had no vocations and who would cause havoc by confusion and bad example. Bella Dodd told the Archbishop that she had personally recruited into the priesthood between 800 and 1200 men who had no vocations. Knowledge such as this was not easy for Archbishop Sheen. Yet it caused him to pray even harder.[33]

Louis Budenz also seemed to be aware of the efforts of the Communists to undermine the Church. He explained that the "Outstretched Hand" initiative was an effort to destroy the Church; "the outstretched hand" was used by the Communists "to infiltrate and manipulate them [Catholics]".[34] In 1937 a paper eventually decoded by the federal government's Venona Project and originally written by the American Communist Party and sent to Moscow, entitled "Confidential Report on Work in Religious and Non-Religious Catholic Organizations", revealed that "a real race was on as to which force will win over the Catholic people in this country—the forces of reaction and fascism represented by the Catholic Church or the forces of progress and democracy [the Communists]."[35] At the time the Party boasted that it had infiltrated the Holy Name Society in a New York parish, as well as the Knights of Columbus and the Catholic trade unions. The Party also had two members on the editorial board of the anti-Communist Catholic Paulist newspaper, *Wisdom*.[36] The former Communist Manning Johnson testified

---

[33] David J. Hartline, "Fulton Sheen, Still a Powerful Witness: An Interview with Fr. Andrew Apostoli", *Catholic Exchange*, February 2, 2008, https://catholicexchange.com /fulton-sheen-still-a-powerful-witness-an-interview-with-fr-andrew-apostoli/.

[34] Louis Francis Budenz, *This Is My Story* (New York: McGraw-Hill, 1947), 341, 355–62.

[35] Herbert Romerstein and Eric Breindel, *The Venona Secrets: Exposing Soviet Espionage and America's Traitors* (Washington, D.C.: Regnery Publishing, 2000), 413.

[36] Ibid., 412–15.

before the House Un-American Activities Committee about the Communist infiltration of the Catholic Church and the efforts of the "Outstretched Hand" to undermine it. In his 1953 testimony, he stated, "The outstretched hand was the new united-front policy of the Communist International applied all over the world. It was the extension of the hand of friendship and cooperation to the church, while in the other hand holding a dagger to drive through the heart of the church."[37] Johnson went on to tell the congressmen:

> The plan was to make the seminaries the neck of a funnel through which thousands of potential clergymen would issue forth, carrying with them, in varying degrees, an ideology and slant which would aid in neutralizing the anti-Communist character of the church and also to use the clergy to spearhead important Communist projects. This policy was successful beyond even Communist expectations.... The Soviet apparatus [was furnished] with a machine which was used as a religious cover for the overall Communist operation ranging from immediate demands to actually furnishing aid in espionage and outright treason.[38]

What Johnson was telling the congressmen was that "if you cannot take over the churches by frontal attack, take them over by the use of deception and guile and trickery, and that is exactly what the Communists practice in order to infiltrate and subvert the church and prepare them for the day when they would come under the hierarchical and authoritarian control of Moscow."[39] Sheen would refer to the "Outstretched Hand" as a Trojan horse. "Citing primary Soviet courses, he [Sheen] called attention to the Popular Front and its tactics of 'boring secretly from within.' 'Communists,' he said, 'are urged to wheel their Trojan Horse into our labor unions, religious organizations, political parties ... under the guise of a peaceful United Front.'"[40] Dodd purportedly spoke of the Communist infiltration of the seminaries when speaking around the country and on college campuses.

---

[37] *Investigation of Communist Activities in the New York Area: Testimony of Manning Johnson to HUAC in 1953* (Washington, D.C.: United States Government Printing Office, 1953), 2165–66, https://www.scribd.com/document/639429677/Manning-Johnson-1953-HUAC-Testimony.

[38] Ibid., 2277–78.

[39] Ibid., 2166–67.

[40] *Positio*, 2.1349.

When asked in 2015 on a live call-in television show on EWTN about the infiltration of the priesthood by Communists, Fr. Mitch Pacwa, S.J., affirmed that there had been efforts by the Communists in the 1930s to corrupt the priesthood but went on to say that he knew of none in the modern Church.[41] George Weigel, writing in the *Wall Street Journal* about the imperiled state of the Catholic Church in Lithuania when Lithuania was under the control of the Soviet Union, noted that the *Chronicle of the Catholic Church in Lithuania* appealed to the Soviet authorities with "requests to end interference in seminaries [and] demands that the efforts of the [Soviet] security services cease efforts to recruit future priests as informants".[42]

While many people dismiss the claims Bella Dodd made about the Communist efforts to undermine the Catholic Church as mere conspiracy theories, there is some corroborating evidence for her claims about the "Outstretched Hand" initiatives and the Communists' success in infiltrating various American religious institutions. She never went back on her assertions that the Communists had infiltrated both the teachers' unions and the Catholic Church, and Bishop Sheen never publicly denied or affirmed her accusations. In a 1970, Rochester, New York, conference for priests and nuns, in speaking about confronting the demonic forces at work in the country, Sheen commented opaquely, "I travel this country from one end of it to the other and I would now tell how I meet the demonic. First of all, we have double agents in the Church, double agents as governments during war have double agents, those who work for one side but actually are working for another. And so in the Church, we have double agents, those that stay in to destroy it."[43]

---

[41] Mitch Pacwa, S.J., *Threshold of Hope*, EWTN, June 30, 2015, video, 52:20, https://www.youtube.com/watch?v=vReHEgsyGY0. In a telephone conversation with the author on February 8, 2022, Fr. Pacwa also pointed to the well-documented connection between the Russian Orthodox Patriarchy, its clergy, and the KGB (the Soviet Union's secret police). For another discussion, see Fr. Pacwa's interview of Paul Kengor, author of *The Devil and Bella Dodd*, on March 29, 2023, hosted at https://www.youtube.com/watch?v=AwLFyq1QKLo.

[42] George Weigel, "Tyrants Can't Tolerate Truth", *Wall Street Journal*, March 18, 2022, A17. *The Chronicle of the Catholic Church in Lithuania* was a dissident journal published on and off for seventeen years. In 1974 its publisher was given a show trial and sentenced to eight years in a labor camp.

[43] Fulton Sheen, "The Power of the Devil in the World Today", *Positio*, 2.1715, https://www.buzzsprout.com/1044874/11343201. For a complete list of Sheen's radio presentations, see FultonSheen.com.

The bishop does not identify the double agents explicitly as Communists or as individuals by name, nor does he identify them as clergy or lay people. Because he prefaces his remarks by stating that he travels America and finds the demonic at work, he is obviously talking about the "double agents" as the demonic elements trying to undermine the Catholic Church. Again, in a retreat for priests in Dallas in the early 1970s, a retreatant said that Sheen referenced Communists: "He said it took a long time for Marxism to enter the Church. Now it finally has crept in.... When the communists entered this time was based on the fact to destroy the faith from within."[44] Sheen does not reference Bella Dodd, but he made claims that appear to vindicate her accusations. As long as she was alive, Bella Dodd continued to insist that the Communists had infiltrated the Catholic Church. She died at the age of sixty-four on April 29, 1969, from complications from a gallbladder surgery. She was buried with Catholic rites in the Gate of Heaven Cemetery in Pleasantville, New York, next to her parents.

The silence Bishop Sheen maintained in the case of Dodd reflects Sheen's principle of charity to all. He remained her spiritual advisor, so their conversations were confidential. He had many converts whom he advised; he never talked about any of them. Dodd promised to live a penitential life following her conversion, and it appears that she was trying to live out her promise.[45] At the same time, Bishop Sheen was going from triumph to triumph with his *Life Is Worth Living* program. *Time* magazine put him on the cover of the April 14, 1952, edition. The cover story mentioned that "Du Mont was overwhelmed by the mail response [8,500 letters in the first week]. The program, [is] now carried by 17 stations.... Wrote *New York World-Telegram & Sun's* Harriet Van Horne: 'It's quite possible that he is the finest Catholic orator since Peter the Hermit.'" The popularity rating of Milton Berle's show had recently dropped ten points, and some columnists attributed this to Sheen. When Bishop Sheen was awarded the Emmy by the Television Academy in 1953 for the "Most Outstanding Personality", he quipped, "I have excellent writers: Matthew, Mark, Luke, and John."[46] Mused Berle, who had been nominated for the same award: "If I'm going to be eased off

[44] *Positio*, 1.410.
[45] Symonds, "Rethinking Bella Dodd", 17.
[46] Testimony of Archbishop Timothy Cardinal Dolan, *Positio*, 1.1059.

the top by anyone, it's better that I lose to the One for whom Bishop Sheen is speaking."[47]

Awards and Celebrity for Fulton Sheen

The Emmy would be the first of many awards made to Bishop Fulton Sheen because of his success on television; it was a success that seemed to take the world by surprise, and it was a success that was sustained. He went on to be nominated for Emmys in 1954 and 1957, which he did not win, but his repeated nominations point to his enduring popularity. In addition to his own program, Sheen was an invited guest on many celebrity shows over the next twenty-four years. He was the "mystery guest" on the game show *What's My Line?* in 1956. He appeared with Jack Parr, Perry Como, Ed Sullivan, Johnny Carson, Jackie Gleason, Merv Griffin, Dean Martin, and Mike Douglas. Bishop Sheen would be interviewed by David Frost, William F. Buckley, the *Today* show, and *60 Minutes.* He was the uncredited technical advisor for the 1953 movie *The Miracle of Our Lady of Fatima.* He would be the narrator for many events and programs, such as the visits of Popes Paul VI and John Paul II to the United States. As late as 2003, almost a quarter of a century after his death, the bishop was featured in a three-part series called *Fulton J. Sheen: His Irish Wit and Wisdom.* In a 1999 survey over a three-month period to determine the "Top 100 Catholics of the Twentieth Century", with almost twenty-five thousand casting votes, first place went to Pope John Paul II, second place to Mother Teresa of Calcutta, third place to Padre Pio, and fourth place to Bishop Fulton Sheen. Fr. Andrew Apostoli said, "It is clear that in the estimation of many Catholics, Archbishop Sheen ranks among the very 'giants' of their Faith."[48] His enduring legacy owes much to his success on television. When he was appointed director of the American office of the Society for the Propagation of the Faith, he remarked, "I have pushed out the classroom walls, and now I can

---

[47] "Bishop Fulton Sheen: The First 'Televangelist' ", *Time*, April 14, 1952, https://content .time.com/time/subscriber/article/0,33009,857161-1,00.html.

[48] Fr. Andrew Apostoli, C.F.R., quoted in Gregory Joseph Ladd, *Archbishop Fulton J. Sheen: A Man for All Media* (San Francisco: Ignatius Press, 2001), 9.

embrace the whole world."[49] With his appearance on television and the ongoing availability of reruns, Sheen is still pushing out the walls and embracing the world.

Celebrity Convert: Virginia Mayo

As a television personality, Bishop Sheen became a celebrity, and as a celebrity, he came in contact with other celebrities. He became a personal friend to many in Hollywood, including many beautiful actresses. When in Los Angeles, he would stay at the home of Irene Dunn (Griffin) and dine at the home of Loretta Young. He graciously said of Irene Dunn, "I sometimes wish that the charming Mrs. Griffin [Dunn] would reveal her true age, so that I might tell at what age women are most beautiful."[50] He was good friends with Jackie Gleason, Bob Hope, and John Wayne, whose wife he had converted to Catholicism. John Wayne converted to Catholicism on his deathbed, likely due to the influence of Fulton Sheen. Jackie Gleason would annually donate $75,000 to the Society for the Propagation of the Faith.[51] The actor Martin Sheen would change his name from Ramón Estévez because he admired Sheen's performances on television. Another Hollywood actress he met came to him in New York desiring instruction in the Catholic faith. Virginia Mayo was in New York City to promote the movie *Giant*, then still in production. Warner Brothers engaged their stars to help promote their films, even if the stars were not in a particular film. While in New York, Virginia Mayo decided to pay a call on Bishop Sheen, whom she had heard on the radio and seen on television.[52]

Virginia Mayo was married to the actor and comedian Michael O'Shea, who was a "slightly fallen away Catholic" who practiced "a slightly watered-down version" of the faith and went to Mass on

---

[49] Fulton J. Sheen, *Treasure in Clay: The Autobiography of Fulton J. Sheen* (Garden City, N.Y.: Doubleday Press, 1980), 353.

[50] Ladd, *Man for All Media*, 33.

[51] Hilary C. Franco, *Bishop Fulton J. Sheen: Mentor and Friend* (New Hope, Ky.: New Hope Publications, 2014), 31.

[52] Virginia Mayo's autobiography serves as the source for her life story and her conversion. Used with permission. Virginia Mayo, *Virginia Mayo: The Best Years of My Life* (Chesterfield, Mo.: Beach House Books, 2002), 89.

occasion.[53] Eventually she started thinking about the larger issues of life. Raised in the Presbyterian Church that her mother attended and overwhelmed with early stardom, she intuited that there was more to life than making movies. But before her life-changing encounter with Bishop Fulton Sheen, Virginia Mayo was a little girl from Saint Louis, Missouri, who was stagestruck at an early age. She was born Virginia Clara Jones on November 30, 1920, to Luke and Henrietta Jones. Her mother was attending a movie when her labor began, and she had to hurry home to deliver her baby, so perhaps baby Virginia was destined for the movies. Her father was a newspaper reporter for the *St. Louis Globe Democrat*, with family roots in Wales, coming to Saint Louis by way of Canada. Two of her relatives on her father's side fought in the Revolutionary War. She proudly followed her grandmother Jones into the Saint Louis chapter of The Daughters of the American Revolution (DAR), whose membership she kept up throughout her life, paying her dues even when she could no longer attend meetings. Virginia Mayo maintained that she was not remarkably pretty or cute as a child. She called herself skinny. Her best physical attributes as a child were her curly blond hair and her green eyes. She wrote, "I never had that 'look' until I hit about seventeen."[54] Perhaps her skinniness was due to having had scarlet fever and diphtheria at the same time around the age of five. The doctor recommended that her mother shave her head, as Virginia's illnesses were making her hair fall out. It was that baldness she seemed to remember best about her convalescence.

At the age of six, Virginia began her lessons in deportment and speech with her father's sister, her Aunt Alice. Aunt Alice had her reciting, "Around the rough and rugged rocks the ragged rascals ran."[55] Soon she was taking lessons in drama, music, singing, and dancing, including tap and ballet, for which Aunt Alice engaged a proper dance instructor. Aunt Alice's School of Dramatic Expression was where the child Virginia blossomed. She wrote, "By the time I was seven, I was completely comfortable on the stage. I loved being there. Every single minute of it."[56] Had it not been for help from her father, who

[53] Ibid., 89.
[54] Ibid., 3.
[55] Ibid., 5.
[56] Ibid.

wrote her papers, and her brother, who did her mathematics home-
work, she probably would never have graduated from high school.
She always regretted her lack of education, but she never regretted
the stage. Her lessons from her Aunt Alice were augmented by an
academy in the Sherman Park neighborhood where children would
be trained in dance and other arts for free during the summer. She
recalled, "I can honestly say there was never a time when I actually
had this big Epiphany or something. It [show business] was my dream
from the time I was able to dream. I absolutely cannot remember
ever giving consideration to any other kind of life.... I was meant for
a life in show business from the moment of my conception."[57]

One of the highlights of Virginia Jones' childhood was witnessing
the take-off of Charles Lindberg in his *Spirit of St. Louis*, on his way
to fly to France in the first transatlantic flight. That brought her a
flight of fancy that added to her fascination for the stage. The stage
was not far distant for her, but the Depression brought great hardship
to her family. Her father lost his newspaper job, and the family lost its
house and had to move in with her aunt and her grandparents. Her
brother dropped out of school to take a job to help the family. She
wrote, "I learned much from my family and father back then, about
the importance of hard work, and the importance of a dependable
salary. These lessons would stand me in good stead for the rest of my
life."[58] Her solid Midwestern background would give her much in
common with Bishop Fulton Sheen, who also learned the value of a
good work ethic from his family.

Rejected at the age of sixteen for a place in the chorus of the out-
door, summertime Saint Louis Municipal Opera Company, the "Muny",
the determined Virginia Jones made herself a short costume to show
off her legs, learned her steps, and auditioned again the following
year. She succeeded and spent the summer playing to the Muny
crowds of ten thousand. For the fall, she organized a group of six
other Muny chorus girls to present an act at the Chase Hotel in Saint
Louis, and while there she was approached by a man who needed a
young woman for his own vaudeville act showing in the same hotel.
His name was Andrew Mayo. His act, she wrote, "consisted of two
men dressed in a horse costume with a pretty girl whipping them,

[57] Ibid., 7, 10.
[58] Ibid., 11.

telling jokes, and dancing a little."⁵⁹ Virginia, with her mother acting as chaperone, joined the act of Pansy the Horse in Columbus, Ohio. Her mother soon moved back home, and the vaudeville act moved on from city to city. Virginia Jones became Virginia Mayo, because the original ringmaster's part was played by Andrew Mayo's wife, who had become pregnant. Mayo and his partner, Norni Morton, billed themselves as the Mayo Brothers, and not wanting the expense of changing the publicity posters and flyers, asked Virginia to adopt the last name Mayo. She agreed; it did not matter to her, she said: "It doesn't matter what your name is as long as you have a sense of self and know who you are. I did then and I do now."⁶⁰

The first time she performed with Pansy, the orchestra was led by Ozzie Nelson with his lead singer, Harriet Hilliard. When the Pansy group performed in the Apollo in Harlem, it shared a billing with Ella Fitzgerald. The big bands of Benny Goodman, Glenn Miller, the Dorseys, Glen Gray, and Artie Shaw all shared billings with the girl from Saint Louis. In New York she shared a dressing room with Dinah Shore and later opened for the Andrews Sisters. Over Christmas of 1940, Pansy ran for seven weeks in Radio City Music Hall. All the while she was sending most of her $50-a-week salary home to help her family in Saint Louis. While Pansy was playing in New York, Virginia met Billy Rose, the theatrical impresario and songwriter, at his nightclub, the Diamond Horseshoe, who immediately hired her away from Pansy the Horse and the Mayo Brothers. She was quite a hit in his review and was featured in a large article in *Look* magazine. After seeing her perform at the nightclub, Samuel Goldwyn, the film producer, asked to see Virginia. She went with Goldwyn to Hollywood in the winter of 1942, where he gave her a "charm coach", along with acting, speech, voice, and dancing lessons. He even put her on a diet and made her brush her hair one hundred stokes each night. She signed a five-year contract with the studio.

Her first movie was a small part in *Jack London*, in which she played the author's first love. The actor who played the part of Jack London, Michael O'Shea, later became her husband. Virginia Mayo's star rose quickly, making her a leading lady playing opposite almost every big-name actor in Hollywood: Bob Hope, Milton Berle,

⁵⁹ Ibid., 24.
⁶⁰ Ibid., 17.

Gregory Peck (whom she thought the best kisser in Hollywood[61]), Ronald Reagan, Alan Ladd, Paul Newman, Burt Lancaster, and Kirk Douglas, among others. Mayo had fifty-six film acting credits to her name from 1943 to 1997. She would add fourteen television credits. In 1947, her five-year contract with Samuel Goldwyn was up, so she went with Warner Brothers for the next stage of her acting career.

Successfully established in Hollywood, Virginia Mayo married Michael O'Shea on July 7, 1947. O'Shea, a Catholic, was divorced, so the couple had to find a Protestant minister to marry them. They did not have a honeymoon, as Mayo had to be on the set of her next film early on Monday morning. Her strong Midwestern work ethic would not allow her to ask for time off, even for a honeymoon. Unknown then to Virginia, she had an obstruction that prevented her from becoming pregnant. After several infertile years, she went to a doctor, who recommended surgery. Not counting solely on medicine, Virginia prayed daily to the Virgin Mary. In 1954, Catherine Mary O'Shea, called Mary, was born to Virginia and Mike. Mary was an only and much beloved daughter. Mike largely stopped acting after their marriage. Virginia said of him, "Mike didn't have the burning desire I had or other actors had. I guess they call it 'fire in the belly'. . . . Police work was his big passion."[62] Some of his happiest times were when he could ride along in the police cruiser as a volunteer with the Los Angeles Police Department. Mike O'Shea was not exactly who he presented himself as being. His big secret was that he was not Irish as he always claimed, but French Canadian and Scottish. He thought wanting to be Irish made him as Irish as any Irishman. He was a good husband and the parent who stayed home with Mary as she grew up. Mayo was the breadwinner in the family, making about $3,500 a week in 1950, but she regretted the great amount of time that her career took away from being the mother she wanted to be. The family moved to a ranch in Encino, California, outside of Los Angeles, where they had a collection of dogs and horses. Mike continued to act on and off in television situation comedies, but his heart was not really in it. He would get overworked, and two times had a nervous breakdown. But she had a family to support. She wrote, "Money was and is very important to me. I worked hard, really very

[61] Ibid., 85.
[62] Ibid., 50.

hard to earn mine.... It was money that motivated me absolutely. The fact that I love being in show business was the icing on that cake!" The moon and the stars may be free, "but remember, you can't eat the moon and the stars."[63]

When Virginia and Mike were in New York City doing promotional work for the film *Giant*, she began to think about Bishop Fulton Sheen, who had greatly impressed her on his television and radio performances.

> I was so taken by the things he said, so incredibly moved by his words and his voice (he was answering questions for me that I had all but buried) that one day I said to Mike "Let's go and try to meet with this man Bishop Sheen".... It wasn't difficult to meet him at all. Maybe my fame helped to open his doors a little more quickly than if I were not famous, but I know he was accessible to all people.
>
> The Bishop was wonderful to us, so gentle. What a sweet, nice man he was. Just brilliant. He had a way of seeing things so incredibly clearly. And he could articulate things about faith and God, religion and spirituality I never could, and probably still cannot. I really do consider, of all the great and famous people I've met, that he was way up at the very top of my "favorite" list. How gentle. How intelligent he was. I miss him terribly.[64]

She asked him for information on the Catholic Church, so Bishop Sheen sent her literature, books, and records for her to study. He would instruct her over the many miles from New York to southern California. She would visit the bishop whenever she was in New York, and according to one of Sheen's staffers, "Virginia Mayo would talk to us with her best profile showing."[65] Mayo was a little cross-eyed, so a side view was always more flattering for her. She could not help being the star she was, but she intuited that there was more to life than the stage.

> I yearned for something special in my life, a religion I could agree with and follow, one that would give me joy and satisfaction.... His [Sheen's] words certainly struck a chord with me. I began to relax. I'd

[63] Ibid., 90.
[64] Ibid., 88.
[65] *Positio*, 1.279.

finally found the Church I had been searching for all my life, either consciously or unconsciously. I don't know, but I knew then that I had been on a long journey to Bishop Sheen's door. I became a Catholic.... I am still, years later after that good man's death, involved in the Catholic Church. I have never looked back and have never once regretted my decision to take instruction, get confirmed, and to join.[66]

Virginia Mayo was consonant with Sheen in their shared anti-Communism: "I am a staunch American and was glad when the government went after the communists, and I was glad about those [congressional] hearings. Why does anyone want to go live in a Communist country when everything here is so perfect", she asked. She would once say, "I do love all things American!"[67]

When her contract with Warner Brothers expired in 1958, Virginia Mayo began to make independent films and television appearances, but without a big studio behind her, her film career was largely over. When in Rome to do an independent picture in Italy, Virginia, Mike, and Mary were whisked off to the Vatican to meet with Pope John XXIII. It was a thrilling experience for Virginia Jones of Saint Louis, Missouri, to be meeting the pope. She said, "It was such an emotional experience for me, one that just can't be duplicated in any way whatsoever!"[68]

Michael O'Shea, the self-proclaimed Irishman, wanted to live in Ireland. They gave it a try for several months, but their daughter wanted to go home to California. Actually, the O'Sheas were terrible businesspeople. They had put their home under the care of someone they thought was trustworthy, only to come home to find that the house had been trashed and their personal belongings, including clothing and furniture, had disappeared. To make things worse, they were largely broke. They had spent their money as quickly as it came in. They somehow managed to scrape together enough money in 1965 to buy a ranch in Thousand Oaks, California. They would live there until the end of their lives; their daughter lives there still.

Michael had not worked in show business for a while when he was approached in 1963 by a member of the Federal Bureau of

[66] Mayo, *Virginia Mayo*, 88–89.
[67] Ibid., 114.
[68] Ibid., 111.

Investigation to do some undercover work: looking into the dealings of Mickey Cohen, a known criminal. The affable Mike O'Shea was to become friendly with Mickey Cohen and relate what he learned about him to the Bureau. A year later, the Bureau came calling again on Mike. Would he spy on the famous patrons of the Friars Club, the all-men club frequented by Hollywood people? The men mostly went to the club to eat, drink, and gamble. Bishop Fulton J. Sheen was the guest of honor at the annual Friars Club roast on October 13, 1973, when he was roasted by Milton Berle, Red Buttons, and Jack Benny, among others.[69] The Friars' patrons were mostly quite respectable, but where there is card playing and gambling, there is likely to be criminal activity nearby. So Mike O'Shea was at the Friars Club on a membership bought for him by the F.B.I. to find out what he could. He must have been successful: the F.B.I. knocked on his door one night telling him to take his family and quickly leave because the Bureau knew of a hitman who had come to town looking for Mike. Eventually Michael O'Shea had to testify at a trial stemming from activities at the Friars Club, something the Bureau had promised him he would never have to do. Suddenly everyone knew that it was O'Shea who had been spying on them. He was involved with the F.B.I. and the trial into 1968, and everyone knew it and could not forget it. Work was almost impossible to come by. Even Virginia Mayo had difficulty finding jobs. After working in the film industry nonstop for thirty years, she found she was no longer offered parts in movies. "I know this activity of Mike's [with the F.B.I. and the trial] had a lot to do with the demise of my career", she wrote.[70] She made only seven more films after the Friars Club trial. While she did a few television programs, her main income came from dinner theater. It was not bad money. She made $100,000 in one year, but it was a far cry from her studio days. She was still supporting her family and needed the work, which often kept her away from home and her family.

She was doing *No No Nanette* in Dallas, and Mike was to also have a part in the play. After a night out to hear Mel Tormé sing, they retired to their apartment. Virginia found Michael O'Shea dead in his bathroom the next morning. It was December 4, 1972, the worst

[69] Ladd, *Man for All Media*, 44.
[70] Mayo, *Virginia Mayo*, 146.

day of her life. Virginia Mayo was convinced that his death had
been caused by his activity with the F.B.I., the Friars Club, and the
ensuing trial. She thought she heard unusual noises that night that
sounded like someone had entered the apartment. She wrote, "The
death has always haunted me ... because of the circumstances. I'll
never know if those people who snared Mike into doing the spying
and other things I'm sure I'll never know about, were somehow
implicated in his death. ... I won't know the answers, ever, but I'll
always know the questions."[71] It does not seem to have occurred to
her that if there was anything nefarious about Mike's death, it could
have stemmed from the criminal element and not the government.

On her own, Virginia Mayo still needed to work. She eventually
began to receive a small pension from the studios for which she
had worked. It was not much, but it helped. In the late 1970s her
agent suggested that she go on various cruises as the paid celebrity
on board. It did not pay very well, but it was easy work and she got
to travel. It was something several movie stars were also doing, such
as June Allyson, Margaret O'Brien, and Ann Miller. The cruises
supplemented her income, along with the various television appearances on talk shows, dramas, and comedies. She remarked, "People
love to have a look at an old former movie diva, and I don't mind
obliging them!"[72]

Virginia Mayo's last acting credit was for a 1997 film, *The Man
Next Door*: she was seventy-seven years old. She continued to live in
her Thousand Oaks home along with her daughter Mary and Mary's
husband and children. For the rest of her life, she displayed a signed
picture of Bishop Fulton Sheen. In thanksgiving for the birth of her
daughter, she maintained a devotion to the Blessed Virgin Mary.
Eventually, she could not drive to Mass any longer and lived in a
nursing home at the end of her life. But her religion always sustained her: "This Church has given me such peace and comfort", she
wrote.[73] Near the end of her life, in her autobiography, she wrote, "I
do believe strongly that everything happens for a reason. I believe in
and trust in God. Sometimes I guess it's not for us to know the reasons
for why things happen in our lives. They just do. I have faith in God

[71] Ibid., 148.
[72] Ibid., 160.
[73] Ibid., 89.

and He's done pretty darned well by me up until now!"[74] Virginia Mayo, a woman who shared so many values with Fulton Sheen, died on January 17, 2005, in Thousand Oaks, California. Near the end, she would say of her life, "I thank God for the gifts He's bestowed upon me.... I am grateful for all the marvelous things that have come my way. It has been the most amazing of lives, fabulous, and magical."[75] Virginia Mayo was to Bishop Sheen one of his children in Christ, and she was always grateful to him for bringing her into the Church. The Sultan of Morocco once called Virginia Mayo tangible proof of the existence of God, and Sheen would have agreed, but for more elevated reasons.[76]

When in the 1950s Virginia Mayo was in her Hollywood heyday, Bishop Fulton Sheen was one of the most popular figures on television. She was an actor's actor, and he was God's spokesperson. When someone offered that he would make a marvelous Shakespearean actor, Sheen replied, "Not on your life, never. I am not an actor. What I speak about I believe in. I can't act, I can only live it."[77] And live it he did. He was genuine and authentic, and his audience knew it. Despite all the worry over whether or not Sheen would succeed on television, his humanity and personality made him such a success. He simply did not fit any preconceived image held by the anti-Catholics.

> Bishop Sheen's phenomenal success on television was a sign that millions of Americans had gone beyond the crude caricature so familiar in the nation's history and were willing to accept Catholics as Christians and friends. A bishop in full regalia who was charming, funny, learned and sensible could win allies, as well as converts, for the Church. It was exceedingly difficult for reasonable people to think of Fulton Sheen as a dangerous and malevolent subversive.[78]

The appearance of such an opinion of Bishop Fulton J. Sheen—that he was a dangerous and malevolent subversive—would have to wait

---

[74] Ibid., 178.
[75] Ibid., 179.
[76] Ibid., 100. From a 1954 fan letter sent to the head of Warner Brothers Studio.
[77] *Positio*, 1.500.
[78] Ibid., 2.1453.

for the rise of the ire of Cardinal Spellman against him. Considering how well the two of them had worked together over the years for the betterment of the Church in America and for the support of the worldwide missions of the Catholic Church, the breach between the two prelates must have caught Fulton Sheen by surprise. Spellman had been his mentor and promoter—and then, quite suddenly in a fit of pique, the eminent cardinal became his fiercest enemy. It need not have happened, but it did. The cardinal's demand for revenge would haunt Sheen for many years to come and present him with the only real failure of his priesthood.

9

The Late 1950s and the 1960s

Triumph and Trials

Falling Out with Cardinal Spellman

Richard Cardinal Cushing introduced Bishop Sheen in Boston in 1955 as "a man who combined the qualities of St. Francis of Assisi and St. Thomas Aquinas":[1] compassion and intellect, which he ingeniously combined with his charm and talent for bringing people to God. That same year the senior class at Notre Dame University voted him the "Man of the Year". Over the years, Fulton Sheen received many such accolades. The *Radio Daily-Television Daily* also ran a nationwide poll that elected Sheen the "Man of the Year". The Advertising Club of New York named him "Our Television Man of the Year". *Look* magazine called *Life Is Worth Living* the "Best Religious Program" for three years in a row. The Catholic Actors Guild would give him its Annual Award. The American Legion gave him its "Golden Mike" award for "bringing about a better understanding of the American Way of Life". The Order of Lafayette gave him its coveted Freedom Award for "distinguished leadership in combatting Communism". The king of Belgium made Sheen a commander of the Order of the Crown of Belgium. The Catholic Radio and Television Association gave him its annual award for his "outstanding contribution to the media". President Eisenhower would invite him to dinner at the White House. Sheen's acclaim and popularity was impossible to miss. He even met with Nikita Khrushchev when the Soviet premier came to the United States in 1957. Khrushchev told

---

[1] *Positio*, 2.1467.

Bishop Sheen, "I have heard of you ... you know more about Marx than I do!"[2] Everybody seemed to know of Sheen and wanted to meet him, even the strongman from Moscow.

It seemed inevitable in hindsight that Francis Cardinal Spellman and the bishop he had promoted, Fulton Sheen, would come into conflict. The New York Archdiocese is large, but not quite large enough for two popular, larger-than-life, strong-willed prelates like Spellman and Sheen. Like a lot of institutional and personal conflicts, it began over money. On May 25, 1955, Spellman requested money from the Society for the Propagation of the Faith that Sheen, as its American director, would not relinquish. It was the first clash between the two. The cardinal asked for funds from the Society to help speed up the post-war recovery in Europe. Sheen insisted that the Society's money was not for European recovery, which was being funded mainly by the United States government, but for the missions, funded by the American Catholic faithful. It was not Sheen's to give. Spellman did not want the Protestant charities to make inroads into European Catholic countries by virtue of their charitable largesse. That was not a compelling argument for Sheen. The cardinal put pressure on Bishop Sheen from many angles: Spellman had delegations of priests visit Sheen to persuade him to release the funds, and he asked Joseph Kennedy, the father of the future President John F. Kennedy, to intervene on behalf of the Europeans. When Kennedy failed to sway Sheen, the Cardinal appealed directly to the General Council of the Society for the Propagation of the Faith in Rome. The Council voted to support Sheen. Eventually, Cardinal Spellman entreated Pope Pius XII to order Sheen to release the funds and to fire Sheen and replace Sheen as director of the American Society with himself. To Spellman's great consternation and utter humiliation, the Holy Father agreed with Bishop Sheen. The Cardinal called Bishop Sheen "a foolish man".[3] Cardinal Spellman did not get the funds he wanted, and he was a man who was not used to anyone telling him no.

Not long after the incident over the mission funds was settled in favor of the missions, Cardinal Spellman again tried to garner funds

---

[2] Ibid., 2.1056 (reported by Timothy Cardinal Dolan).
[3] Ibid., 2.1470–72.

from the Society headed by Sheen to pay for surplus powdered milk the federal government had been donating free of charge to be distributed to the world's poor by the Catholic missions. Spellman was requesting millions of dollars he claimed to have paid the government for the powdered milk. Documents Sheen was able to present to the Holy Father proved that the milk had come free from the government and that Spellman had paid nothing for it. Cardinal Spellman had lied to Sheen and lied to Pope Pius XII, so of course the pope again sided with Sheen against Spellman. Cardinal Spellman was furious with Bishop Sheen, who had twice humiliated him before the pope. Spellman was famous for his temper and his stubbornness, and he vowed to get even with Fulton Sheen. He offered Sheen a wealthy parish if he would resign from the Society. He then engaged investigators to look into Sheen's private affairs in hopes of turning up something incriminating. Spellman raged at Sheen, "I will get even with you. It may take six months or ten years, but everyone will know what you're like."[4] Spellman went so far as to tell seminarians at Saint Joseph's Seminary that Fulton Sheen was "the most disobedient priest in the country" and said, "I want none of you to turn out like him."[5] His was a very personal and public vendetta against Fulton Sheen.

Bishop Sheen, for his part, was much more discreet. He never mentioned the Spellman falling-out in his autobiography. While he may have confided his trials with the cardinal to a few priest friends, he did not share them with any lay people, even his best friends like Clare Boothe Luce. Thomas Reeves reported that in 1966, Bishop Sheen told a Byzantine Rite bishop that he was indebted to him, "for you are the one friend who stood by me in the dark, dark days of the not too distant past".[6] At one point he was said to have told a priest friend of his, "Jealousy is the tribute mediocrity pays to genius."[7] But for the most part, Sheen was always outwardly polite and cordial to the Cardinal. He even helped plan the celebration for Spellman's twenty-fifth anniversary as a bishop and personally created the flowery invitations to the events in Yankee Stadium. At the end of his life, Sheen still did not discuss his contentious relationship with

[4] Thomas C. Reeves, *America's Bishop: The Life and Times of Fulton J. Sheen* (San Francisco: Encounter Books, 2001), 254.

[5] D.P. Noonan, *The Passion of Fulton Sheen* (New York: Dodd, Mead & Company, 1972), 82.

[6] Reeves, *America's Bishop*, 256.

[7] Noonan, *Passion*, 80.

Cardinal Spellman. He did not wish to score points over something twenty years in the past.

But Cardinal Spellman found ways of getting even with Sheen. He had Sheen barred from preaching his Lenten homilies at Saint Patrick's Cathedral, which had always attracted such throngs that the crowds spilled out of the cathedral and onto Fifth Avenue, causing the avenue to be temporarily closed for the events. Perhaps worse yet, Cardinal Spellman saw to it that Bishop Sheen was pulled off the television airwaves. In October of 1957, the cardinal used his power to retire the bishop from television. In thwarting Sheen, Spellman was cutting off an important avenue of funding for the Catholic missions around the world, but he could be satisfied because it was a way to punish Fulton Sheen. The funds for the missions mattered less to Cardinal Spellman than to Bishop Sheen, and they mattered very much to Bishop Sheen. So the cardinal of New York wrote directly to the president of the Admiral Corporation, which sponsored *Life Is Worth Living*, to inform him that Fulton Sheen was no longer permitted to perform on television.

Bishop Fulton Sheen lost his main public platform for raising monies for the missions and for maintaining his celebrity status, although most Catholics knew nothing of the conflicts between Spellman and Sheen. Sheen would say, "One must occasionally retire from the lights of TV to the shadow of the cross where one is refreshed and strengthened."[8] Sheen merely announced he was leaving television to spend more time raising money for the missions, which probably sounded plausible to most people until they stopped to think about it. Sheen had been making $26,000 a night for his show, with the entirety of it going directly to the missions.[9] He had worked it out with the Internal Revenue Service that his television salary would bypass him altogether and go directly into the mission coffers and that he, therefore, would not pay income tax on it—it was never counted as income. He would find his way back onto television eventually, but his popularity and impact never again matched that of the period of 1952 to 1957 and the original *Life Is Worth Living* series. Over the course of his sixteen-year tenure as the director of the American branch of the Society for the Propagation of the Faith, an average of $18,000,000

[8] Ibid., 78.
[9] Reeves, *America's Bishop*, 239.

flowed annually to the Society's coffers, supplying up to 70 percent of the Church's total annual expenditure for its worldwide missions.[10] His successful fundraising efforts on the part of the missions were a tremendous tribute to his dedication and hard work. The *New York Times* reported that Sheen had raised more than $100,000,000 for the missions, but in reality it was closer to $200,000,000.[11]

He still had his monthly mission magazines and weekly newspaper columns to plead for the missions. He had other books to publish, including his very popular *Life of Christ*, which came out the year following the cancelation of his weekly television show. In studying the life of Christ, Fulton Sheen would confide to his secretary and friend, Fr. Michael C. Hogan, that he was "pondering the suffering and crucifixion [of Jesus] to help his own situation".[12] It was his ongoing crucifixion to live with the frequent hostility and harassment from Cardinal Spellman. Later Sheen would say, "During those days when my life was backed up against the cross, I began to know and love it more."[13] Sheen would refer to the experience only obliquely: "In the dark days in which the *Life of Christ* was written were hours when ink and gall did mix to reveal the mystery of the crucifix."[14] Yet his niece Jean Sheen Cunningham, who lived and traveled with the bishop as a young girl and knew him very well, would say of him, "He never criticized [Spellman] ... I think he was very disappointed that he had to get into that position. He didn't like confrontation."[15] The most he would say, even to a member of his family, Clarys Cleary Souter, was "Now Clarys, pray for me. The Cardinal [Spellman] is very hard on me."[16]

More Wrangling Over Money

Cardinal Spellman was only one of Fulton Sheen's problems in the mid-1950s. At the same time that the cardinal was trying to get funds

[10] *Positio*, 1.889. See also Reeves, *America's Bishop*, 261.
[11] *Positio*, 2.1571–72.
[12] Reeves, *America's Bishop*, 258, from Reeves' interview of Hogan.
[13] Fulton J. Sheen, *Life of Christ* (New York: Popular Library Edition, 1960), 9–10.
[14] Fulton J. Sheen, *A Priest Is Not His Own* (San Francisco: Ignatius Press, 1963), 9.
[15] *Positio*, 1.347.
[16] Ibid., 1.720.

from the Society for the Propagation of the Faith for the war recovery effort in Europe, Gertrude Algase, a Sheen convert from Judaism and Sheen's literary agent as well as Spellman's, was demanding 10 percent of his royalties, which she estimated in 1955 had reached $800,000 since she had begun to represent him in 1942, and 10 percent of his television earnings, which at $26,000 a program were considerable. Bishop Sheen claimed to have turned all his royalties and fees over to the Church and kept nothing for himself. He personally kept no financial records and was famously disorganized about such details. Algase hired a lawyer and appealed to Cardinal Spellman against Bishop Sheen, threatening to make a public scandal out of her charges and to open a court case against Sheen. The diocese suggested that Sheen give Gertrude Algase 5 percent instead of the 10 percent she was demanding. Sheen approached the Holy Father with the problem. Gertrude Algase was paid off and the embarrassing situation went away. It is not known how much she was paid or the source of the funds used to pay her.[17]

Despite his personal trials, most people continued to see Sheen as optimistic and as a continuing source of funds for the missions. In 1958, Sheen personally contributed $1,000,000 to the Society for the Propagation of the Faith.[18] He wrote book after book, with the proceeds always going to the missions. Some of his books were largely written by others and compiled from his previous works. *This Is the Mass* and *This Is Rome* both came out in 1960, followed by *This Is the Holy Land* in 1961. To all appearances, Bishop Fulton Sheen was still his scintillating, charming self. But his suffering at the hands of the vindictive Cardinal Spellman did not go unnoticed in the Vatican. Pope John XXIII, who genuinely liked Sheen and had twice invited him into his ancestral home to meet his family, told the bishop, " 'You have suffered much, which will bring you to a high place in Heaven. Is there anything that I can do for you?' Sheen told him there was nothing he wanted except to do the will of God. The Pope replied, 'That makes it very easy for me.' "[19] Even Pope Paul VI was aware of his travails with Spellman and amazed at Sheen's continuing

---

[17] Reeves, *America's Bishop*, 249–50.

[18] Ibid., 261.

[19] Fulton J. Sheen, *Treasure in Clay: The Autobiography of Fulton J. Sheen* (Garden City, N.Y.: Doubleday Press, 1980), 232. See also Reeves, *America's Bishop*, 263.

success with the missions. Timothy Cardinal Dolan recalled running into Sheen after one of Sheen's private audiences with Pope Paul VI. When asked what had transpired between them, Sheen answered, "The Holy Father looked at me, took my hand, and said, 'Fulton Sheen you will have a high place in Heaven'.... Well, I replied, 'Your Holiness, would you mind making that an infallible statement?'"[20]

The Second Vatican Council

Pope John XXIII appointed Bishop Fulton Sheen to a number of pre-Conciliar commissions leading up to the Second Vatican Council. The pre-Conciliar commissions would help set the agenda for the Council by recommending topics to be discussed. As a measure of the pope's affection for Sheen, Sheen was one of twenty-six of the American hierarchy who participated in a total of ten pre-Conciliar commissions. Most prelates worked on no pre-Conciliar commissions or just one or two at the most. The pre-Council meetings took place over the three years preceding the Council, which opened on October 11, 1962, and lasted until December 8, 1965.

The Council convened with 2,600 bishops in attendance. Reeves wrote, "Sheen saw himself as a centrist who wanted both fidelity to historic and biblical teaching, and at the same time a commitment to rectifying social injustice."[21] For instance, Bishop Sheen argued for the insertion of a chapter on women in the Constitution on the Church in the Modern World, *Gaudium et spes*. He explained, "I had a strong conviction that the feminine principle in religion had been neglected. Many world religions were without the feminine principle and we were beginning to live in an age when women were coming into their own."[22] He thought a society, even an entire civilization, should be judged by how well it treated its women: "To a great extent the level of any civilization is the level of its womanhood. When a man loves a woman, he has to become worthy of her. The higher her virtue, the more noble her character, the more devoted she is to truth, justice, and goodness, the more a man has to aspire to

[20] Timothy Cardinal Dolan, foreword to *Bishop Fulton J. Sheen: Mentor and Friend*, by Hilary C. Franco (New Hope, Ky.: New Hope Publications, 2014), xiv.

[21] Reeves, *America's Bishop*, 269.

[22] Ibid., 267.

be worthy of her. The history of civilization could actually be written in terms of the level of its women."[23]

The Virgin Mary to Fulton Sheen was the embodiment of the perfection of womanhood. His affection for the mother of Jesus and the truth, beauty, and goodness he found in her spilled over into his estimation of all women. Edythe Brownette, his personal secretary, herself a beautiful woman, said of Sheen, "He liked to have a good time, lovely looking women, but that was as far as it went. He knew his place." Her sister Marlene Brownette, a nun who had traveled with the bishop, added, "He loved beautiful women; he saw them as a gift from God.... Everyone was God's and spoke God to him."[24] "He always thought it a mistake that the council chose not to accept his proposal."[25]

Over the three years of the Second Vatican Council, there were 4 sessions, 168 general meetings, 10 plenary meetings, 147 reports issued, and a total of 2,212 speeches made. Sheen attended all the meetings of the Council and was the only American to be on the Commission on Missions for the entirety of the Council. There was complete freedom of speech at the Council providing the speaker spoke in Latin, adhered to the point, and disciplined himself with a ten-minute limit for each speech. Of the American delegation to the Council, Cardinal Spellman spoke more frequently than any other American prelate. Bishop Fulton Sheen of the United States did not speak or present an oral intervention at all during the first three sessions, although he made written interventions, especially on ecumenism and religious freedom, but it is obvious that he was thrilled just to be there. He wrote to Marlene Brownette, "It is marvelous to be a part of the infallible Church teaching. I thank God I live in these times.... It will be a different world at the end of the Council. The Spirit is everywhere over us, as at Pentecost."[26]

For the most part, it was a very congenial group that met to set the course for the Catholic Church for years to come. Sheen would say, "To be part of that Council, to mingle with more than two thousand bishops of different nationalities and cultures, and to sing the Creed together with them each morning is a Council of Nations which would make the United Nations blush for want of a common

---

[23] Fulton J. Sheen, "Women Who Do Not Fail", *Life Is Worth Living*. See also *LIWL*, 255.
[24] *Positio*, 1.155.
[25] Reeves, *America's Bishop*, 267.
[26] Fulton J. Sheen to Marlene Brownett, November 8, 1962, Marlene Brownett File, Sheen Archives.

commitment."[27] It was not a doctrinal council, but a pastoral council. In the mid-1960s there were no doctrines in dispute. There were four bishops in attendance who did not believe that a council should even be held at all and who voted "no" on every issue that came before the bishops. Bishops could respond to a proposal by voting "yes", "no", or "yes with reservations".[28] At the time, the world was waking up to the idea of social justice, something whose existence the First Vatican Council did not even acknowledge. The challenging aspect of the Second Vatican Council, Sheen thought, was to balance the extremes "between evangelization and human progress, between soul-winning and society saving, between divine salvation and human liberation.... Those of us who were at the Council knew the balance was being struck between being in the world and not of the world, but it was very difficult to convince either of the two extremes—the conservatives and the worldlings—of how the spiritual and the social were combined."[29]

It was during the Second Vatican Council that Bishop Fulton Sheen got to know Krakow's auxiliary bishop, the young Karol Wojtyła. The Polish bishop, who was to become Pope John Paul II and a saint of the Church, greatly admired Fulton Sheen. Karol Wojtyła learned to speak English at least partially by listening to tapes of Fulton Sheen and by reading his many books.[30] Sheen was something of a celebrity at the Council, especially for the bishops from missionary territories, many of whose attendance at the Council he was financially subsidizing, so impoverished were their dioceses. Sheen not only subsidized the poorer bishops at the Council, but perhaps more importantly, he lived with them in a small Roman convent, demonstrating his solidarity with the poor and dispensing advice and spiritual consolation.[31] The bishops came running back to their seats to hear Sheen when he gave his last spoken intervention on the missions; it was the longest and most detailed intervention by an American.[32] He began

[27] Sheen, *Treasure*, 293.

[28] Ibid., 286.

[29] Ibid., 290.

[30] *Positio*, 1.153.

[31] Ibid., 1.882.

[32] Kathleen L. Riley, *Fulton J. Sheen: An American Catholic Response to the Twentieth Century* (New York: Alba House, 2004), 260.

by asking not what the missions are, but where the missions are. Sheen insisted that missions are the poor people of the world wherever they are found. He told the Council fathers that if all the poor of the world lined up single file to march past Saint Peter's Basilica, the line would encircle the globe twenty-five times, and it would take thirty years for them all to pass by.[33] It is not a territory that defines a mission, but the people in need. Sheen believed that the burden of the missions should fall on the entire Church and not only on the Propagation of the Faith. For instance, Karol Wojtyła told him that in Poland, which was not a mission territory, there were young men who wanted to become priests, but there were no seminaries. That was a need that the Society for the Propagation of the Faith could help if the definition of "mission" included the needs to be met in the entire world, not just in designated "mission territories". Sheen would tell the Council, "It is souls, not territories, that make the mission." The idea of "mission" was becoming identified with white people of European extract serving the needs of Black, brown, and yellow people, but in effect colonizing them. Sheen saw needs above and below what was called the "hunger line" of the globe's thirtieth parallel.[34] Many of the Council's bishops and cardinals were uncomfortable discussing poverty, but Sheen was unrelenting on the topic. He said, "I beg you most earnestly, Venerable Fathers, that the notion of poverty be strongly affirmed in this council.... We live in a world in which 200 million people would willingly take the vow of poverty tomorrow, if they could live as well, eat as well, be clothed as well, and be housed as well as I am.... As only a wounded Christ could convert a doubting Thomas, so only a Church wounded by poverty can convert a doubting world."[35] Sheen was the last to speak

---

[33] Franco, *Bishop Fulton J. Sheen*, 153–54.

[34] Riley, *Fulton J. Sheen*, 262.

[35] Fulton J. Sheen, speech to the Vatican Council II on the Missions, November 9, 1964, https://vaticaniiat50.wordpress.com/2014/11/10/text-of-bishop-fulton-sheen-on-draft-document-on-missions/; Franco, *Bishop Fulton J. Sheen*, 153. Fulton Sheen could have been a very wealthy priest if he had not given away nearly all of his earnings. Sheen was a diocesan priest, who did not belong to a religious order like the Jesuits or Benedictines. Secular priests serve the diocese where they are incardinated and do not take a vow of poverty. Sheen was "on loan" from the Diocese of Peoria to the Society for the Propagation of the Faith, the Archdiocese of New York, and later the Diocese of Rochester. He always remained a priest of the Diocese of Peoria, Illinois, where he had been ordained. He could have asked for a formal transfer from Peoria, but he never did.

for the missions and was the only speaker to be allowed more than the usual ten minutes to make his case. After Sheen spoke, there was thunderous applause that lasted longer for Sheen than for any other speaker at the Council, despite applause being discouraged. Cardinal Spellman must have seethed at Sheen's ongoing celebrity, especially at the Council and among his brother bishops.

Spellman found that he could not keep Bishop Fulton Sheen off television. Between Council sessions, Fulton Sheen was almost immediately again on the small screen visiting people in their homes over their TV dinners. In 1962, after the end of his *Life Is Worth Living* series, Sheen did a series on the life of Christ, and two years later the series *Quo Vadis America*, which challenged Americans to ponder where they were going as a nation. He challenged his audience: Would Americans be a God-centered, moral, and holy people or grasping materialists following the secular spirit of the age and indifferent to God? The themes of *Quo Vadis America* would be reprised as *What Now, America?* in a thirteen-part series in 1974–1975; for this series he no longer wore his full bishop's regalia, but only a clerical suit without even a pectoral cross. In 1966 the seventy-one-year-old Bishop Sheen made another television series based on the original *Life Is Worth Living*. It was in color and is widely available today for sale in video or streaming formats. That series, too, is now called *Life Is Worth Living*, but at the time it was called *The Bishop Sheen Show*. The color makes Sheen's episcopal regalia all the more dramatic, but not enough to make up for what many consider a lesser series than the original. Even his mostly sympathetic biographer, Thomas Reeves, wrote that "Fulton's timing was off; there were long pauses, and the physical posing often seemed artificial.... The jokes were feeble.... Sheen came across as nice, positive, and humorous. But the magic was nearly gone."[36] What Reeves neglects to say is that audiences and the country had changed in the intervening years; their expectations for entertainment were more sophisticated and their worldviews skewed by the spirit of the age. Sheen mostly had not changed in his presentation style or his Christian message. What had been new and fascinating in the relatively quiet early 1950s was not enough to hold the attention of audiences in the middle of the tumultuous

[36] Reeves, *America's Bishop*, 285–86.

1960s. The Sixties were the time of *The Feminine Mystique*, unrest on college campuses, civil rights marches, and race riots across the nation, all with the war in Vietnam as the backdrop. John Lennon of the Beatles famously commented in March of 1966 that "we [the Beatles] are more popular than Jesus now."[37]

Fulton Sheen continued his fundraising efforts on behalf of the Society for the Propagation of the Faith. (It is interesting to note that Sheen tried unsuccessfully to get the Second Vatican Council to change the name of the Society because "propaganda" had an unfortunate connotation.) He traveled around the globe meeting with bishops, priests, nuns, and recipients of the Society's largesse. He even visited various leper colonies in Africa where he found Christ in the ravaged faces of the lepers he encountered as he pressed rosaries into their mangled hands. At first, he simply dropped rosaries into open, maimed hands, but in a moment of illumination, he knew he loved the afflicted souls and then, he said, "I dug my fingers into his leprosy, took out the cross and pressed it into his hand."[38] In China he learned of the horrific martyrdom of Bishop Ford at the hands of the Communist government. In New Guinea he met the young man who would become the world's first "cannibal" priest. The Bishop in Kenya asked for $600 for a clinic for his people, who wore no clothes at all. When Sheen and the bishop he had just consecrated drove into the village, the chief ran to meet them wearing nothing but the feathers on his head. Fulton Sheen quoted Saint Augustine, "The world is a book and those who do not travel read only a page", and went on to add, "Travel depends on what you bring to the places you visit."[39] Fulton Sheen carried with him the Gospel and a love of the Eucharistic Lord, with whom he convened daily in his Holy Hour, and the Virgin Mary. He was always in good company. His travels brought him into contact with the poorest of the world's poor, who taught him the importance of the Church being for the poor, wherever they are found. On a flight returning to the United Stated from

---

[37] John Lennon made this statement on BBC Radio 4's *Today* program on March 4, 1964. It was picked up by the media and repeated many times. See "The Beatles in America (1966)—'More Popular Than Jesus'", https://www.youtube.com/watch?v=4lGVGdhHSxc; Reeves, *America's Bishop*, 283.

[38] Sheen, *Treasure*, 121.

[39] Sheen, *Treasure in Clay*, 127.

one of his missionary journeys, he told the attending stewardess how moved he was by his experience in the African leprosarium. A few months later, the young woman knocked on his office door to ask for his blessing. She had resigned from her position with the airline and was on her way to be a missionary sister in Africa. In retelling the story to an audience in Tulsa, Oklahoma, Sheen described the stewardess as a "ravishing beauty". When the audience gasped at the bishop's description, he paused a beat or two and responded, "Celibacy doesn't blind us, you know."[40] Bishop Sheen could move one person at a time or a whole group of people. He told the bishops assembled in Saint Peter's Basilica, "Let the Spirit of Poverty be the fruit of the Second Vatican Council."[41] He warned, "We must become the Church of the Poor, or else we will become the poor Church."[42]

Sheen's Bittersweet Three Years as Bishop of Rochester

In April of 1966, Bishop Sheen was called to the Vatican for an audience with Pope Paul VI, where he was told he was being reassigned from the American Society for the Propagation of the Faith to become the bishop of a diocese. Sheen later reported that he had been given his choice of several positions, including two archdioceses and five dioceses. He chose the diocese of Rochester, where he was installed on December 15, 1966. For those who wondered why the celebrity bishop was being sent to an outlier like Rochester, Sheen enthusiastically replied, "I am a soldier. I go where the general sends me.... I'm overjoyed.... What I wish to do would be the task of implementing and putting into action, the decrees of the Ecumenical Council. Today the people come to the Church. Tomorrow the Church must go to the people."[43] It must have seemed to Sheen like some romantic ideal to be the shepherd of his own flock. Unfortunately, it did not quite work out the way Fulton Sheen had hoped. The good news for him was that he was out from under the harassment of Cardinal Spellman. Reeves explained, "Rochester was the revenge

[40] Beth Macklin, "Round the Clock", *Tulsa World*, December 1, 1971.
[41] Noonan, *Passion*, 41.
[42] Ibid., 49.
[43] Riley, *Fulton J. Sheen*, 271.

Spellman had promised all those years ago."[44] Many had expected Sheen to replace Spellman as cardinal in New York, but Spellman did not want Sheen to succeed him and, Joan Sheen believed, wrote Reeves, that "Spellman wanted her uncle out of New York entirely. There was great jealousy."[45] Sheen was well aware that he had been banished by Spellman, but, on the other hand, he wrote a bishop friend, "I will be going to Rochester on December 15th. The snare is broken and the bird is free."[46] It was a relief to be out from under the cardinal and a challenge to be the ordinary of a diocese. In appointing Sheen to Rochester, Pope Paul VI pointed to Sheen's past successes and looked to future triumphs: "Everything that you have so tirelessly accomplished in the past, by deed and by the spoken and written word to feed the sheep of Christ's flock ... has won for you universal acclaim. We now nourish the fond hope that in the future you will vigorously undertake even greater things."[47]

Bishop Fulton Sheen had never been a pastor before, and now he was about to be the leader of a diocese, shepherding the laity, succoring the clergy, and being the face of the Catholic Church in the upstate New York city of Rochester. He was pleased to be their bishop. He said, "I'll be just a bit closer to the people than I was before.... I love souls. In fact, souls are the only reality in the world."[48] Cardinal Spellman was on hand for Sheen's installation and was the first to speak at the celebratory luncheon following the ceremony. The cardinal could be charming when he chose, and he chose to be so at that moment; he then left Rochester as soon as he politely could. Bishop Sheen asked the people of Rochester to write to him and to pray for him. He also announced that all the installation gifts would be given to the missions.

Bishop Fulton J. Sheen, with no real pastoral or administrative experience, intended to make his new see a "microcosm" of the post–Vatican II Church. He was eager to institute the reforms of the Council in his new diocese. A *New York Times* interviewer wrote, "Sheen left

[44] Reeves, *America's Bishop*, 286.

[45] Ibid., 287.

[46] Ibid., 289.

[47] "Thousands Welcome Sheen in Rochester", *New York Times*, December 16, 1966.

[48] Sheen in an interview with Robert Considine, "Bishop Sheens's Great Joy—The Privilege to Serve", *World Journal Tribune* (New York), November 8, 1966. See also Noonan, *Passion*, 160–61.

the lingering impression that he was 'set to remold Rochester into a demonstration diocese of his Church in America.'"[49] He saw Rochester as presenting him with a chance to take up "the sweet burden of pastoral care".[50] Sheen was most keen on serving the poor of Rochester and of fostering strong ecumenical ties with both Protestants and Jews. He announced that he was now in a position to "put into practice many of the ideas which I have cherished through the decades".[51] It was a promising start to the next phase of his career, but its glow of the moment was just that—a moment. After the ceremonies were over, Sheen spent his first night at Saint Bernard's Seminary to emphasize his closeness to the priests of his diocese, then took up residence in an apartment over a store and below the diocesan offices. In a typically gracious move, he left the bishop's more lavish residence to the much-loved retiring Bishop James Kearney, who had guided the Diocese of Rochester since 1937.

Rochester had suffered a serious race riot just two years prior to Sheen's arrival. The rioting had lasted for three nights, requiring the National Guard to quell the violence that left 4 dead, 350 injured, 750 arrested, and millions of dollars in property damage. The lay Catholic Interracial Council, which had been formed in 1960, had been dissatisfied with Bishop Kearney's response to the riot and to the plight of Rochester's Black community. The local board of the ecumenical Urban Ministry funded the known radical, Saul Alinsky, to come to Rochester in 1965 to set up FIGHT, which stood for "Freedom, Integration, God, Honor, Today." Alinsky's fee was $100,000. The inner-city Saint Bridget's parish, the Loretto House, a Catholic lay-funded preschool for Black children, and a few diocesan priests also joined FIGHT. That same year the diocese funded a Head Start program in the inner-city, and the Sisters of Mercy opened a social services center for Black children. The Black community blamed its poverty on the Eastman Kodak Company, the largest employer in Rochester. There were few Blacks in Kodak's forty-one-thousand-person workforce. While many people in the diocese did not approve of FIGHT, Sheen met almost immediately after his installation as bishop with the

[49] "Sheen Seeks Aid for World Poor", *New York Times*, November 8, 1966.

[50] Sheen, letter to the Most Rev. Cornelius Lucey, Bishop of Cork, November 10, 1966, in the Correspondence Files, Sheen Archives.

[51] Ibid.

management at Kodak to mediate between FIGHT and the company. His actions may have won him a few friends, but more enemies, especially after he appointed as his Vicar for the Urban Poor a white priest who was a FIGHT member. Rochester was a fairly conservative city; it generally liked the status quo. Bishop Sheen alarmed parents when he closed and combined schools in the diocese and raised the age for Confirmation to seventeen or eighteen, when most dioceses confirmed children between the ages of nine and twelve.

Fresh from the Vatican Council, Sheen wanted to do too much too fast. He shook up the local seminary in an effort to improve the education of priests. He brought in European professors, lay people, non-Catholic professors, a married ex-Anglican priest convert, and even the ex-Communist editor of the London *Daily Worker*, who taught the seminarians about Christian-Marxist dialogue. Sheen engaged a Protestant minister to teach homiletics to the seminarians, on the basis of the idea that Protestants did a better job of preaching than most Catholic priests. Perhaps most upsetting to the seminary's faculty was Sheen's invitation to a newly converted former rabbi to join the faculty.[52] Sheen required the seminarians to have experience working in the Rochester slums. He proposed a cooperative agreement between the Catholic seminary and the local Protestant divinity school. He appointed a lay board to review applications to the diocesan seminary. The new bishop, in the wake of the Second Vatican Council, sought to have more lay participation in a variety of diocesan areas, including priestly assignments to parishes. "In the past the parish accepted the priest sent to them by the bishop. Now the laity will have a voice in determining the type of priest to be sent."[53] The lay board of four men and three women would assist the seminary authorities in selecting the candidates most fit to be priests. He did all this largely without consulting the seminary rector, Fr. Joseph P. Brennan, who heard about the lay board after it had been publicly announced. After the first meeting of the lay seminary board, the bishop called only the male members to its next meeting, and then he never again called the group together. It was an idea that flashed and then immediately fizzled.

[52] *Positio*, 1.946.
[53] Sheen, quoted in the *National Catholic Reporter*, May 24, 1967.

All these changes in the seminary education of priests, most of which were instituted within a few months of Bishop Sheen's installation, were more than upsetting to the rector and the long-standing regular faculty and pointed to Sheen's lack of administrative skills. He was used to running the American Society for the Propagation of the Faith as his own fiefdom, making all the decisions and expecting his loyal staff to carry them out. A diocese, especially one governed for nearly thirty years by the same bishop, needs time to adjust to new leadership, but Sheen was used to being decisive and quick in his decisions. Perhaps it was his age and what he knew would be a short tenure in Rochester. He was in a hurry to make what he saw as necessary changes to bring the Diocese of Rochester into the model of the *aggiornamento* envisioned by the Second Vatican Council.

The new bishop wanted to implement a more horizontal, decentralized type of organization in his diocese. He formed the Priests' Council, similar in concept to the Roman Curia, but elected by the priests (with a few members appointed by himself), and then he divided the diocese into geographic vicarates to be overseen by various vicars he would appoint. He assigned a few priests not to parishes but to seek out and assist the poor wherever they were to be found in the diocese. Sheen traveled throughout the diocese visiting rural parishes, talking to the laity and priests in the countryside, and saying Mass in homes, hospitals, jails, and prisons. He was serious about ecumenism, visiting Protestant churches and Jewish synagogues and preaching to their congregations.

What Bishop Sheen found out was that he was personally unsuited to long meetings and taking the measure of the ideas presented at the meetings. He would often ask his priests for input in a decision to be made and then dismiss their ideas and go ahead with what he had wanted to do all along. A few priests were open to what their new bishop was trying to achieve, but most were recalcitrant and unhappy. They would have been pleased to return to the relaxed ways of Bishop Kearney. Sheen was fairly popular with those outside of the Catholic Church in Rochester, with the exception of the local journalists who wanted to see the famous bishop cut down to size, probably because, as was his habit of old, he sent his press releases to the *New York Times*, not the local Gannet press. He also alienated some of the elites in the city when, in reference to the poverty and hopelessness of its Black, Cuban, and Puerto Rican residents, he likened the city of Rochester to "a beautiful woman with a pimple on her nose"—racial discrimination.[54] Without consulting anyone, the new bishop once tried to close the school at Most Precious Blood, an Italian parish, only to be met with vile names and dirt clods thrown at his car. He retracted his decision the next day. It must have been shocking for a man accustomed to adulation from the masses to be pelted with mud. He could not even get out of his car until it was inside the garage and the garage door closed.[55]

Sheen shocked many people in Rochester and across the country by his July 30, 1967, homily at Sacred Heart Cathedral when he denounced the Vietnam War. It was the first public anti-Vietnam sermon by a Catholic prelate. Despite Pope Paul VI's vehement declaration at the United Nations, "No more war, war never again" and his inveighing against the Vietnam War specifically, the American hierarchy, especially Cardinal Spellman, were ardent supporters of the war in Southeast Asia.[56] In a surprising sermon, Sheen called on President Johnson to immediately withdraw all United States troops from South Vietnam. "May we plead only for a reconciliation between blacks and whites, and not between blacks, whites, and yellows? ... to paraphrase the gospel ... go and be reconciled to your northern Vietnam brothers, then come back and offer your prayers." Reeves comments that "the statement was wholly consistent with Sheen's view on war and peace and race, with what he had written and preached all of his life."[57]

Sheen thought the money spent on armaments of war would be better spent alleviating the sufferings of the poor. But Cardinal Spellman told the American forces engaged in the war in Vietnam that they were "holy crusaders" fighting "Christ's war against the Vietcong and the people of North Vietnam". Cardinal Spellman told the U.S. troops in Da Nang that "less than total victory was inconceivable".[58] However, the war in Vietnam was very unpopular, especially among

[54] Noonan, *Passion*, 164; Reeves, *America's Bishop*, 301.

[55] Reeves, *America's Bishop*, 303–4.

[56] Ibid., 309, quoting the pope's speech to the United Nations in 1965.

[57] Reeves, *America's Bishop*, 308; Sheen, press release, July 30, 1967; "Sermon of Bishop Sheen", *Eight Month Report*, Diocese of Rochester Archives.

[58] "Spellman Sticks to His Guns", *National Catholic Reporter*, January 4, 1967, 5.

the youth of America. Young men signed up for the military draft on their eighteenth birthdays and, if called up, were subject to two years of mandatory service in the armed forces. They could volunteer for the Army, Navy, Air Force, Marines, Coast Guard, or National Guard, but it was usually the Army that filled many of its ranks with draftees. One could get a draft deferment for several reasons, such as attendance at college, being married with children, being a member of the clergy, or having expertise in select technical occupations. In effect, the pool of the draftees was filled with young men who did not attend college, those who tended to be poor, less educated, and not well connected. This led to glaring social inequities. Wealthier and well-connected young men seemed to find any number of ways to avoid the draft; for instance President Gerald Ford's son, Steve, was given a deferral. Some young men fled the country to Canada rather than serve in the Army with the unhappy prospect of going to Vietnam, and others entered graduate or professional schools to prolong their higher education in hopes of running the clock out on the war. There were riots on college campuses to protest the war. Universities canceled their Reserve Officers' Training Corps (ROTC) programs. Protestors burned American flags, draft cards, and even their military medals. Celebrities like the popular actress Jane Fonda even went so far as to go to Communist North Vietnam to support its cause against the South and, especially, against the United States, while the disadvantaged youth of America served in the war. The draft was a flash point for anger and frustration, despite the fact that the vast majority of those Americans serving in Vietnam were volunteers. In 1969 a draft lottery system went into effect with far fewer possible deferments allowed. The active conscripting of men into the services ended in 1973, when the all-volunteer military went into effect.[59]

When Sheen became the ordinary of Rochester, "Sheen's poor" were no longer to be found in mission territories around the world, but in the slums of his diocese. But he was not ignoring the missions by any means. In May of 1967, the ambitious bishop announced a tax to be imposed on new construction in the diocese. The proceeds

[59] Men are still required to register with the Selective Service System as a contingency in case of a national emergency that would require a general mobilization.

from the tax would be split between the missions and the needs of Rochester's poor. The tax ranged from 1.25 to 3.00 percent, depending on the total cost of the building project. Sheen hoped that the tax would "not only cut down on extravagances in building, but also ... make the local Church conscious that it is part of the Mystical Body throughout the world".[60] He devised a way for wealthier parishes to help support the parishes and schools in the inner city, which were homes to Black and immigrant families from the American South and from abroad. His plan was so successful that not a single inner-city school was closed during his tenure. He also wanted to improve the salary levels of parochial schoolteachers when they were earning between $2,000 and $3,000 annually in 1967.

All his new ideas, especially about social justice and civil rights, were costing the diocese a great deal of money that was added to the considerably large debt he had inherited from Bishop Kearney, and, for God's Microphone, fundraising suddenly became difficult. He made other financial reforms by appointing a layman as the diocesan comptroller, saying that priests did not know how to handle money (perhaps he was speaking of himself). But Bishop Fulton Sheen was less worried about the money than about the poor. He said, "Today bishops are often criticized for a wrong reason.... The danger today may be the primacy of administration over love."[61] Sheen supposedly told an audience of priests, "For the love of Christ, stop being administrators and start being shepherds of souls."[62] While some of his administrative moves may be justly criticized, nobody could ever doubt Fulton Sheen's great love for souls. He must have been thinking about himself as well as Clare Boothe Luce when he later wrote to her, "The more you love, the more you suffer."[63]

Bishop Sheen was probably relieved to be invited by Pope Paul VI to join 187 other bishops for a month-long synod in Rome in October of 1967. There Sheen was part of the progressive wing in that he wholeheartedly endorsed the documents of Vatican II. Rochester's diocesan historian, Fr. Robert McNamara, said of Sheen, "His one constant fear was that Catholicism would be judged by other

[60] Fulton Sheen, "Spirit of Poverty", *Eight Month Report*, Diocese of Rochester Archives.
[61] Sheen, *Treasure*, 100.
[62] Quoted in Noonan, *Passion*, 150.
[63] Sheen, letter to Luce, January 12, 1972, Sheen Archives, Rochester.

Americans as behind the times or irrelevant."[64] Sheen gave three talks at the synod, mostly emphasizing the need to involve the laity in almost every layer of the Church. He also suggested that the seminary training of priests be extended by two years because he found young men of the 1960s too immature for the job for which they were training. He was energized by the synod and especially by the friendship of the pope, who said to him, "I am your friend. Do not kneel[;] let me embrace you as one I trust."[65] Friendship with the pope and progressive ideas at the synod earned the bishop from Rochester more jealousy and enemies among his priests at home.

Sheen's nemesis, Francis Cardinal Spellman, died of a stroke on December 2, 1967. There were many accolades for the deceased cardinal. His funeral was attended by the president of the United States Lyndon Johnson; New York mayor John Lindsay; Senator Robert F. Kennedy, himself six months away from an assassin's bullet; Cardinal Cushing of Boston; and a host of priests, prelates, and dignitaries. Bishop Sheen was there as well. His remarks were typically gracious. He said of the man who had promoted him and then sought to crush him, "The battlefields and soldiers will mourn, for they lost their chief chaplain. The missions will grieve, for they have lost their open-handed friend.... The death of a great man like Cardinal Spellman gathers up all humanity into one heart shedding one common tear. In life he claimed our attention, our respect, and our love. That does not deny him in death the more beautiful tribute of our prayers."[66] While he could beautifully eulogize his former friend and mentor, he found that administering a diocese left him almost no time at all to do what he loved most. He was so busy with charities, preaching, teaching, and attending to individual priests and lay people that his time was consumed with the mundane. He wrote to Clare Boothe Luce that while he loved what he was doing, he had been kept so busy "that I have done little instructing of converts, but somehow or other I feel that nothing

---

[64] Reeves, *America's Bishop*, 313. See also Robert F. McNamara, *The Diocese of Rochester in America, 1868–1968* (Rochester, N.Y.: Diocese of Rochester, 1968), 519.

[65] Sheen related this scene in a letter to Marlene Brownett, October 27, 1967, Marlene Brownett File, Sheen Archives.

[66] "Francis J. Spellman: New York Archbishop and Dean of American Cardinals", *New York Times*, December 3, 1967.

is more important. Anyhow, to be at peace I must find more sheep for his green pastures."[67]

The catastrophe that Cardinal Spellman wished on Sheen came over Saint Bridget's parish, an inner-city parish with fewer than one hundred members. The ensuing bruhaha, only fifteen months into Sheen's tenure as bishop, would bring the revenge that Cardinal Spellman had promised Sheen in 1957. Bishop Sheen, always in pursuit of social justice, observed that there had been fewer than fifty low-income housing units built in Rochester over the previous five years and that affordable housing was a major problem for many of the city's poor.[68] His solution was to donate diocesan property to the federal government on which to build housing for the poor. First, as canon law required, he had to consult with the Vatican and the apostolic delegate to the United States about his (at the time) inchoate idea. He was vague about his plan with his urban vicar, Fr. David Finks. He did not consult the Rochester Housing Authority. Also, as required by canon law, he called a board of consultors, whom he appointed to discuss turning an inner-city parish property into low-income housing. Only once the parish to be closed was selected did he tell pastor Fr. Francis H. Vogt of Saint Bridget's parish. It was only a few days before its public announcement, and Vogt was upset. The bishop had not consulted with the people of the parish, as that would have taken too long. Bishop Sheen, a man in a hurry, was determined to see the project through expeditiously.

On November 8, 1967, the bishop of Rochester had written directly to the United States secretary for housing and urban development, Robert Weaver, to offer a yet-to-be-named parish property to the government:

Sometimes the right to property is preserved in the midst of the property-less.... We now want to give away a church. We do not do this because we do not need it, nor because we are not finding new expressions of apostolate in a tightly circumscribed environment, nor because it is a burden on our budget, but because the poor are a greater burden on our conscience. We are under the Gospel-imperative not to be just a receiving Church, but a giving Church.

[67] Quoted in Reeves, *America's Bishop*, 314–15.
[68] Sheen, *Treasure*, 178.

We are under the necessity to be not just a ministering Church, but a surrendering Church. We are moved by the Spirit to do this.... Would you, therefore, be willing to accept from the people and clergy of the Diocese of Rochester the free, total and unqualified gift of one of our parishes in the inner city? We will pass the Church and all the property attached to it, to you or any person whom you designate, so long as on that property is built within the shortest possible time, housing for the poor.[69]

Bishop Sheen went to Washington to confer directly with Secretary Weaver, who then presented the idea to President Johnson. President Johnson was pleased with the proffered donation. Officials from HUD went to Rochester to select the property, and it was they, not Bishop Sheen, who chose Saint Bridget's. News of the donation of Saint Bridget's was leaked to the public, largely by its pastor, Fr. Vogt, who thought the bishop too progressive, and by the bishop's urban vicar, FIGHT member Fr. David Finks, who thought the bishop too conservative.[70] Bishop Fulton Sheen issued a press release, once again to the *New York Times*, announcing the donation of Saint Bridget's to the federal government for housing for the poor on Ash Wednesday, February 28, 1968. The Diocese of Rochester had to learn about the donation from the national media. It was the beginning of Lent, and to Sheen's mind the diocese was making a sacrificial, Lenten gift, a kind of almsgiving to the poor. "The Diocese of Rochester has chosen Ash Wednesday as the day on which to make a symbolic and real sacrifice for the poor.... The Diocese ... and its people have offered Church property to the propertyless."[71]

It was a dramatic gesture, and it received a dramatic response. Sheen believed that the opposition to the transfer of the Church property to the federal government was artificially stimulated. Immediately young people were outside of the pastoral offices of the diocese protesting with printed placards condemning the bishop. His car was pelted with rocks by an angry crowd. It was far worse than the demonstrations over the closing of the school at Most Precious Blood

[69] Sheen, *Treasure*, 179.
[70] Reeves, *America's Bishop*, 315.
[71] Riley, *Fulton J. Sheen*, 295.

Parish.[72] Twenty-two of his priests wrote an open letter to Bishop Sheen expressing their "sheer disappointment and disillusionment" with how Sheen had gone about the transfer of the property.

> We ... are aware of and share your concern for the people of the inner city, and especially their need for adequate housing. At the same time we feel that ... precipitous decisions could fail to achieve the good they intend.... This decision has completely bypassed the principle of collegiality. Neither the lay people affected not the priests were involved [or] participated in this decision.... Therefore, we recommend that your decision be withdrawn.[73]

Later, other priests would sign the letter, bringing the number of signatories to 139 priests, including several of the consultors who had originally approved the donation. Fr. Vogt publicly asked the bishop to retract his offer of Saint Bridget's. He noted that his parish was largely made up of poor Black people and Puerto Ricans and that Saint Bridget's school "was the most important thing in the neighborhood. There is enough empty property around without taking down the church and school."[74] But an empty lot would not have served the bishop's ends. An empty lot would not have had the benefit and impact of the world seeing a Catholic church and school taken down in order to raise up housing for the poor. Unfortunately, Sheen was in serious contravention of his own stated desires to have a diocesan administration that was formed by dialogue and democratic consensus. There were hurt feelings and anger all around, and Bishop Fulton Sheen rescinded his offer of the property to the government four days later. Because it was a public announcement, its rescission was a public humiliation for Fulton Sheen. Fr. Vogt told his happy parishioners on March 3, 1968, that Saint Bridget's would remain open.

Bishop Sheen never publicly referred to the contretemps over Saint Bridget's; that was not his way. For all his celebrity and notoriety, Fulton Sheen was a very private man. Not surprisingly, those

---

[72] Sheen, *Treasure*, 180.

[73] Letter to Bishop Sheen signed by twenty-two diocesan priests, March 1, 1968, in the St. Bridget's Case File, Diocese of Rochester Archives.

[74] Ibid.

outside of Rochester were more forgiving, and even supportive, of his desiring housing for the poor. Fr. John Reedy, C.S.C., was quoted in the Jesuit magazine *America* calling it an "imaginative and edifying gesture".[75] According to Riley, *America* would later label the Saint Bridget's episode "a brilliant blunder".[76] Even the pastor of Saint Bridget's appreciated the nobility of the bishop's desire to house the poor; he just did not want it in his backyard. Journalist Douglas Roche wrote of Sheen in 1968, well after the unfortunate episode of Saint Bridget's, "The ecumenical movement blessed by Vatican II went forward in Rochester by leaps and bounds.... In every action he took, Sheen revealed an intense commitment to conciliar thought as formulated in ... the Council documents.... The conciliar revolution, launched by Pope John, was brought down to earth and planted in local soil by Fulton Sheen."[77]

After the Saint Bridget's fiasco, the bishop of Rochester was never quite the same again. His priests even thought he looked different. The bishop never again put forth any bold or innovative ideas for the diocese. He was defeated and hurt by the vehemence of the outpouring against him personally. The letters against the transfer of Saint Bridget's were less aimed at the idea of giving away the parish and more at the bishop personally. A man who had grown up in the ranks of parish priests would have known the necessity of bringing people along slowly and would have developed the adroit skills to do so. Sheen did not have the experience or the temperament to proceed in that way.

In his autobiography, he does not dwell on his time in Rochester, but does refer to himself as the weak clay that is found in a compromised treasure.[78] In fact he would title his autobiography *Treasure in Clay*. Sheen said of his administration of the diocese, "This is an agony we would be glad to share." Later he noted, "No one wants authority these days—those who do are inviting untold difficulties."[79] Even though he was an enthusiastic supporter of the Second Vatican Council, in his mind the Church was still the same Church it had always been, based on authority and obedience. Fr.

[75] Quoted in *America*, April 13, 1968.
[76] Riley, *Fulton J. Sheen*, 298–99.
[77] Douglas Roche, *The Catholic Revolution* (New York: David McKay Co., 1968), 70, 79.
[78] Sheen, *Treasure*, 177.
[79] Riley, *Fulton J. Sheen*, 303.

Robert McNamara said of Sheen, "His churchmanship was basically 'old fashioned'; he was too mercurial to seek advice readily; and his prime gift was as a monologist, not a dialogist."[80] So disillusioned and shattered was Bishop Sheen that on the night the picketing and taunts began, he decided to resign. He knew he could no longer be an effective leader in Rochester. The laity was upset, his priests were in revolt, and the local media sided with the protestors. It was an untenable position for a bishop who had so many talents but lacked what he needed most in Rochester: administrative talent.

Fulton Sheen was never really out of ideas, and he never lost his interest in housing for Rochester's poor. A mere six weeks after the agony of Saint Bridget's, Bishop Sheen announced the creation of the Bishop Sheen Housing Foundation. The foundation was funded by seventy lay people who would donate ten dollars a week for twenty-four weeks to establish a housing fund that would grow over time. It was but a drop in the bucket in terms of numbers and immediate return when compared to what newly built housing on the grounds of Saint Bridget's would have accomplished. But before Bishop Sheen left the diocese, eighteen indigent families became homeowners because of the foundation, not including one poor family for whom he personally purchased a home. In 1980, one of Sheen's successors, Bishop Matthew H. Clark, joined the Sheen Housing Foundation with a commission run by the Episcopal Diocese of Rochester to form the Bishop Sheen Ecumenical Housing Foundation (called Sheen Housing), which is still operating today. In this quieter way, Fulton Sheen was able to accomplish something good and long-lasting for the poor of Rochester. Saint Bridget's would eventually be closed and stand empty for many years, and Bishop Sheen would go back to New York City for the rest of his life, but the Sheen Housing Foundation went on serving the poor decade after decade.

The turmoil over Saint Bridget's was to plague Sheen for some time. In 1974 he told Fr. Patrick Collins about the events surrounding the attempted donation of the parish.

The pain was still palpable as he related the incidents to me that night.... Said Sheen 'that night, that very night, I resigned as Bishop of Rochester. It took Pope Paul VI some time to accept it. But that

---

[80] McNamara, *Diocese of Rochester*, 540–41. See also Reeves, *America's Bishop*, 315.

night, as far as I was concerned, I left Rochester.' My sense was that he was still badly bruised by the experience and felt deeply the rejection and hurt. It seemed clear to me also that he failed to understand that he had brought the trouble on himself by failing to be a consultative bishop.[81]

He may have had his difficulties in his own diocese, but Fulton Sheen was still an important prelate in the Catholic Church and a good friend to the pope. Pope Paul VI appointed Sheen to several more synods in Rome. Being in Rome near the Holy Father must have been a welcome respite for Rochester's bishop. Shortly after Sheen's sermon against the Vietnam War, the pope appointed him to a synod on world peace. He also made a long trip to Ireland, where he visited his ancestral home in the village of Croghan; ostensibly, he was on a mission to recruit Irish men to become priests in his diocese.

Leaving Rochester

While Bishop Fulton Sheen was emotionally detaching himself from his diocese, it was not until May of 1969 that he was able to meet in Rome with Pope Paul VI to discuss his desire to retire from the Diocese of Rochester. He was then into his seventy-fifth year, the usual age for bishops to present their retirement requests to the pope. Popes may accept or deny the retirement requests from their bishops. Sheen had wanted to date his retirement from Rochester to September 20, 1969, which was the fiftieth anniversary of his ordination to the priesthood, but popes do not necessarily keep to the timetables of others. The Vatican announced the retirement of Fulton Sheen in mid-October. He left the diocese of Rochester on November 29, 1969. His friend Pope Paul VI elevated Sheen to the titular see of Newport in Wales as its archbishop. As was his wont, Sheen made light of his new see, saying that "being the archbishop of an ancient Christian seat 'is very much like being made a Knight of the Garter. It is an honor to have the Garter, but it does not hold up anything.' "[82] The pope also honored Sheen by making him an assistant at the

---

[81] Reeves, *America's Bishop*, 320. From an interview by Reeves of Fr. Collins.
[82] Sheen, *Treasure*, 184–85.

Pontifical Throne. As if trying to make the hurts of Rochester go away, Pope Paul VI appointed Archbishop Sheen to the Papal Commission for Non-Believers. Sheen was also part of the papal commission that brought about the end of the mutual excommunication between the Byzantine and Roman Catholic Churches. Sheen was even allowed to be bi-liturgical. He could say Mass in English in Eastern rite Catholic churches, the first American priest to do so. Additionally, the pope allowed Bishop Sheen the privilege of naming his own successor. Sheen chose Fr. Joseph L. Hogan to succeed him as bishop of Rochester. Fulton Sheen knew he was leaving the diocese in good hands.

Archbishop Sheen told his priests in his farewell address to them, "I am not resigning work. I am not retiring. I am regenerating." He asked for forgiveness "for the things I said and should have left unsaid, for the things I left unsaid and should have said; for the times I monologued when I should have dialogued."[83] His remarks to the priests of Rochester were an apology and a great show of humility on Sheen's part. Most people do not associate celebrity with humility, but the two were well combined and in tension in Fulton J. Sheen. Even the outspoken Fr. Finks, who often clashed with his bishop, would later write of Sheen:

> My respect for Bishop Sheen remains. My subsequent experience convinced me that for all his autocratic faults, Sheen honestly tried to meet the problem of the times head-on, and that was a rare occurrence for a Catholic bishop.... Bishop Sheen had no administrative experience.... He thought he could move ahead by preaching and example. It is enough that he helped when he did. In a time of ambiguity, he did some good things. That is not a bad epitaph, for a man or a bishop.[84]

Another of his priests would write of him, "Fulton J. Sheen was essentially an idea man and a prophet, and as such he set his diocese in the right direction. If he had had more experience in administration, he would have seen more of his dreams for Rochester come true."[85]

[83] Riley, *Fulton J. Sheen*, 304.

[84] P. David Finks, "Crisis in Smugtown" (Ph.D. diss., Graduate School of Union of Experimenting Colleges and Universities, 1975), 210.

[85] Fr. McNamara, typescript dated December 19, 1079, Diocese of Rochester Archives.

Bishop Fulton Sheen would probably agree with the assessments of his priests, but it is too bad that they were rendered so far after the fact. Fortunately, Sheen was not one to dwell on the past; he was always future oriented and ready for action. He was trusting in the Lord to open new doors for him.[86]

He asked his niece Joan Sheen Cunningham to locate a small apartment for him in Manhattan. He was going "home" to New York City. Before he left Rochester, he gave away most of his books and the things he had accumulated over the years. Some he gave to the Diocese of Rochester and others went to Saint Bernard's Seminary for what would become the Sheen Archives. His would be a new start in New York. He did not even have any furniture to take. His niece helped him outfit his upscale two-bedroom apartment overlooking the East River at 500 East Seventy-Seventh Street. He turned the second bedroom into his chapel, carpeted in blue for the Virgin Mary. At the age of seventy-six he was learning to cook and clean up after himself. He referred to his dishpan hands, the making of his own bed, and all the hamburgers he cooked and ate. He did not mind the dust. Every Good Friday, Catholics are reminded that from dust they come and to dust they shall return. He told close friends, "It is not an unhappy adventure."[87] Edythe Brownette once again became his personal secretary, arranging his appointments, speaking engagements, and travel. He had left Rochester, but he was not fading away. He opined, "If we live intensely, I believe that somehow or other we can work up until the day God draws a line and says, 'Now it is finished.' "[88] Archbishop Fulton J. Sheen had ten more years ahead of him for living intensely. He threw himself headlong into the last decade of his life when his main foci would be on the holiness of priests and the humbling of himself.

[86] Riley, *Fulton J. Sheen*, 311.
[87] Reeves, *America's Bishop*, 329.
[88] Sheen, *Treasure*, 183.

10

The 1970s

Living Life Intensely to the End

Retiring into a More Secular and Materialistic World

Archbishop Fulton J. Sheen meant it when he told the people in Rochester that he was not retiring. Relieved of the administrative duties of a diocese, Sheen arrived in New York with a full schedule of speaking engagements, television interviews and programs, books to write, converts to instruct, and retreats to give, especially to priests. For instance, almost immediately after leaving Rochester, he gave an interview to David Frost, where he defended the pope for his insistence on priestly celibacy and the sinfulness of artificial contraception and his opposition to the war in Vietnam. He told Frost that Christian war is never justified, and that secular war could only be engaged in if one's country was invaded, and then only to repel the invaders. He said, "I think we must begin to make wars against war."[1] Into his late seventies and early eighties, Sheen's schedule was enough to undo a younger man. He was often away from home for three weeks out of each month. In just the first two months of 1974, he traveled more than thirty thousand miles, giving talks and retreats. He had kept himself fit by his abstemious eating habits and his twice-weekly tennis games, along with a stationary bicycle he kept in his apartment. He insisted, "My legs and my lungs must be kept strong, just as my mind must be kept alert."[2] That regimen paid great dividends to the

[1] On-air interview of Archbishop Sheen on the *David Frost Show*, December 18, 1969, episode 2, quoted in Thomas C. Reeves, *America's Bishop: The Life and Times of Fulton J. Sheen* (San Francisco: Encounter Books, 2001), 338.

[2] Quoted in Reeves, *America's Bishop*, 340–41.

aging bishop who depended on God alone to tell him when "it is finished." He expected to work until the end of his life, and upon retiring he still had a lot of life to live.

The United States of Sheen's so-called retirement was a very different country from the country that had welcomed Sheen into its homes in the early 1950s via television. If he thought of the Diocese of Rochester as a microcosm of the post-Conciliar Church, Rochester itself was in fact a microcosm of the entire country. It was a country that was experiencing a rapid transformation in directions that would make Bishop Sheen and others like him very uncomfortable. Its youth were disillusioned with their elders and rejected the status quo, including what they considered to be outdated modes of thought and expression. It was a less civil society, much more casual, sloppy, and, occasionally outrageous in dress, and degraded in morality. Bishop Sheen thought the student radicals of the Sixties and Seventies essentially no different from those with radical revolutionary impulses in the 1930s, only their shirts were colorfully tie-dyed and not the brown, red, or black shirts of the earlier era. The Supreme Court decision *Roe v. Wade* legalized abortion; no-fault divorce tore apart families. Student antiwar protests became more violent, blowing up university buildings and killing people. At Kent State University, the National Guard fired on protesting students, killing four and injuring nine. Militant Black Panthers were robbing and murdering in the name of civil rights for African Americans, as was the anarchistic, bomb-building, antiwar Weather Underground. New Left scholars like Professor Howard Zinn at Boston University were reinterpreting America through a Marxist lens—Zinn's textbook, *A People's History of the United States*, is still widely used across the country. Mainline Protestant churches were accepting of divorce, contraception, abortion, and gay rights. Society as a whole was moving left, accepting and giving in to challenges to tradition and authority at every level.

The Catholic Church was not immune to the zeitgeist; in fact many in the Church happily embraced it. Liturgical norms were being overthrown in the "spirit of Vatican II". It may be apocryphal, but perhaps not too farfetched, that there were priests dressed as Easter bunnies processing for Easter Masses. Reeves wrote, "The National Council of Catholic Bishops, created in 1966 ... fell under liberal control, sanctioning and encouraging an assortment of liturgical novelties and in general pushing the American Church to the left."[3] Tabernacles were moved from the main altars to side altars, or even to the rectory down the hall. The Mass in the vernacular, while welcomed by most Catholics, including Bishop Sheen, used the new missals whose translations were not always the best. The language could be clunky and, according to Sheen and the traditionalists, it was not particularly elevating or beautiful. Churches were stripped of statues and other works of art. Newly built Catholic churches were sparse, sterile, and bare compared to the traditional Gothic or Romanesque architecture of older churches with their soaring heights, many statues, and beautiful stained-glass windows. The new buildings were all glass, steel, and concrete, without the warmth one associates with a church.

While not all nuns were leaving the life of a religious, many who remained in their orders were wearing polyester pants suits instead of habits and asking to be made priests. Bishop Fulton Sheen was not in sympathy with women who wanted to be priests—they might one day become deaconesses, but never priests. "If the Lord wanted women to be priests, instead of symbolizing the Church, He would have made His Immaculate Virgin Mother a priest."[4] Many priests, along with the nuns, were leaving their vows behind, and the loss was tremendous. Schools were shuttered without priests and nuns to teach the children. Priests were vocal about desiring an end to the celibate priesthood. Parishes were consolidated or closed for want of priests. While many men were leaving the priesthood, there were also far fewer young men entering the seminaries. As the bishop of the Diocese of Rochester, Sheen had refused laicization to the priests who requested it. The priest shortage would become acute in some dioceses. Reeves noted, "The price for abandoning authority and tradition and embracing the world has long been known to be expensive for Christian churches."[5]

The loci for the push left could be found in the seminaries and universities, among the Church's intellectual elites. The Jewish scholar Will Herberg took Catholics to task when he addressed a

---

[3] Reeves, *America's Bishop*, 331.
[4] Sheen interview by *Catholic Standard and Times*, August 12, 1976.
[5] Reeves, *America's Bishop*, 332.

Catholic convention: "I say just the opposite: in all that is important, the Church must stand firm in its witness to the truth that is eternal and unchanging; it needs no updating.... If it is to be true to its vocation, it must take a stand against the world, against the age, against the spirit of the age—because the world and the age are always, to a degree, to an important degree, in rebellion against God."[6] But many Catholics were not listening to voices such as Herberg's. They were swayed not by a Herberg, but by the popular and liberal Fr. Theodore Hesburgh, president of Notre Dame, who was much more accommodating to the spirit of the age. In 1972, the ex-priest T. Joseph O'Donoghue boasted:

> Liberal Catholics have a lock-tight grip on the publication of catechisms and religious formation texts, and a similarly tight grip on university religious education departments which train religious teachers for all levels.... Liberal Catholics have mastered the technique of designing structures and liaison patterns to multiply total impact.... Pity the poor establishment which sees the once docile Catholic populace of its area now constantly infused by liberal itinerants whose words endure in small but solid liberal movements.[7]

This statement by O'Donoghue could have come directly out of a Communist training manual in the 1930s, when it taught that a committed few with a single-minded worldview were willing to take on the important institutions of government, education, and religion and clandestinely bend them to their purpose. Sheen understood well the power of a united and determined creative minority to effect change in society, for good or for ill. And to Sheen, the communists wanted to produce havoc in every institution in America.

It was not only the Catholic Church in America that suffered in the leftward lurch of society. The mainline Protestant denominations found that the more they accommodated the demands of the Left, the more their congregants abandoned their churches. It could all be traced, as Reeves wrote, to "the intellectual elites who controlled

---

[6] Quoted in Roger Finke and Rodney Stark, *The Churching of America, 1776–1990: Winners and Losers in Our Religious Economy* (New Brunswick, N.J.: Rutgers University Press, 1992), 258.

[7] "Ratifying a Victory", editorial, *National Catholic Reporter*, March 24, 1972, 8.

major seminaries, religious periodicals, and denominational machinery. More rapidly than the society at large, they were moving to the left, challenging tradition, and authority, and often the very basics of the Christian faith itself."[8]

Every institution in America was impacted by the upheavals of the time. Fulton Sheen, however, was not dismayed or negative about the prospects of the Catholic Church. He always supported the decrees of the Second Vatican Council even when he was not in full approval of the implementations that occurred. He thought the English translations from the Latin for the missals and the sacramentaries were less than felicitous and aimed at the least literate. Thomas Reeves believed that Sheen was distressed over society's "fascination with sex divorced from love and marriage".[9] It could not possibly lead to anything good. He did not like the stripped-down churches that did not, in his estimation, project a sense of the sacred. Archbishop Sheen was so critical of nuns abandoning their habits that he refused to recognize un-habited sisters or to give retreats in convents where the sisters no longer wore traditional habits.

He was appalled when his Jewish jeweler friend, Herbert Trigger, called him to ask what he should do with the hundreds of crucifixes in his possession. Trigger explained that Roman Catholic nuns were coming by and hocking their sterling silver crucifixes. The sisters no longer wanted to wear the crucifixes because they felt the crucifix separated them from the people they were serving. The bishop asked Trigger to craft for him a pectoral cross with an attached corpus to wear from some of the crucifixes the nuns had abandoned to remind him of their apostasy and of the imperative to love the cross of Jesus whereupon the economy of salvation was enacted. The rest of the crosses Sheen bought from Trigger to give away. The nuns' rejection of their crosses made both Trigger and Sheen very sad. Sheen felt a righteous anger at the sisters for turning their backs on the crucifix, a symbol of Christianity's most basic tenet.[10] Monsignor James Malone called Sheen's anger "Holy anger; he was upset that the nuns had

---

[8] Reeves, *America's Bishop*, 330. See also Fulton Sheen, *Guide to Contentment* (New York: Macau, 1967), 38; "Babies and Children", season 3, episode 1, *Life Is Worth Living*.

[9] Reeves, *America's Bishop*, 336.

[10] Fulton J. Sheen, *Treasure in Clay* (Garden City, N.Y.: Doubleday Press, 1980), 275–76.

given up their crosses."[11] Trigger told Sheen he had paid the nuns thirty pieces of silver for their crucifixes.

Sadder yet for Sheen was the refusal of priests and theologians to discuss sin, Satan, hell, or repentance. Eventually, many even in the Church would reject the idea of the "absolute" and the "divine". It would be the tyranny of relativism rampant in the world, and Sheen believed that the "demonic is always most powerful when he is denied".[12] He always thought that the country did not suffer from a lack of tolerance, as many claimed; it was too tolerant—tolerant of bad, wrong, and dangerous ideas, tolerant of sin and loose morals, tolerant of greed, violence, and war. He pointed out that "tolerance is not always right, and intolerance is not always wrong."[13] According to Fulton Sheen, properly understood, "tolerance never refers to people", and "tolerance always refers to evil, real or imaginary, never to good."[14]

Sheen's Eternal Optimism

But there was a silver lining to be found in the chaos regnant in the modern world. Even though the Church may become smaller, it will become stronger because the Holy Spirit is its guardian. Sheen wrote:

> It is a historical fact that whenever there is an outpouring of the Holy Spirit as in a General Council of the Church, there is always an extra show of force by the anti-Spirit or the demonic. Even at the beginning, immediately after Pentecost and the descent of the Spirit on the Apostles, there began a persecution and the murder of Stephen. If a General Council did not provoke the spirit of turbulence, one might almost doubt the operation of the Third Person of the Trinity over the Assembly.[15]

Sheen, always the optimist, thought it a wonderful time to be a Catholic. Twenty or thirty years earlier it had been easy to be a proud

---

[11] *Positio*, 1.561.

[12] Fulton Sheen, *Through the Year with Fulton Sheen: Inspirational Readings for Each Day of the Year*, ed. Henry Dieterich (San Francisco: Ignatius Press, 2003), 192.

[13] Fulton J. Sheen, *Life Is Worth Living* (New York: McGraw Hill, 1954), 107 (hereafter *LIWL*).

[14] Ibid., 105–11.

[15] Sheen, *Treasure*, 202–93.

Catholic and a patriotic American, because most of the country supported those values. With those values in decline, it was more difficult to be Catholic or even Christian. He thought God was testing his people, and the Lord tests those whom he loves. With pragmatism taking hold in the Western world, public virtue declined when utility was becoming the highest good. It becomes more difficult to live the virtuous life when those around one have abandoned virtue. According to Reeves' analysis, Bishop Sheen believed that society and the Church would right themselves in time, giving up "secularism and hedonism and returning to the faith and objective moral standards it once had".[16] The clock is still running on that prognostication, but it is never a good idea to bet against the intuition of Fulton Sheen. He truly believed that "evil may have its hour, but God has His day."[17]

In the fight against the collapse of the sense of the sacred and the importance of virtue, Sheen looked for allies wherever he could find them. In 1972, he spoke in the evangelical Robert Schuller's gigantic Garden Grove Community Church, better known as the Crystal Cathedral.[18] When Sheen spoke, in addition to the two thousand seats inside the church, there were four thousand folding chairs set up on the lawn for people to hear Sheen's sermon. The next year, Bishop Sheen addressed an enormous audience of Lutheran young people. He was determined to live his life intensely. In 1975, he spoke to seventy-five thousand Catholics at the New Orleans Holy Year Rally. That same year he preached a three-hour service in Los Angeles, where his friend Loretta Young was in the congregation. The following year, Sheen spoke to over six thousand in the Las Vegas Convention Center. In March, he preached to the Hibernian Society in Savannah. In August, he preached to the Eucharistic Congress in Philadelphia. He had written in 1939, "Burning the candle at both ends for God's sake may be foolishness to the world, but it is a profitable Christian exercise—for so much better the light!"[19] Sheen took energy from being with like-minded Protestants, as he did from

---

[16] Reeves, *America's Bishop*, 337.

[17] Fulton J. Sheen, "Three Times in a Nation's History", *Life Is Worth Living*. See also *LIWL*, 276–81.

[18] The Crystal Cathedral of Rev. Schuller was subsequently purchased by the Catholic Diocese of Orange, California, in 2010, when it became Christ Cathedral.

[19] Reeves, *America's Bishop*, 339.

the Catholic laity and from the priests to whom he gave numerous retreats in the 1970s.

Getting Closer to His Brother Priests

Giving retreats for priests was possibly the most important and satisfying work Archbishop Sheen did in his later years. He wrote:

> I have loved every work to which I have been called or sent. But perhaps the most meaningful and gratifying experience of my life has been giving retreats to priests, not only because they brought me into contact with the priesthood, but because the very review one makes of his own spiritual life in order to speak to others helps oneself too. I wonder if the priests who made the retreats received as much from me as I did from them.... The word "retreat" connotes a series of sermons, exhortations, and meditations given over a period of time varying from three days to over a week—the purpose of which is to remind diocesan priests that their own pastoral life, whatever it may be, is intrinsically related to their sanctification, that the horizontal relationship to neighbor is inseparable from the vertical love of God; that the triple work of the priest is to teach, sanctify, and shepherd, for those are three forms in which the holy life manifests itself.[20]

The elderly archbishop knew well what he was speaking about, for he lived a deep spirituality in his own life. His personal holiness was the source of his strength and inspiration. Not only did he keep a daily Holy Hour throughout his life, but he also accomplished much of his thinking and writing in his chapel before the Blessed Sacrament. He wrote, "All my sermons are prepared in the presence of the Blessed Sacrament. As recreation is best nourished and profitable in the sun, so homiletic creativity is best nourished before the Eucharist. The most brilliant ideas come from meeting God face to face."[21] He was utterly devoted to Christ in the Eucharist and to the Blessed Virgin Mary. That is why he admonished priests to think less of administration and to love more fully.

[20] Sheen, *Treasure*, 216.
[21] Ibid., 75.

Once when giving a retreat to the monks down the coast from Big Sur at California's Camaldolese Monastery, the Bishop brought enough fresh oranges for each monk because he knew that their regular fare was very meager. The prior passed out the oranges, but as the men came for confession to the bishop, each one brought him an orange, so great was their detachment from even the smallest luxuries of life. He went home with as many oranges as he had brought. In this case, he wrote, "It was I who was edified, inspired and challenged."[22]

Being a retreat master was an exhausting business. Sheen usually gave five or six conferences a day every day for three days to a week. Each conference was thirty to sixty minutes long and occasionally longer. He always stood when speaking and he never used notes, so it was physically and intellectually draining. He insisted that his retreats be given in the chapel before the exposed Sacrament. Once he showed up to give a retreat in a monastery to find that the Blessed Sacrament was not in the church, but down the hall in the former prior's room. Bishop Fulton Sheen would not commence the retreat until the Blessed Sacrament was in its proper place on the altar. He insisted that everyone who was making a retreat with him as the retreat master spend a continuous hour of meditation each day in front of the consecrated Host in the monstrance. His retreats for priests, nuns, and bishops took him around the country and abroad. Soon after his eightieth birthday, he flew the almost seventeen thousand miles across the Pacific Ocean and back to give a retreat to the bishops in the Philippines.[23]

Sheen also gave retreats to college men and women and to prisoners. He found that the college students wanted to hear about Christ and his love; prisoners wanted to hear about forgiveness and reconciliation and Christ's salvific sacrifice on the Cross. The bishop would often begin his prison retreats, "Gentlemen, there is one great difference between you and me. You have been caught; I was not. In other words, we are all sinners."[24] Prisoners were not required to attend his retreats, but about 95 percent would show up to listen

---

[22] Ibid., 219.
[23] Ibid., 215–27. See also Reeves, *America's Bishop*, 343.
[24] Sheen, *Treasure*, 224.

to Fulton Sheen. Many prisoners converted to the Catholic faith. They would write to him for advice and consolation. Sheen contacted the governor about parole for an inmate who had completed twenty-six years of a life sentence. When the man was released from prison, he called Bishop Sheen. The bishop asked him what work he had done in prison and, when told that his prison job had been in the kitchen, Sheen asked him to become his cook. Of retreats for prisoners, Sheen wrote, "It is easy to give retreats and conduct spiritual exercises for men like this, for they know that they are not so good—and this is always the condition of entering the Kingdom of Heaven."[25] Fulton Sheen understood this from his sixty years as a priest and from his encounter with Kitty, as expressed in his *Life Is Worth Living* episode on "Nice People". The Bible teaches that the first shall be last and the last shall be first (Mt 20:16).

Sheen's experience in Rochester, his only real failure and, in retrospect, where he also in truth had many successes, made him more introspective, self-critical, and humble. He told one of his audiences, "I have been a priest for fifty-five years, for which I thank God. I was doing much better thirty years ago in my own mind than I am now. Now I feel as if I have done so little."[26] He wrote, "The Church is not made up of saints, but of sinners who are trying to be saints. This is true of the bishops."[27] And it was true of Fulton J. Sheen.

Many people believed that it was the roar of the audience and the din of the applause that propelled Fulton J. Sheen into his celebrity status and kept him there year after year. Indeed, Sheen fully recognized the peril of his celebrity: "Radio and television greatly satisfy me because they give a larger pulpit than any other activity. But they can be the most dangerous to a priestly soul."[28] Thomas Reeves called Sheen a "supernatural man". By that he meant that Bishop Sheen was moved by God to love the sinner, to seek the convert, and to defend his Church against the onslaught of the increasingly secular age.[29] With his inspiration from above, Sheen's influence in America and beyond was tremendous. He reached millions of viewers

---

[25] Ibid., 227.
[26] Reeves, *America's Bishop*, 341. See also Sheen, *Treasure*, 329–30, on the difficulties in the priestly vocation.
[27] Sheen, *Treasure*, 99.
[28] Ibid., 216.
[29] Reeves, *America's Bishop*, 348.

on his weekly programs, first on radio and then on television. His sixty-six books were read by multitudes. Someone estimated that he had converted forty-two thousand individuals, but he was never one to count. Only God knows the total count of Fulton Sheen's converts. The converts were gifts from God and never of his own making. Sheen was a man on fire for God. He said, "If I were asked if I had to live my life to live over again, would I live the priesthood as I have, the answer is: 'No, I would try to love Christ more. The only sorrow in my life, or any life, is not to have loved Him enough.'"[30] That would not be the estimate of those who knew him well. One of his converts testified for the *Positio* that Sheen did not have excessive self-esteem. "I think he was like, here I am, an instrument and whatever God wants." Another said "His love of people was that he wanted so badly to bring people to God and to make them understand the importance of why we are here, where we are going.... He loved people so much that he devoted his entire preaching to trying to bring them to the Lord." His great-nephew said of him, "He saw Christ in each and every person."[31] Fulton Sheen loved God and people, and no doubt he loved his celebrity, but he loved God more. After Rochester, wrote Reeves, "he particularly regretted his fine clothes, his Cadillacs, his love of clerical titles and privileges."[32] Sheen wrote:

> While many young priests sought ways to imitate the way I preached, was I inspiring anyone to imitate Christ in the daily carrying of His Cross? I knew it was not right. I knew I should be giving away more than I gave. I should have resembled more closely Christ, Who had nowhere to lay his head. I should have fled from the applauding mobs as the Lord fled from the enthusiasms at Capharnaum after the multiplication of bread; maybe I was like Peter, who at one point "followed the Lord far off."[33]

In his autobiography, he goes on in the same vein: "I loved creature comforts. I dressed well and I excused myself for this, saying that the ambassador of Christ should always present himself as a gentleman to the people and one of whom they could be proud."[34]

[30] Ibid., 35.
[31] *Positio*, 1.101–8.
[32] Reeves, *America's Bishop*, 358.
[33] Sheen, *Treasure*, 336–37.
[34] Ibid., 337.

Interestingly, Sheen goes on to tell the story of how he came to have a new Cadillac year after year. The owner of the local Cadillac agency complained to him that he was having trouble with his workers. Sheen listened to the man's problems and then proposed that to make the workers happier and more productive, the agency should give the workers not just their salaries, but also a one-half share of the company's year-end profits. The owner was so pleased with the result of the profit sharing that he gifted Sheen with a loan of a new Cadillac every year for twenty-five years. So Bishop Sheen, on the one hand, apologized for driving a Cadillac luxury car and, on the other, explained away how that had come about, demonstrating his ongoing struggle between humility and pride.

A good antidote for Sheen's tendencies to worldliness was always a trip to Lourdes, where he was able to prostrate himself once again before the Virgin Mother to pray for her guidance and support for his priesthood. Every time he made a trip to Europe, he tried to include a personal side visit to Lourdes. He was attracted to Fatima in Portugal too, but Lourdes is where he felt closest to the Mother of Christ. In his autobiography, Bishop Sheen devoted an entire chapter to the Mother of God, the Theotokos, which he entitled "The Woman I Love". Ever since his ordination, Sheen had offered the Eucharistic Sacrifice each Saturday to the Virgin, "renewing my feeble love of her and invoking her intercession".[35]

Bishop Sheen's devotion to the Blessed Mother and his lifelong meditation on the seven sorrows of Mary gave him insight into the sacredness of suffering. At the time he was suffering exquisite and constant pain, and with his doctor and a nurse in the front pew, he looked back over his life while preaching a Good Friday sermon in 1979 at Saint Agnes Church in New York City; the bishop told the congregation, "I've had a great deal of suffering in the eighty-three years of my life. There has been physical suffering. And other kinds ... but as I look back over the years, I have never received the punishment I deserved. God has been easy with me. He has never laid on me burdens equal to my faith."[36] It would be his last Good Friday sermon, and when he got up slowly to approach the pulpit and before he had even said

[35] Ibid., 317.
[36] Sheen's Good Friday Sermon at St. Agnes Church in New York City, April 13, 1979, https://www.dailymotion.com/video/x8dhler.

a word, the crowd gave him a standing ovation. He felt that the Lord had not pierced him with the slings and arrows of suffering, such as the distressed and anguished people he met on his missionary travels to remote villages in the midst of famine or to the leprosaria he visited in Africa and Asia experienced. He did not have on his hands scars like those of the crucified Christ, but he did comment seriously that the scars from his open-heart surgery gave him a chest scar like that of Jesus. That scar was the visible sign of his close identification with Jesus Christ. "Oh what joy is mine just to have endured minuscule imitation of His suffering on the Cross by having a wounded side. Maybe He will recognize me from that scar and receive me into His Kingdom."[37]

The priest, Sheen would assert, is also a victim. "It is not enough to be a priest; one also had to be a victim", he wrote.[38] To be a victim is to suffer. To identify more closely with Christ, the priest must recognize himself as both priest and victim, as Christ is the High Priest as well as the Victim sacrificed on Calvary and re-presented on every Catholic altar throughout the world. The recognition of the victimhood of the priest was always part of Sheen's retreats to his fellow priests. Fulton Sheen worried about himself and all priests: "I was the priest; was I the victim?"[39] Was he thinking about himself as victim when he told Mike Wallace of CBS in an interview, a mere two weeks after leaving Rochester, that he might have gone higher in the Church's hierarchy, "But I refused to pay the price"?[40] Was the price he refused to pay the loss of his integrity had he given into Cardinal Spellman's demands not once, but twice? Sheen did not elaborate. In his autobiography, Sheen quotes Euripides: "Silence is wisdom's first reply."[41] He went on to remark, "I have resolved in this book not to touch on any sufferings that came from others."[42]

[37] Sheen, *Treasure*, 339–40.

[38] Ibid., 340.

[39] Ibid., 335.

[40] Reeves, *America's Bishop*, 327. Mike Wallace, interview with Bishop Sheen, October 28, 1969, transcript in the Sheen Archives in Rochester. See also a photo of Sheen on the set with Wallace in D.P. Noonan, *The Passion of Fulton Sheen* (New York: Dodd, Mead & Company, 1972), 88.

[41] Euripides, *Euripides Dramatic Fragments*, ed. Jeffrey Henderson, #977 (Cambridge: Harvard University Press, Loeb Classical Library, 2008), 560, https://www.loebclassics.com/view/euripides-dramatic_fragments/2008/pb_LCL506.561.xml; Sheen, *Treasure*, 343. Sheen uses a loose translation of the Greek.

[42] Sheen, *Treasure*, 312.

Over time, Fulton Sheen came to recognize that all suffering comes from the direct will of God or through the permissive will of God and that God offers either a sweet or a bitter remedy. Sheen wrote that in "chewing the cud of resentment, licking the wounds and the memories of how we received them, the playing of the tapes of injustices real or imagined, were so many proofs that I had not thoroughly digested what my Faith taught me and my lips confessed, that all trials come from the Hands of the Loving God."[43] Even the trials at the hands of Cardinal Spellman were really sufferings sent to him by God; Spellman was merely the instrument. It was better for Sheen and for his beloved Church, that he keep silent about his unpleasant interactions with Cardinal Spellman. He wrote, "Silence is recommended because any discussion of conflicts within the Church diminishes the content of the Christ . . . . Silence is also imperative in order to avoid the danger of self-justification . . . . Finally, silence is recommended because if I judge not, I will not be judged."[44] Interviewers were always interested in two things when face to face with Fulton Sheen—the contretemps with Spellman and the brouhaha over Saint Bridget's—but he would never take their bait. He would never discuss the sufferings brought to him by others. Physical suffering was in a different category.

The Beginning of the End

It was not lost on Bishop Sheen that much of the physical suffering he endured at the end of his life came on three of the Virgin Mary's feast days. He had told friends that he wanted to die on a feast day of the Virgin Mary or on a Saturday, the day he always dedicated his Mass to her, and he wanted to die before the Blessed Sacrament. He was just back from a trip to Lourdes, accompanied by Sister Marlene Brownette and his nurse friend, Cathy Yetman, when on the feast of Our Lady of Mount Carmel on July 16, 1977, he had open heart surgery, the oldest person at that time to undergo the operation. When Clare Boothe Luce learned of his impending

---

[43] Sheen, *Treasure*, 345.
[44] Ibid., 312–13.

heart surgery, "she remarked, 'I am stricken of course, but I'll also be astounded if the surgeons find a heart, since he's been giving it away for so long.'"[45] It took more than seventy pints of blood for Sheen's surgery to be successful, and there were many moments that the surgeons were nearly in despair for his life. In the recovery room after surgery, a priest friend came to say Mass on an altar set up over Sheen's bed, and when it came time for the consecration of the Host, Fulton Sheen found the energy to sit up, move his hands and say the words of a concelebrant.

Later that same summer on August 15, 1977, the Solemnity of the Assumption of Our Lady, he underwent prostate surgery and remained in the hospital until November 3. While he was in the hospital, Pope Paul VI wrote the ailing bishop twice and called once. President Jimmy Carter also called twice. Sheen was visited by Terence Cardinal Cooke of New York and Mother Teresa of Calcutta. Victim he may have been, but a priest always and always on the lookout for a soul in need of conversion or consolation. In the intensive care unit after surgery, he heard a nurse say that a man in a neighboring bed was about to die. Sheen was too weak to speak or to move, but minutes before the other patient died, the bishop prayed to God to take his own suffering for the salvation of his neighbor's soul and then managed to raise his finger to bless the man with the sign of the Cross and to give him conditional absolution from his sins. A few months later, the widow of the deceased man came to visit Bishop Sheen to ask what he had done for her husband, and when he confirmed that her husband had been blessed and absolved of his sins, the widow was greatly comforted. She presented the bishop with a Jewish long-life medal, grateful that, in the midst of his own suffering, the bishop had cared for her husband.

While Sheen was still in the hospital recovering, another Jewish man visited him daily. When he missed a few days, he told the bishop that his wife had been diagnosed with cancer and was to be operated on the next day. Sheen gave him a small silver crucifix that had been blessed by Pope John XXIII, saying, "I am going to give you something which is Jewish and for that reason I know that you will receive

[45] Hilary C. Franco, Bishop Fulton J. Sheen: Mentor and Friend (New Hope, Ky.: New Hope Publications, 2014), 111.

it. It is the death of Christ on the Cross. I will only tell you that He was Jewish on His Mother's side. Who was His Father, you will have to find out from Heaven. But if you throw your trust with the well-being of your wife into His Hands, you may one day discover who His Father is." The man returned to Sheen a few days later wearing the crucifix on a chain around his neck. The man's wife did not have to have the surgery; it turned out to be unnecessary. He told Sheen, "I found out Who Christ's Father was."[46]

First and foremost, Archbishop Fulton Sheen was always a priest. At the impromptu press conference outside as Archbishop Fulton Sheen was leaving the hospital, he told the reporters, "I was never afraid to die because God is with me ... wherever I go. At no time did I have any fear."[47] In his autobiography, he wrote, "I know that I am not afraid to appear before Him. And it is not because I am worthy, nor because I have loved Him with deep intensity, but because He has loved me. That is the only reason any one of us is really lovable. When the Lord puts His love into us, then we become lovable."[48]

Nonetheless, dying was much on his mind toward the end of his life. He told a *New York Times* interviewer who was interviewing him on his eighty-fourth birthday, "As long as I live Christ is with me. When I die I will be with Him."[49] It was not that he wished to die, just that he was looking forward to seeing Jesus no longer as through a glass darkly but at last face to face (see 1 Cor 13:12). On the other hand, Fulton Sheen always felt that he had more to do in this life. He wrote, "I am so happy ... that I sometimes feel that when I come to the Good Lord in Heaven, I will take a few days' rest and then ask Him to allow me to come back again to this earth to do some more work."[50]

His first public appearance when leaving the hospital after his prostate surgery was to receive the Catholic Actors Guild Award. Sheen, always gracious, began his acceptance talk by introducing the doctors who had saved his life. A white-haired Clare Boothe Luce, all the way from Hawaii, was on hand to "roast" the recipient of the award. She accused him of "envy (he envied those who could carry

---

[46] Sheen, *Treasure*, 346–47.
[47] *New York Daily News*, November 4, 1977.
[48] Sheen, *Treasure*, 39.
[49] Reeves, *America's Bishop*, 355. Sheen letter to Mr. and Mrs. Chester Baker, June 3, 1979.
[50] Sheen, *Treasure*, 61.

a tune), covetousness (he coveted souls), anger (against those who were uncharitable and unkind to others), a sort of reverse gluttony (he lived largely on canned pears), and sloth (he refused to read the newspapers)." She ended by calling him "my beloved archbishop".[51] Later in the evening, young Andrea McArdle, who was playing the lead in *Annie* on Broadway, went up to the archbishop to sing "You Light Up My Life".

Less than a year later, in 1978, on the day the Church celebrates the birth of the Mother of Jesus, September 8, Sheen was back in the hospital with a serious kidney ailment. While he was recovering, a nurse told him that a man down the corridor had tried to commit suicide by slashing his throat. Sheen asked that the man be allowed to visit him if he wanted. Later, a nurse wheeled the man down the hall in his bed to Sheen's room and arranged their beds side by side. On questioning the man, Sheen found out that the man had been a Catholic, but that he no longer believed in the divinity of Christ or in his Church. Sheen talked to the man of his debts, all of which the man claimed to have paid. When pressed on his moral debts, the man was silent. Sheen pulled out a crucifix and said, "He paid your debts—every one of them." Then he talked of Jesus' redemption for sin. That same day, Sheen heard the man's confession and gave him his first Communion in forty-five years. Sheen had prayed to the Lord to let his suffering do some good for a soul in need, and again the Lord heard him.[52] At age eighty-two, he would comment that, along with Saint Paul, he was determined to preach the Gospel, to preach Christ Crucified for the redemption of sins. "I have taken a resolution all the rest of my life to preach nothing but Christ and him crucified."[53] Sheen wrote to his cousin in early 1979 saying that he was on bed rest and flat on his back: "I have no complaint whatever about my condition because I firmly believe that the Lord often puts us on our back so that we will keep looking up to heaven."[54] He would also comment, "The horizontal apostolate may sometimes be

[51] Reeves, *America's Bishop*, 351–52. From a recording of the event in the possession of Marlene Brownett.

[52] Sheen, *Treasure*, 348.

[53] "Bottom-Line Theology: An Interview with Fulton J. Sheen", *Christianity Today*, June 3, 1977, 8.

[54] Sheen, *Treasure*, 353.

just as effective as the vertical."[55] Whatever his condition, he would preach Christ until the very end. Even when he was in and out of the hospital for various ailments and, often, just plain exhaustion, he kept on going.

His February schedule included the 1979 National Prayer Breakfast in Washington, D.C., attended by President Jimmy Carter and his wife, Rosalynn, along with other governmental officials and dignitaries. Sheen was the featured speaker, with the Reverend Billy Graham on hand as a substitute for Sheen should Sheen be unable to show up. Against the advice of his physicians and with them in tow, Fulton Sheen not only showed up, but he amazed the attendees with the power of his talk. He famously began by turning his piercing eyes to President Carter to begin his talk: "Mr. President, you are a sinner." Then he paused with one of those famous Sheen pauses, and, pointing to himself, he continued, "I am a sinner. We are all sinners, and we all need to turn to God." Graham contended that Sheen "went on to preach one of the most challenging and eloquent sermons I have ever heard". President Carter wrote later of the event, "It was a real pleasure and an unforgettable experience to meet him in person, and I especially appreciated his coming to the National Prayer Breakfast while I was president."[56]

Again, Fulton Sheen received a standing ovation for just stepping into the pulpit of Saint Patrick's Cathedral in New York, where he was a surprise guest preacher for the cathedral's one hundredth anniversary on May 12, 1979. His friend Rabbi Marc Tanenbaum got Sheen a job narrating a biblical movie, and the Society for the Propagation of the Faith had Sheen as a narrator for its film *The Great Inheritance*. At the end of the summer of 1979, Sheen filmed a half-hour program for a New York television studio for the impending visit to the United States by Pope John Paul II. When the pope arrived in New York City on October 2, 1979, Fulton Sheen would narrate his visit for national television. Amid this flurry of activity and despite his frailty, Bishop Sheen instructed four converts and officiated at two weddings. Feeling that his end was near, Archbishop Fulton Sheen was writing his autobiography, which he wrote out longhand until he was too weak to hold the pencil; then he committed his memoirs

[55] Ibid., 350.

[56] Reeves, *America's Bishop*, 353–54. Carter's letter is now in the Carter file in the Sheen Archives.

to dictation while holding the Dictaphone mic in one hand and a crucifix in the other.

He celebrated his sixtieth anniversary as a priest on September 20, 1979, in his apartment chapel with five of his closest friends. He even gave a brief homily. Reeves wrote, "He acknowledged that the exact day on which he died did not really matter, because he knew he belonged to Jesus and the Blessed Virgin. Fulton hoped that when he appeared before the Lord, He would say, 'Oh, I heard my Mother speak of you.' "[57] His sixtieth priestly anniversary did not go unnoticed by the Holy Father in Rome. Pope John Paul II wrote him a warm congratulatory letter:

I am one with you in giving thanks to God for your sixty years in the priesthood of Our Lord Jesus Christ. God called you to proclaim in an extraordinary way his dynamic word. With great zeal you accepted this call and directed your many talents to spreading the Gospel of Jesus Christ. Thus, in your six decades of your priestly service, God has touched the lives of millions of men and women of our time. They have listened to you on radio, watched you on television, profited from your many literary achievements and participated in spiritual conferences conducted by you. And so with Saint Paul, "I thank my God whenever I think of you; and everytime I pray for ... you, I pray with joy, remembering how you have helped spread the Good News (Phil 1.3–4)".... I ask you to pray for me ... and I shall pray for you, asking our Lord Jesus Christ to give you peace and to sustain you in his love.[58]

Fulton Sheen responded to the Holy Father in kind, saying:

I am still, thank God, blessed with the Psalmist's promise, "Vigorous in old age like a tree full of sap (92.14)".... I bow in humble gratitude for the Pontifical approval of my ministry of the Word.... Pray for your Holiness? That I always do for the Vicar of Christ.... Every night when silence gives vision scope, I pray to Our Lord in the Blessed Sacrament for the Chief Shepherd of our souls, and the only moral authority left in the world.... I wish I were younger to enjoy the blessings to come.[59]

---

[57] Reeves, *America's Bishop*, 356, quoting Sheen's September 20, 1979, homily transcript in the possession of Marlene Brownett.

[58] Sheen, *Treasure*, 242.

[59] Ibid., 243.

Despite Sheen's insistence on being like a tree full of sap, he was privately speaking to friends of his impending death. "It's not that I do not love life; I do. It is just that I want to see the Lord. I have spent hours before Him in the Blessed Sacrament. I have spoken to Him in prayer, and about Him to anyone who would listen, and now I want to see Him face to face."[60]

This was not the first letter Bishop Fulton Sheen received from Pope John Paul II. The pope wrote him a lengthy letter on the occasion of the twenty-fifth anniversary of Sheen's elevation to the episcopacy. They were old friends from the heady days of the Second Vatican Council, so the pope wrote to Sheen recalling their prior friendship:

> We have the most happy remembrance of you, Venerable Brother; We cherish with the highest esteem your life and manifold activities, and We seek at this present moment to amplify that most sweet joy We bear you.... For no other than the Lord Jesus Himself is the One Who has poured out to others, through your ministry, such an abundance of graces.... We greatly rejoice and give thanks to God, for neither age nor state of health has impeded you, but always with a joyful spirit, with pastoral devotedness and good manners, even now you draw many men to Christ and to the Church; particularly the priests you have given spiritual admonitions and help; to vast assemblages you have sown the truths of the Gospel.... We beseech the Most Benign Redeemer to invigorate you and strengthen you in your fruitful work, and rejoice you with the consolation of a strong faith. Then when it pleases Him, may He make you happy in the clear vision of Himself in Heaven.[61]

When the Holy Father made his first visit to the United States, only the second by a pope, he saw many of the sights in New York City, where he arrived on October 2, 1979. Sheen had narrated the visit when Pope Paul VI arrived on October 4, 1965, and would do the same for Pope John Paul II when the Polish pope arrived almost exactly fourteen years later. There was a ticker-tape parade down Fifth Avenue for the Holy Father. Pope John Paul II preached to

[60] Ibid., 354.
[61] Ibid., 241.

eighty thousand when he celebrated Mass in Yankee Stadium and to another fifty-two thousand waiting in Shea Stadium. There was also a Mass, mostly for the bishops, priests, and religious, but also laity, in Saint Patrick's Cathedral. Archbishop Fulton Sheen, greatly weakened by illness and age, was assigned a seat off to the side. When the pope entered the cathedral, the congregation erupted with applause. When Pope John Paul II looked about himself, he did not see Archbishop Sheen, so he asked for his old friend. The infirm archbishop, led by his secretary, made his way slowly to the sanctuary and, when he fell to his knees before the pope, John Paul II lifted him to his feet and embraced him. The applause was crashing and went on for several minutes. It would be the last thunderous applause Fulton Sheen was to hear. It was the highlight of his life to be told by his friend, the Holy Father, "that I had written and spoken well of the Lord Jesus, and that I was a loyal son of the Church".[62] The pope gave Archbishop Fulton J. Sheen one of the best epitaphs a priest could have. On the last page of his autobiography written in his own hand, Sheen rejoiced in his sufferings, the "thorn in the flesh" given him by God, but said, "The greatest gift of all may have been His summons to the Cross, where I found His continuing self-disclosure."[63]

The archbishop made out his will on the 4th of December. He left small amounts of money to his three best friends, Bishop Edward O'Meara, who succeeded him as director of the American Society for the Propagation of the Faith, Fr. Vincent Nugent, and Fr. Michael Hogan. He left his manuscript files, kinescopes, and videotapes to the Sheen Archives in Rochester. To the Society for the Propagation of the Faith he left his publication rights. His personal effects were to be distributed by Bishop O'Meara as Sheen's executor according to a document never made public. The one possession he valued highly, an antique Russian chalice of great beauty, he gave to Saint Patrick's Cathedral. Over the next few days that Fulton Sheen had to live, he was in daily contact with friends and relatives. On December 9, 1979, he entertained a young couple and gave them part of a sermon he was working on for Midnight Mass at Saint Patrick's. He also wrote

---

[62] Archbishop Edward T. O'Meara, Homily at the funeral Mass for Fulton J. Sheen, New York, Saint Patrick's Cathedral, December 13, 1979, quoting Sheen in the epilogue to Sheen, *Treasure*, 354.

[63] Sheen, *Treasure*, 350.

a letter, the last he would ever write, to thank Ann O'Connor for a blanket she had sent him. He wrote, "My heart has to be elastic—otherwise it would break with gratitude for your friendship and gifts during the year."[64] He was ever grateful for any kindness done him. Ann O'Connor had been a child of five when he met her in London alone on a street corner when he was a student priest away from his studies at Louvain. Little Ann invited him to tea at her home the next day, and, to the amazement of her parents, he showed up and the two remained fast friends across the decades and the expanse of the Atlantic Ocean.

Sometime that Sunday evening, December 9, the day after the feast of the Immaculate Conception, Archbishop Fulton J. Sheen collapsed and died in his chapel before the Blessed Sacrament. His body was received into Saint Patrick's Cathedral by Terence Cardinal Cooke the following day. The coffin was placed in the Lady Chapel on the 11th and viewed by thousands of Sheen's friends, converts, and fans, including Martin Sheen, who had met the bishop in 1965. Family and friends came from around the country to honor him in death. There were three Masses at the Cathedral for Fulton J. Sheen. On December 11, there was a Mass at the request of the Society for the Propagation of the Faith. On the 12th there was a Mass at the request of the Diocese of Rochester, where Sheen had been its ordinary for three short years. The funeral Mass was held on the 13th with Cardinal Cooke as the main celebrant. In attendance were four cardinals, forty-eight bishops, the governor of New York, Hugh Carey, and the mayor of New York City, Ed Koch, along with Sheen's family members, friends, and thousands of admirers. The homily was delivered by Fulton Sheen's good friend Bishop O'Meara, who concluded his talk most poignantly:

> Last Sunday, at 7:15 P.M. God called Archbishop Fulton Sheen to himself by name. It was a moment known to God, and fixed by Him from all eternity, a call to perfect life and truth and love, a call to a life he will never tire of, that can never be improved, and which he can never lose.
>
> Dear friend, Archbishop Sheen, we are all better because you were in our midst and were our friend. We trust you to the care of your

---

[64] Reeves, *America's Bishop*, 360, letter in Ann O'Connor's possession.

"Lovely Lady dressed in blue." We pray that Jesus has already said:
"I've heard My Mother speak of you."

Bye now, Fulton Sheen, and God Love You Forever![65]

The Legacy of Fulton J. Sheen

Archbishop Fulton Sheen belongs to God and to his Church, and, through them, to everyone. The Diocese of Peoria, Sheen's diocese, began exploring the cause for his sainthood in 2002. In 2012 Pope Benedict XVI approved the official opening of Fulton Sheen's cause for sainthood; Sheen is now venerated by the Church for his heroic virtues and his life of great faith. In 2019, one hundred years after his ordination as a priest, Pope Francis approved a miracle attributed to the intervention of the Venerable Fulton Sheen. A newborn baby, apparently stillborn without a pulse for sixty-one minutes, suddenly started breathing after the parents and others sought the direct intercession of Fulton Sheen:

> On Sept. 15, 2010, Bonnie Engstrom went into labor after a healthy, low-risk pregnancy. What no one knew at the time was that her son, James, had a true knot in his umbilical cord that had tightened during labor and cut off his oxygen supply. When he was delivered, he was lifeless. James was without a pulse for 61 minutes. Just as the medical staff at the OSF Health Care St. Francis Medical Center in Peoria, IL. were preparing to call time of death, James's heart started beating. And, in his mother's words, "it never stopped again."
> The family asked for the intercession of Archbishop Fulton Sheen for their son's life and for the complete healing of any damage to James's body, and the answer to their prayers was recently approved as a miracle.[66]

Travis Engstrom, the baby's father, had baptized the lifeless infant, and the hospital chaplain had given the child the Sacrament of Confirmation. The doctors at the Peoria, Illinois, hospital were amazed that baby James Engstrom came to life after his traumatic entrance

---

[65] Ibid., excerpt, 362, and Sheen, *Treasure*, 351–55, full transcript of O'Meara's homily.
[66] Haley Smith, "She Prayed to Fulton Sheen and Her Baby Was Saved. Meet Bonnie Engstrom", *America Magazine*, July 25, 2019, https://www.americamagazine.org/faith/2019/07/28/she-prayed-fulton-sheen-and-her-baby-was-saved-meet-bonnie-engstrom.

into this world, but they predicted that James would die soon from organ failure brought on by the hour-long lack of oxygen or, if he lived, he would suffer from major brain damage. Contrary to the doctors' predictions, today James Fulton Engstrom is a healthy little boy in every way, a gift from God at the intervention of the Venerable Fulton Sheen.

Miracles for the cause of sainthood are always medical cures, and each is rigorously investigated by the Vatican. First a panel of doctors, some of whom are non-Catholic, must attest that there is no medical explanation for the cure. If the medical panel finds the cure medically inexplicable, that is, miraculous, then the case is turned over to a panel of theologians who seek to discover if the miracle was effected by the intervention of a single individual. It takes two certified miracles for an individual to be declared a saint in the Catholic Church. The Venerable Fulton Sheen is well on his way to sainthood. His beatification, an important step on the way to being named a saint, has been held up, first over a squabble between the Dioceses of New York and Peoria over where Sheen's mortal remains should reside. Sheen's will stipulated that he preferred to be buried in Saint Patrick's Cathedral, and when he died, Cardinal Cooke assigned him a place in the crypt of the Cathedral, ironically opposite that of Cardinal Spellman. After a long court battle, the archbishop's body was disinterred from Saint Patrick's crypt and transferred to Saint Mary's Cathedral in Peoria, Illinois, Sheen's home diocese, and interred there on June 27, 2019, nearly one hundred years after his ordination at St. Mary's on September 20, 1919. The Venerable Sheen's beatification date was announced and then the date was canceled without comment after a request from the Diocese of Rochester, which wanted to wait until the statute of limitation had run out on a claimant's legal ability to make an accusation of clergy sexual abuse against a perpetrator or an administrator who somehow mishandled the complaint. After exhaustive investigations by the Vatican, the Diocese of Rochester, and the Diocese of Peoria, nothing has been found to implicate Rochester's former bishop in any wrongdoing. For whatever reason, the Vatican continues to "pause" the process of canonization for the Venerable Fulton J. Sheen, but the Diocese of Peoria, as it awaits a second certified miracle wrought by the intervention of

Sheen, is confident that its native son will eventually become Saint Fulton Sheen.

Saint or not, Fulton Sheen changed the lives of his countless converts and continues to do so to this day. For every one of his newsworthy converts like Heywood Broun, Louis Budenz, Clare Boothe Luce, or Bella Dodd, there were hundreds and thousands of people who converted to or returned to the Catholic Church under the influence of the Venerable Sheen. Most of his converts were anonymous individuals who were moved by his radio and television addresses or by the plethora of his publications. They never actually met the man who helped to convict them of the truths of the Catholic faith. They were, nonetheless, his spiritual children, as dear to him as any father's children, even if he did not know them personally. People wrote to him from all over the world asking for his advice, counsel, and prayers. Some asked for written materials. He or his staff would always respond to these requests. Many would write to tell him that they had been converted to the Catholic Church by something he said or did. One woman told him she had converted because of one of his television programs. When asked which program, she replied that it was the one where Sheen had famously read Shakespeare's death scene of Caesar, substituting the names of Stalin and his circle of friends for Caesar, Brutus, Cassius, and the other conspirators. Sheen was surprised at her response. He wrote, "There was absolutely nothing in that telecast that would draw a soul to the Church. God just used it as an instrument."[67] Sheen denied that he used his electronic pulpit to proselytize: "Never once was there an attempt at what might be called proselytizing."[68] He would just lay out the truths of the faith and let God do the rest at the invitation of the individual. God would never force himself on a person; a conversion was at the grace of God and the will of the individual. Sheen would say, "The audience is always there, the opportunities ever present."[69] He was God's instrument in converting them in great and grateful numbers. Even his Jewish jeweler friend Herbert Trigger and his six daughters converted—Herbert on his deathbed.

---

[67] Sheen, *Treasure*, 74.
[68] Ibid., 73.
[69] Ibid., 75.

Among those who influenced Fulton Sheen, he specifically credits G. K. Chesterton as the greatest influence on his writing style. Chesterton "never used a useless word [and] saw the value of a paradox and avoided what was trite". C. S. Lewis also influenced Sheen for being "concrete, pedestrian, full of examples, analogies, parables and always interesting". Malcolm Muggeridge was another influence, "always sparkling, brilliant, explosive, humorous". Sheen also loved poetry, "especially the poems of ... Francis Thompson".[70] He committed many poems to memory and would recite them at will and to good effect. On reading his published works and watching his videos, it is obvious that the Venerable Sheen was concise, never trite; he employed analogies, parables, and a plethora of examples; he certainly was interesting, brilliant, full of good humor, and always challenging.

The breadth of his knowledge was encyclopedic, but his love of God was what drove him throughout his long career. His audiences loved him then and they are loving him now. His influence may not be what it was fifty years ago, but it is still felt by many today. American seminaries assign his books to their students, especially *A Priest Is Not His Own*. These young men become priests and in their homilies from the pulpit they scatter Sheen's quotations and words of wisdom to their parishioners. Among younger, traditional Catholic parents, the name Fulton is given to sons. The popular Bishop Robert Barron made Fulton Sheen the subject of one of his televised episodes in his series *Pivotal Players* in 2020. Fulton Sheen and Flannery O'Connor were the only Americans to be profiled in the twelve-part series.

Bishop Barron came to Sheen somewhat through the back door. He had not been catechized into the keeping of a daily Holy Hour as a young priest and did not know much about Fulton Sheen. It was under the influence of the next generation of priests that Bishop Barron came to keep the Holy Hour, and through the Holy Hour he came to know and love Fulton J. Sheen. With his photogenic and poised presence, Bishop Barron is often called the "next Fulton Sheen". With his Word on Fire platform, regular podcasts, many publications, and frequent talks around the country, Bishop

---

[70] Ibid., 79.

Barron has become a media darling in much the same way Bishop Fulton Sheen was over seventy years earlier. But with all due respect to Bishop Barron and others like him, with all their talents and wisdom, there will never be another Fulton J. Sheen, because the importance of Sheen comes from the man and his message plus his times. The genius of Bishop Barron comes with his message properly attuned to our time. Sheen was unique—the right man at the right time with the right message.

Today there are many more voices clamoring for attention, many with messages that need to be heard, like the eloquent Bishop Robert Barron's. When Fulton Sheen first went on the radio and then on television, he had the intellect, the talent, the personality, and the empathy necessary to the task at hand. The post–World War II growing television audience was hungry for the messages that Sheen was so brilliantly delivering week after week—and he was the only one offering his particular message, that the way to personal peace and love was through the crucified Christ. Sheen asserted that it is not so much that we love Christ, but that he first loved us and made it possible for us to love him. There can never be another Fulton J. Sheen, as there will never be a mid-twentieth century United States that so appreciated him. Archbishop Timothy Dolan praised Fulton Sheen in a letter: "As an historian of the Catholic Church in America, I can say without any fear of contradiction that he [Sheen] was the most effective evangelist we have ever generated!"[71]

It was Archbishop Sheen who inspired and paved the way for men like Bishop Barron to use whatever media are available to spread the word of Jesus Christ and to present his Church to a nation that has drifted away from Christianity and is in need of healing and reconciliation. The influence of Archbishop Fulton J. Sheen cannot be overestimated. He remains a towering figure in American Catholicism. His tapes and books are still making converts to this day. Young priests want to emulate him. The laity are drawn to him. God willing, he will soon be a canonized saint in the Roman Catholic Church.

[71] *Positio*, 2.1049.

11

A Coda

On Conversion

What Is Conversion and Who Converts?

Nobody calls it a conversion when an individual changes from the Baptist Church to the Methodist Church, or from the Presbyterian Church to the Unitarian Church. It is merely a change in group membership or picking up a new label. The same cannot be said when an individual joins the Roman Catholic Church from any other church or religion, or from none. G. K. Chesterton wrote of the Catholic Church, "It does not merely belong to a class of Christian churches. It does not merely belong to a class of human religions."[1] The Catholic Church is not a denomination of Christianity, one denomination among many; it is not a denomination at all. It is the Church founded by Jesus, not as an institution, but as his Body with himself as its head. The person who joins the Catholic Church, from whatever background, is called a "convert". The Greek word for a religious conversion is *metanoia*. It indicates a complete change of heart, as when God spoke through the prophet Ezekiel, saying, "A new heart I will give you, and a new spirit I will put within you" (Ezek 36:26). Metanoia brings about a profound change in character, making one a new man. To convert is to begin walking in another direction—with and toward Jesus, away from one's former life, away from sin and false beliefs and following the Way, the Truth, and the Life. It is clearly seen in the companions of

[1] G. K. Chesterton, *The Catholic Church and Conversion* (San Francisco: Ignatius Press, 2006), 93.

Jesus, the first twelve apostles who left their families and livelihoods and, eventually, their ancient Jewish laws and rituals to follow the Lord wherever he might lead or send them. They were following the person of Jesus, compelled by his teachings, his miracles, and his personality. They knew they were following Jesus the man; only later did it dawn on them that their master was in fact divine, the true Son of God come down to earth to bring salvation to mankind. They were shocked and distressed at the Passion and death of Jesus, still not comprehending what he had told them about raising the destroyed Temple in three days. It was not until the post-Resurrection appearances of Jesus and the coming of the Holy Spirit upon them at Pentecost that the scales fell completely from their eyes so that they could apprehend the full truth of their Lord and what their mission now entailed. They were called to love as Jesus had loved them, bring sinners to repentance, spread his message of divine love and mercy to the ends of the earth, and make disciples of all nations—to make converts of Jews and gentiles alike, holy ones and sinners, to bring all to the Lord.

Modern converts have the benefits of having the death and Resurrection of Jesus well documented and behind them for almost two thousand years, the accumulated Holy Scriptures and writings of the Church Fathers, and a Church organization structured to protect the deposit of faith. New catechumens (those preparing to become Catholic) and converts can see the entire economy of salvation laid out before them, unlike the original apostles for whom the faith, the truth of Jesus, was slowly revealed. Converts have the assurances of well-developed doctrines and the graces available to them as they complete their journey into full communion with the Church, the Body of Christ.

The Unfolding of Conversions

Converts' journeys into the Catholic Church are as varied as the individuals who eventually receive Baptism (if not already validly baptized), make a Profession of Faith, and receive the sacraments of Reconciliation, the Eucharist, and Confirmation. There is not one single avenue into the Church. G. K. Chesterton said, "The

Church is a house with a hundred gates; and no two men enter at exactly the same angle."[2] This is proved by the conversion stories of well-informed, articulate men and women. Some approach the Church with doubt, rage, despair, fatigue, disillusionment; some are initially intellectually drawn, others are emotionally or aesthetically brought to the Church doors. Converts often think their personal road into the Church is the only road. The insights and the graces may come slowly or all at once. Those desiring to know more about the faith eventually come to realize that they seek Truth; they seek Jesus. They can come to the Church because Jesus first loved them and the grace of the Holy Spirit inspired them to recognize Christ in his Church, and to believe that the Catholic Church is the one, true Church to which they must belong. The Spirit and Truth compel them to convert.

The priests who guide converts into the Church are only the instruments of God, not the cause of anyone's conversion. Bishop Fulton J. Sheen was well aware that it was God who made the converts, not he. Chesterton noted, "Catholicism is not spread by any particular professional tricks or tones or secret signs or ceremonies."[3] Practical knowledge of Christ comes only through the gift of the Holy Spirit, as Sheen wrote, "Who leads us to accept Jesus as Lord and Savior".[4] Despite understanding himself as an instrument, Sheen acknowledged that conversion could be a hard process on all concerned. Some converts brought him joy, and others reminded him that the priest is also a victim. Most, but perhaps not all, who came to Sheen for instruction in the faith were in some kind of crisis, a point in their lives when they simply could no longer go on as in the past. Sheen believed that all converts come out of one type of crisis or another: "Every conversion starts with a crisis: with a moment or situation involving some kind of suffering, physical, moral or spiritual; with a dialectic, a tension, a pull, a duality or a conflict. This crisis is accompanied on the one hand, by a profound sense of one's own helplessness and, on the other hand, by an equally certain conviction that God alone can supply what the individual lacks."[5] Fr. Donald

[2] Ibid., 38.
[3] Ibid., 71.
[4] Fulton J. Sheen, *The Priest Is Not His Own* (San Francisco: Ignatius Press, 2004), 118.
[5] Fulton J. Sheen, *Peace of Soul* (New York: Whittlesey House, 1949), 232.

Haggerty writes, "God meets a soul at a crossroad of life and in some unexpected way makes His real presence known."[6]

Saint Augustine's famous line underscores what the convert seeks: "For thou hast made us for Thyself and our hearts are restless till they rest in Thee."[7] Converts seek the peace of soul that only God can provide when they finally turn to him. One of England's famous converts whose restlessness persisted through years of spiritual turmoil and crisis was John Henry Newman, who wrote of this ultimate tranquility: "From the time that I became a Catholic ... [I] have had no anxiety of heart whatever. I have been in perfect peace and contentment; I never have had one doubt."[8] It was not that he understood completely everything Church doctrine holds. For instance, he grew up in a tradition that did not teach transubstantiation and found it a difficult teaching, yet, he wrote, "I made my profession [of faith] upon my reception with the greatest ease, and I have the same ease in believing them [the tenets of the Faith] now."[9] Despite whatever difficulties he had with transubstantiation or any other doctrine, he could maintain his equanimity, writing, "Ten thousand difficulties do not make one doubt."[10] He explained, "I did not believe the doctrine [of transubstantiation] till I was a Catholic. I had no difficulty believing it, as soon as I believed that the Catholic Roman Church was the oracle of God, and that she had declared this doctrine to be part of the original revelation."[11] Newman's crisis lasted for almost two decades of intense intellectual struggle to remain in the Church of England where he was a priest and enjoyed a benefice at Oxford. He would go on to be a cardinal in the Catholic Church.

For Clare Boothe Luce, the crisis was living with the death of a daughter she felt she had neglected. Fritz Kreisler needed a lifeline near the end of his illustrious career and in the midst of terrible physical suffering from a tragic accident. Louis Budenz, a former Catholic and Communist Party member, finally came to see the Communist Party for the evil it represented and intended, and he

---

[6] Donald Haggerty, *Conversion: Spiritual Insights into an Essential Encounter with God* (San Francisco: Ignatius Press, 2017), 24.

[7] Augustine, *Confessions*, trans. F.J. Sheed, 2nd ed. (Indianapolis: Hacket Publishing, 2006), 3.

[8] John Henry Newman, *Apologia pro Vita Sua* (New York: W.W. Norton, 1968), 184.

[9] Ibid., 155.

[10] Ibid.

[11] Ibid., 156.

was appalled by what he had participated in. Heywood Broun had a premonition of an early death and did not want to die in his sins. Ada "Bricktop" Smith felt alone in a hostile and racially discriminatory world. Elizabeth Bentley was bereft after the death of her Communist lover and pressured by the Communist Party to do things she did not want to do. Bentley's Russian handler wanted to "eliminate" her by poison. Bella Dodd, also a Communist, finally saw the darkness at the heart of the Party and the need to extricate herself from its tentacles. Her life, too, was in danger. Virginia Mayo was at loose ends after having lost her husband when her film career was nearly at its end. All needed the love and support Fulton J. Sheen was able to offer them when the Holy Spirit moved them to seek instruction in the Catholic faith. As Christ promised, "The Spirit of truth ... will guide you into all the truth" (Jn 16:13). Fulton Sheen emphasized the "three rules of dealing with those who come to us: 1. KINDNESS, 2. KINDNESS, 3. KINDNESS".[12] Kindness, above all, presented with his heroic generosity and deep faith, was what Bishop Sheen offered the seekers after the truth, along with the doctrines of the faith. The Holy Spirit did the rest, provided they came to seek the truth of the Catholic faith with an open mind and an open heart. For not all who seek instruction in the faith will ultimately convert, and not all who convert will remain within the walls of the Church—note, for example, the failed conversion of Henry Ford, who threw over the Catholic Church for a new bride. One of Bishop Sheen's converts, journalist Gretta Palmer, had been given the assignment by her magazine to do an article on Bishop Sheen focusing on his converts. He refused to give her the requested interview, as he generally avoided publicity. In order to get to see him, she told him she had been baptized a Catholic but had fallen away. He would see her, but only off the record and only to give her instruction in the faith. She agreed, more out of curiosity than anything else. Gretta Palmer had been an atheist since her teenage years, but was always searching for ways to improve the lot of humans. She greatly believed in progress, the perfectibility of man, and science. When Gretta first met Sheen, she told him to not bother with the rational arguments for the Church.

---

[12] Fulton Sheen, "Instructing Converts", in *Winning Converts*, ed. James A. O'Brien (South Bend, Ind. Notre Dame Books, 1957), 179.

His answer surprised her. He told her, "You can't abandon your reason. That's the mistake the followers of Hitler made. That's the kind of thing that makes people believe a man in Moscow, Idaho, is God, because he claims to be. Let me tell you what we Catholics believe, and if your reason rejects it, go away with my blessings. But I beg you, my friend, don't throw in the sponge on using your intellect."[13] One does not abandon reason in converting to the Catholic Church; on the other hand, reason, although necessary, is not sufficient to bring about a conversion. As the novelist Robert Hugh Benson wrote, "The puzzle which God had flung at me ... needed ... not the head only, but the heart, the imagination, the intuitions; in fact the entire human character had to deal with it."[14]

Accordingly, Sheen told Palmer to read the Gospels very slowly. She discovered that "if Christ is truly God, then everything else must follow." Sheen instructed her from July to December, when she became a Catholic. She wrote, "I became a Catholic because I was looking for the truth, and I had found it."[15] Interestingly for Gretta Palmer and for many others, at her conversion she did not yet understand all that the Catholic Church had to offer, but in accepting that Christ is God and that it is the Catholic Church that he founded, she could accept all that the Church teaches about the Virgin Mary, the papacy, purgatory, indulgences, saints, and the foundations of morality. For Gretta Palmer, "The Catholic's universe is thus a universe that makes sense, and the only one that does."[16] She had already tried all the other possibilities, but, in the end, only the Catholic Church could satisfy her. Gretta Palmer was forever grateful to Fulton Sheen for shepherding her into the Church. She sent him fresh flowers three times a week to decorate his chapel.[17]

Robert Hugh Benson, not a Sheen convert but one who came to the Catholic Church through a great deal of personal turmoil as the son of the Archbishop of Canterbury, was also convinced of the truth of the Catholic faith. He wrote of his conversion, "There

---

[13] Gretta Palmer, "Escaping from an Atheist's Cell", in *The Road to Damascus*, ed. John A. O'Brien (Garden City, N.Y.: Doubleday, Image Books, 1949), 32.

[14] Robert Hugh Benson, *Confessions of a Convert* (Notre Dame, Ind.: Christian Classics, 2016), 64.

[15] Palmer, "Escaping", 33.

[16] Ibid., 39.

[17] *Positio*, 1.484.

seemed nothing within me at all except an absolute certainly that I was doing God's Will and was entering the doors of His Church." Of the doctrines of the Church he wrote, "I was quite sure that I perfectly believed them, as indeed everything else which the Church proposed to my faith."[18] He was seeking the Truth: "I did not want the broad ways of pleasantness, but the narrow Way that is Truth and Life."[19] What kept him out of what he had come to believe was the one true Church for so long was his unwillingness to cause distress to his mother and friends, who discouraged his conversion—he was an ordained minister of the Anglican Church. His friends, many of whom were also clergy in the Church of England, were convinced that religious beliefs were no more than matters of taste and individual choice. For his defection to Rome, they called Benson "a deliberate traitor or ... an infatuated fool, or ... an impatient, headstrong, ungrateful bigot."[20] Benson was not attracted to Rome because he was attracted to her customs and rituals, but because "I believed the Church to be the Church of God."[21] He was convinced of the truth of Catholic doctrine, especially in light of his conviction that the Roman pontiff was indeed the successor to Saint Peter, but for a time he lacked the will to make the change. He would make that choice eventually and find peace and happiness as a priest in the Catholic Church.

Clare Boothe Luce was also convinced of the truths found in the Church, yet she too lingered outside its doors, until she could say, "The Catholic doctrine seemed to me the solid objective truth."[22] That objective truth was revealed to her by the Holy Spirit. She wrote, "As every convert knows, Faith is a gift of Grace, received by an act of the free will."[23] Luce was grateful to Fulton Sheen: "God intended me to be a Catholic or He would not have sent me to Father Sheen, the one best equipped to rid my mind of nonsense and fill it with the sense of Our Lord Jesus."[24] Fulton Sheen would reply, "No man could go to Clare and argue her into the faith. Heaven had

[18] Benson, *Confessions*, 88–89.
[19] Robert Hugh Benson, quoted by Dawn Eden, foreword to Benson's *Confessions*, ix–x.
[20] Benson, *Confessions*, 92.
[21] Ibid., 80.
[22] Clare Boothe Luce, "The 'Real' Reason", Part One, *McCall's*, February 1947, 118.
[23] Clare Boothe Luce, "The 'Real' Reason", Part Three, *McCall's*, April 1947, 80.
[24] Ibid., 85.

to knock her over."[25] It was not his arguments that won her over; it was heaven—the Holy Spirit—who convicted her. Luce wrote, "So in the end, all conversions are effected through love. The mind is hungry for the truth, but the soul is athirst for love. And it is the soul that must be touched. If the Catholic cannot successfully argue the word of love, all his other arguments fail."[26] Fulton Sheen underlined the Catholic's relationship to Jesus: "It is first and foremost a love relationship."[27]

The Process of Conversion

As can be seen from the examples of Robert Hugh Benson and Clare Boothe Luce, conversion is a process that can be discerned. There is a beginning, a middle, and an end. But before there is even the beginning, the convert's entire life is a prologue to his conversion. All his life experiences, for better or for worse, are a preparation for that first encounter with whoever will be providing instruction in the faith. Donald Haggerty wrote, "Conversions are never entirely sudden, coming out of nowhere, even when they seem to ignite an explosively new force within a life. The hidden chiseling of the hand of God has usually been at work for an unknown time; concealed touches have been laid upon the heart."[28] Clare Boothe Luce agreed: "Every convert agrees on this: his conversion was the end of a process that had his whole life for its beginning. In retrospect, he sees all the days of his non-Catholic years as a preparation for the divine act of grace which called his soul from darkness into light."[29] What amazed Mrs. Luce was that God, who knew everything about her, could still love her. That is because, as Sheen noted, "He sees us with a Father's eye and loves us, wanderers though we may be, with a Father's heart."[30] The Holy Spirit will have been at work all along,

[25] Stephen Shadegg, *Clare Boothe Luce: A Biography* (New York: Simon & Schuster, 1970), 211, quoting from an interview with Sheen twenty-two years after Luce's conversion.

[26] Clare Boothe Luce, "The Right Approach", in *Winning Converts: A Symposium on Methods of Convert Making*, ed. John A. O'Brien (San Diego, Calif.: Catholic Answers, 1996), 70.

[27] Fulton J. Sheen, *Preface to Religion* (New York: P.J. Kennedy & Sons, 1946), 120.

[28] Haggerty, *Conversion*, 24.

[29] Clare Boothe Luce, "Under the Fig Tree", in *Road to Damascus*, ed. O'Brien, 196–97.

[30] Fulton J. Sheen, *Guide to Contentment* (New York: Macau Publishing, 1967), 26.

moving the individual gradually to be open to what the Catholic Church teaches about Jesus and his Church. Conversion is not made by one big decision at the Profession of Faith, but by an accumulated store of decisions over the course of instruction and period of seeking the truth.

Chesterton viewed conversion as a tripartite process. He called the first phase of conversion "patronizing the Church". This is a time when the seeker begins to learn that at least some of what the Church proposes is true or at least plausible and to acknowledge that what is said about the Church by those on the outside may not be true or fair. The second phase of conversion is "discovering the Church", a digging into the doctrines of the faith and finding them to be true. This second phase can be short or long. Chesterton's third phase is "running away from the Church".[31] This is when the honest seeker after religious Truth believes the doctrines of the faith but is overwhelmed by that Truth and what it will mean for him.

Ultimately, "God is the only convert maker", however one labels the stages of conversion, for God the Holy Spirit is at work throughout.[32] When the conversion comes, "The convert is discovered by grace, and not grace by the convert."[33] And it is the grace of the Holy Spirit that, in the end, makes the assent of intellect and will possible. The conversion is a supernatural event. An individual cannot merely will or assert his conversion on his own power without first being moved by the Holy Spirit. A conversion is the submission of one's will to God. Faith is ultimately a gift from God that brings about such a submission. But if one desires and prays for a conversion, God will respond. "God never refuses His grace to those who sincerely ask," held Bishop Sheen, "but many souls cringe at the thought of such grace changing them"—hence Chesterton's third phase of conversion is running away from the Church for those who cringe.[34] The catechumen finds that the Church had been right where he had been wrong, and that is a challenge to his pride. The honest seeker finally makes his assent to the truths of the faith and finds that he is where

[31] Chesterton, *Conversion*, 90.

[32] John A. O'Brien, "The Contemporary Scene in America", in O'Brien, ed., *Winning Converts*, 5.

[33] Luce, "Fig Tree", 203.

[34] Sheen, *Peace of Soul*, 250.

God wants him to be and where he is finally at home, at peace. Conversion is due to the personal assent of the intellect and will all along the path to enter the Catholic Church.[35] True conversion cannot be forced, but once convicted of the truths of the Catholic faith, one must convert. Fulton Sheen emphasized, "Grace will aid, direct, and perfect your human actions, but only on condition that you freely cooperate with it. God breaks down no doors."[36]

A new convert may be surprised that the Profession of Faith is but the beginning of his journey into becoming a new creation in the Lord. To comprehend fully the richness and the complexity of the Catholic faith takes a lifetime. Conversion, therefore, is an ongoing process; it does not end with one's reception into the Church, but, rather, as Sheen would say, it is a lengthy process of perfectibility that entails "being re-created, re-made and incorporated into the Risen Christ, so that we live His life, think His thoughts and will His love".[37] One of the best discussions of the importance of ongoing conversion is found in chapter five, "The Universal Call to Holiness in the Church", of *Lumen gentium*, the Second Vatican Council's Constitution of the Church. Leviticus 11:45 charges God's people to "be holy, for I am holy." If being holy seems daunting, the Lord calls his people to perfection. *Lumen Gentium* tells us, "The Lord Jesus, the divine Teacher and Model of all perfection, preached holiness of life to each and everyone of His disciples of every condition. He himself stands as the author and consumator of this holiness of life: 'Be you therefore perfect, even as your heavenly Father is perfect.' "[38]

How is it possible to be holy as God is holy, to be perfect as the Father is perfect? It is an enveloping process whereby one is docile to the will of God as illumined by the presence of the Holy Spirit within. When one listens for the will of God and cooperates with the grace of the Spirit, one becomes more and more conformed to Jesus, the exemplar of all holiness and perfection. The Holy Spirit gives graces to all who ask in the measure of their abilities, and their abilities

---

[35] For a full scholarly discussion on this topic, see John Henry Cardinal Newman's *An Essay in Aid of a Grammar of Assent* (Monee, Ill.: Veritatis Splendor Publications, 2016).

[36] Sheen, *Preface to Religion*, 105.

[37] Ibid., 65.

[38] Vatican Council II, Dogmatic Constitution on the Church *Lumen gentium* (November 21, 1964), no. 40, quoting Matthew 5:48.

increase as they become more and more conformed to Christ. It is the will of God that each individual should become ever more like Jesus, giving witness to Christ's charity, devoting his life to glorifying God and serving his neighbor. This universal call to holiness does not demand that all abandon the world, but that through their actions the people of God elevate the world and make it more truly human; their task is to be the leaven in the world, that others, through the Catholic's life lived in mercy, kindness, meekness, and patience, will be drawn to Jesus in his Catholic Church. If Catholics live as saints, others may be brought to Christ through the examples of his people. *Lumen gentium* proclaims, "In this temporal service, they [God's people] will manifest to all men the love with which God loved the world."[39] Converting to the Catholic Church is not a change in lifestyle; it is a change in life, life finally lived as it is meant to be. One of the most famous sayings of Irenaeus of Lyon is "The Glory of God is man fully alive."[40] Only in Christ can one be fully alive. One's life in Christ is a new reality, as God meant it to be. It can be ours because God wills it and because the Holy Spirit is our guide. *Lumen gentium* tell us, "It is charity which guides us to our final end. It is the love of God and the love of one's neighbor which points out the true disciple of Christ."[41] Conversion moves the individual to a new beginning and provides a second chance to live life to the fullest.

Bishop Sheen was extremely fond of the poem by Francis Thompson "The Hound of Heaven". In the poem the soul runs, hides, and flees from God, who continuously and relentlessly pursues it. Sheen wrote, "The two greatest dramas of life are the soul in pursuit of God and God in pursuit of the soul. The first has less apparent urgency, for the soul that pursues God can do it leisurely, as Peter followed the Savior from afar. But when God pursues the soul, He proves a Relentless Lover, Who will never leave the soul alone until He has won it or been conclusively denied."[42] It is the Holy Spirit that Christ sent into the world after his ascension into heaven who pursues the souls on earth. *Lumen gentium* again: "The Spirit dwells in the Church and

[39] Ibid., no. 41.

[40] Saint Irenaeus of Lyon, *Against Heresies, Books 4 and 5*, trans. Dominic Unger and Scott Moringiello (New York: Newman Press, 2024), 4.20.7.

[41] *Lumen gentium*, no. 42.

[42] Fulton J. Sheen, *Lift Up Your Heart* (Liguori, Mo.: Liguori/Triumph, 1997), 260.

in the hearts of the faithful as in a temple. In them he prays and bears witness to the fact that they are adopted sons."[43] In their divine adoption, the faithful are brothers and sisters of Jesus the Lord and are called to imitate him, growing more like him in his self-giving love and holiness throughout the rest of their lives. Their Profession of Faith is just the beginning of becoming truly holy. Holiness is a lifelong ambition and enterprise. Bishop Fulton J. Sheen would tell converts that now that they have joined the Church, "There are no limits to the truth you can know, to the life you can live, to the love you can enjoy, and to the beauty you can experience."[44] By the light and life of Archbishop Fulton J. Sheen, the greatest and best journey is still ahead for the newly converted.

[43] Lumen gentium, no. 4.

[44] Fulton J. Sheen, Simple Truths: Thinking through Life with Fulton J. Sheen (Liguori, Mo.: Liguori/Triumph, 1998), 48.

ACKNOWLEDGMENTS

Even a monograph is a collaborative work. Many thanks go to those at Ignatius Press who first believed in the project and who worked to bring it to a publishable conclusion. Thank you also to Dr. Donald Prudlo for his help and interventions at key points along the way. I want to recognize my first readers, Msgr. Patrick Gaalaas and my daughter, Christine Hughes, for their corrections and encouragement, as well as my sons, Robert and Alexander, for their enthusiasm. Most of all, my gratitude goes to Bill Hughes, my devoted husband, chef extraordinaire, and my biggest fan. "Thank you one and all" does not say quite enough. You are every one in my heart.

BIBLIOGRAPHY

Alsop, Joseph. "The Strange Case of Louis Budenz". *Atlantic Monthly*, April 1952, 29–33.

American Bishops. "Statement on Secularism". In *Pastoral Letters of the American Hierarchy, 1792–1970*. 2nd ed. Vol. 2, edited by Hugh Nolan. Washington, D.C.: United States Catholic Conference, 1984.

Apostoli, Andrew. Introduction to *The Enduring Faith and Timeless Truths of Fulton Sheen*, by Mark J. Zia, xiii–xiv. Cincinnati: Servant Books, 2015.

Augustine. *Confessions*. 2nd ed. Translated by F.J. Sheed. Indianapolis: Hacket Publishing, 2006.

Barron, Robert E. "The Priest as Bearer of the Mystery". *Furrow* 46, no. 4 (April 1995): 203–9.

Bates, Ernest Sutherland. "A Champion of Reason". *Commonweal*, January 13, 1926.

Benedict XVI. "The Church's Alter Christi". General Audience, June 24, 2009.

Benson, Robert Hugh. *Confessions of a Convert*. Notre Dame, Ind.: Christian Classics, 2016.

Bentley, Elizabeth. *Out of Bondage*. Auckland: Muriwai Books, 2018.

Biancolli, Amy. *Fritz Kreisler: Love's Sorrow, Love's Joy*. Portland: Amadeus Press, 1998.

"Bottom-Line Theology: An Interview with Fulton J. Sheen". *Christianity Today*, June 3, 1977.

Bricktop (Ada Smith DuCongé) and James Haskins. *Bricktop*. New York: Atheneum, 1983.

Budenz, Louis Francis. *This Is My Story*. New York: McGraw-Hill, 1947.

"Catholic Hour Speaker Honored and Broadcast Blessed by Holy Father". *Catholic Action* 16, no. 8 (August 1934).

Chambers, Whittaker. *Witness*. New York: Random House, 1953.

Chesterton, G.K. *The Catholic Church and Conversion*. San Francisco: Ignatius Press, 2006.

Congregatio de Causis Sanctorum. *Beatificationis et Canonizationis Servi Dei Fultonii Ionis Sheen*. Vatican City: Libreria Editrice Vaticana, 2011.

Conniff, James C.G. *The Bishop Sheen Story*. New York: Fawcett Publications, 1953.

Connor, Charles P. *Classic Catholic Converts*. San Francisco: Ignatius Press, 2001.

—. *The Spiritual Legacy of Archbishop Fulton J. Sheen*. New York: Alba House, 2010.

Considine, Robert. "God Love You". *Cosmopolitan*, July 1952.

Cooke, Alistair. *A Generation on Trial: U.S.A. v. Alger Hiss*. New York: Alfred A. Knopf, 1950.

Coolidge, Calvin. First Annual Message to Congress, December 6, 1923. https://www.presidency.ucsb.edu/documents/first-annual-message-20.

Cutié, Albert. *God Talk: Preaching to Contemporary Congregations*. New York: Church Publishing, 2012.

Dodd, Bella V. *School of Darkness*. New York: Devin-Adair, 1963.

Dolan, Jay P. *In Search of an American Catholicism*. New York: Oxford Press, 2002.

Dolan, Timothy Cardinal. Foreword to *Bishop Fulton J. Sheen: Mentor and Friend*, by Hilary C. Franco, xiii–xiv. New Hope, Ky.: New Hope Publications, 2014.

Duquin, Lorene Hanley. *A Century of Catholic Converts*. Huntington, Ind.: Our Sunday Visitor, 2003.

Ellis, John Tracy. *American Catholicism*. Chicago: University of Chicago Press, 1956.

—. *Catholic Bishops: A Memoir*. Wilmington, Del.: Michael Glazier, 1983.

Ernest, Edward Sutherland. "A Champion of Reason". *Commonweal*, January 13, 1926.

Euripides. *Euripides' Dramatic Fragments*. Edited by Jeffrey Henderson. Cambridge: Harvard University Press, 2008.

EWTN Live. "Communism in the Church: Interview with Paul Kangor by Mitch Pacwa, S.J." Aired March 29, 2023, on EWTN.

Finck, Henry T. "Lion of the Musical Season". *The Nation*, March 18, 1915.

Finke, Roger, and Rodney Stark. *The Churching of America. 1776–1990: Winners and Losers in Our Religious Economy*. New Brunswick, N.J.: Rutgers University Press, 1992.

Finks, P. David. "Crisis in Smugtown". Ph.D. diss. Graduate School of Union for Experimenting Colleges and Universities, 1975.

Flesch, Carl. *The Art of Violin Playing*. Translated by Frederick H. Martens. New York: Carl Fisher, 1930.

Franco, Hilary C. *Bishop Fulton J. Sheen: Mentor and Friend*. New Hope, Ky.: New Hope Publications, 2014.

Freud, Sigmund. *The Future of an Illusion*. New York: Horace Liveright, 1928.

"Fulton J. Sheen: The First Televangelist". *Time Magazine*, April 14, 1952.

Gaffey, James P. *Francis Clement Kelley & the American Catholic Dream.* Vol. 2. Bensenville, Ill.: Heritage Foundation, 1980.

Gannon, Robert J. *The Cardinal Spellman Story.* Garden City, N.Y.: Doubleday, 1962.

Glazier, Michael, and Thomas Shelley, eds. *The Encyclopedia of American Catholic History.* Collegeville, Minn.: Liturgical Press, 1997.

Haggerty, Donald. *Conversion: Spiritual Insights into an Essential Encounter with God.* San Francisco, Ignatius Press, 2017.

Hartline, David J. "Fulton Sheen, Still a Powerful Witness: An Interview with Fr. Andrew Apostoli". *Catholic Exchange*, February 2, 2008. https://catholicexchange.com/fulton-sheen-still-a-powerful-witness-an-interview-with-fr-andrew-apostoli/.

Hayes, Patrick Cardinal, "N.C.C.M. Inaugurates Weekly 'Catholic Hour'". *NCWC Review* 12, no. 3 (March 1930).

International Commission on English in the Liturgy (ICEL). *The Rites of the Catholic Church as Revised by the Second Vatican Ecumenical Council.* New York: Pueblo Publishing, 1976.

Investigation of Communist Activities in the New York Area: Testimony of Manning Johnson to HUAC in 1953. Washington, D.C.: United States Government Printing Office, 1953. https://www.scribd.com/document/639429677/Manning-Johnson-1953-HUAC-Testimony.

Irenaeus of Lyon. *Against the Heresies, Books 4 and 5.* Translated by Dominic Unger and Scott Moringiello. New York: Newman Press, 2024.

Jackson, Jeffrey. *Making Jazz French: Music and Modern Life in Interwar Paris.* Durham: Duke University Press, 2003.

Kessler, Lauren. *Clever Girl.* New York: Harper Collins, 2003.

Kossmann, Patricia. "Remembering Fulton Sheen", *America*, December 6, 2004.

Kreisler, Fritz. *Four Weeks in the Trenches.* New York: Houghton Mifflin, 1915.

———. "The Great Kreisler Hoax". As told to Louis Biancolli. *Etude*, June 1951.

Ladd, Gregory Joseph. *Archbishop Fulton J. Sheen: A Man for All Media.* San Francisco: Ignatius Press, 2001.

Levin, Daniel. "Smith Act". In *Encyclopedia of American Civil Liberties*, edited by Paul Finkelman. Boca Raton, Fla.: CRC Press, 2008.

Lewis, John L., et al. *Heywood Broun as He Seemed to Us.* New York: Random House, 1940.

Lochner, Louis P. *Fritz Kreisler.* New York: Macmillan, 1950. Reprinted by St. Claires Shores, Mich.: Scholarly Press, 1977.

Lonergan, William I. Review of *God and Intelligence in Modern Philosophy*, by Fulton J. Sheen. *America*, June 19, 1926.

Luce, Clare Boothe. *Europe in the Spring*. New York: Alfred A. Knopf, 1940.
―――. "The 'Real Reason' ". Pts. 1–3. *McCall's Magazine*. February–April 1946.
―――. "The Right Approach". In *Winning Converts*, edited by John A. O'Brien, 63–76. El Cajon, Calif.: Catholic Answers, 1996.
―――. "Under the Fig Tree". In *The Road to Damascus*, edited by John A. O'Brien, 213–29. Garden City, N.Y.: Doubleday, Image Books, 1949.
Lynch, Christopher Owen. *Selling Catholicism: Bishop Sheen and the Power of Television*. Lexington, Ky.: University of Kentucky Press, 1998.
Martens, Frederick H. *Violin Mastery: Talks with Master Violinists and Teachers*. New York: Frederick A. Stokes, 1919.
Martin, Ralph G. *Henry and Clare: An Intimate Portrait of the Luces*. New York: Perigee Books, 1992.
Mayo, Virginia. *Virginia Mayo: The Best Years of My Life*. Chesterfield, Mo.: Beach House Books, 2002.
McAlmon, Robert. *Being Geniuses Together: A Binocular View of Paris in the '20s*. Revised by Kay Boyle. New York: Doubleday, 1968.
McMahon, Charles A. "The First Year of the Catholic Hour", *NCWC Review*, no. 13 (March 1931): 9–11.
McNamara, Robert F. *The Diocese of Rochester in America, 1868–1968*. Rochester: Diocese of Rochester, 1968.
McSweeney, Thomas J. "Sheen, Fulton John". In *The Encyclopedia of American Catholic History*, edited by Michael Glazier and Thomas J. Shelley, 1285–88. Collegeville, Minn.: Liturgical Press, 1997.
Midnight in Paris, directed by Woody Allen. New York: Gravier Productions, 2011.
Miller, Spencer Jr. "Radio and Religion". In the *Annals of the American Academy of Political and Social Science*, no. 117 (January 1935): 135–40.
Monahan, Patrick. "To Bricktop on Her Belated Birthday". *Paris Review* (blog), August 15, 2011. https://www.theparisreview.org/blog/2011/08/15/to-bricktop-on-her-belated-birthday/.
Morris, Charles R. *American Catholic: The Saints and Sinners Who Built America's Most Powerful Church*. New York: Vintage Books, 1997.
Morris, Sylvia Jukes. *The Price of Fame*. New York: Random House, 2014.
―――. *Rage for Fame*. New York: Random House, 2014.
Newman, John Henry. *Apologia pro Vita Sua*. New York: W. W. Norton, 1968.
―――. *An Essay in Aid of a Grammar of Assent*. Monee, Ill.: Veritatis Splendor Publications, 2016.
Nolan, Hugh, ed. *Pastoral Letters of the American Hierarchy, 1792–1970*. 2nd ed. Washington, D.C.: United States Catholic Conference, 1984.

Noonan, D.P. *The Passion of Fulton Sheen*. New York: Dood, Mead & Company, 1972.

Novak, Michael. *The Open Church*. Milton Park, Abingdon, U.K: Taylor & Francis, 2017.

O'Brien, John A. "The Contemporary Scene in America". In *Winning Converts*, edited by John A. O'Brien. South Bend, Ind.: Notre Dame Books, 1957.

O'Connor, Richard. *Heywood Broun: A Biography*. New York: G.P. Putnam's Sons, 1975.

Olmsted, Kathryn S. *Red Spy Queen*. Chapel Hill, N.C.: University of North Carolina Press, 2002.

Palmer, Gretta. "Escaping from an Atheist's Cell". In *The Road to Damascus*, edited by John A. O'Brien, 29–55. Garden City, N.Y.: Doubleday, Image Books, 1949.

———."Why All These Converts? The Story of Monsignor Fulton Sheen". *Look*, June 14, 1947.

Pius XI, Pope. *Quadragesimo anno* (The Fortieth Year), May 15, 1931.

"Present at the Demolition: An Interview with Dr. Alice von Hildebrand". *Latin Mass Magazine*, Summer 2001. http://www.latinmassmagazine.com/articles/articles_2001_SU_Hildebran.html.

Reeves, Thomas C. *America's Bishop: The Life and Times of Fulton J. Sheen*. San Francisco: Encounter Books, 2001.

Riley, Kathleen L. *Fulton J. Sheen: An American Catholic Response to the Twentieth Century*. New York: Alba House, 2004.

Roche, Douglas. *The Catholic Revolution*. New York: David McKay, 1968.

Romerstein, Herbert, and Eric Breindel. *The Venona Secrets: Exposing Soviet Espionage and America's Traitors*. Washington, D.C.: Regnery Press, 2000.

Rooney, Dennis. "Instinctive Partnership: Franz Rupp Reminisces about Playing with Fritz Kreisler". *The Strand*, January 1987.

Rorty, James, and Moshe Decter. *McCarthy and the Communists*. Boston: Beacon Press, 1954.

Rosenberg, Harold. *Discovering the Present*. Chicago: University of Chicago Press, 1973.

Rothe, Anna, and Helen Demarest, eds. "Kreisler, Fritz". In *Current Biography 1944*. New York: H.W. Wilson, 1945.

Roy, Basanta Koomar. "The Personality of Kreisler". *The Mentor*, December 31, 1921.

Shadegg, Stephen. *Clare Boothe Luce: A Biography*. New York: Simon & Schuster, 1970.

Sheed, Wilfrid. *Clare Boothe Luce*. New York: Berkley Books, 1982.

Sheen, Fulton J. *Communism and the Conscience of the West.* Indianapolis: Bobbs-Merrill, 1948.

———. *Communism Answers Questions of a Communist.* New York: Paulist Press, 1937.

———. *Crisis in Christendom.* 3rd ed. Washington, D.C.: National Council of Catholic Men, 1952.

———. *God and Intelligence in Modern Philosophy.* Garden City, N.Y.: Image Books, 1958.

———. *Guide to Contentment.* New York: Macau Publishing, 1967.

———. *The Holy Hour: Readings and Prayers for a Daily Hour of Meditation.* Washington, D.C.: Council of Catholic Men, 1946.

———. "Instructing Converts". In *Winning Converts,* edited by John A. O'Brien, 160–70. South Bend: Notre Dame Press, 1957.

———. *Life Is Worth Living.* New York: McGraw Hill, 1954.

———. *Life of Christ.* Garden City, N.Y.: Doubleday, 1977.

———. *Lift Up Your Heart.* Liguori, Mo.: Liguori/Triumph, 1997.

———. *Missions and the World Crisis.* Milwaukee: Bruce Publishing, 1963.

———. *The Mystical Body of Christ.* New York: Sheed and Ward, 1935.

———. *One Lord, One World.* Huntington, Ind.: Our Sunday Visitor, 1944.

———. *Peace of Soul.* New York: Whittlesey House, 1949.

———. *Peace: The Fruit of Justice.* Huntington, Ind., Our Sunday Visitor, 1940.

———. *Preface to Religion.* New York: P.J. Kenedy and Sons, 1946.

———. *The Priest Is Not His Own.* San Francisco: Ignatius Press, 2004.

———. *Simple Truths: Thinking Life Through with Fulton J. Sheen.* Liguori, Mo.: Liguori Publications, 1998.

———. "Spirit of Poverty". *Eight Month Report.* Diocese of Rochester Archives.

———. *Through the Year with Fulton Sheen: Inspirational Readings for Each Day of the Year.* Edited by Henry Dieterich. San Francisco: Ignatius Press, 2003.

———. *Treasure in Clay: The Autobiography of Fulton J. Sheen.* Garden City, N.Y.: Doubleday, 1980.

———. *Whence Come Wars.* New York: Sheed and Ward, 1940.

Sheen, Joseph F. "My Brother's Vocation". *Missionary Youth,* 1954.

"A Sheen Moment". *Archbishop Fulton J. Sheen Foundation Newsletter.* Summer 2022.

Sherwood, Timothy H. *The Preaching of Archbishop Fulton J. Sheen: The Gospel Meets the Cold War.* New York: Lexington Books, 2019.

Skousen, W. Cleon. *The Naked Communist.* Salt Lake City: Ensign Publication Company, 1960.

Smith, Haley. "She Prayed to Fulton Sheen and Her Baby was Saved. Meet Bonnie Engstrom". *America Magazine*, July 25, 2019.

Stewart, Kenneth. "An Interview with America's Outstanding Roman Catholic Proselytizer and Philosopher". *PM Magazine*, June 16, 1946.

———. "Monsignor Fulton J. Sheen". *PM Magazine*, June 23, 1946.

Stidger, William L. *The Human Side of Greatness*. New York: Harper and Brothers, 1940.

Symonds, Kevin. "Rethinking Bella Dodd and Infiltration of the Catholic Priesthood". *Homiletics and Pastoral Review*, December 24, 2021. https://www.hprweb.com/2021/12/rethinking-bella-dodd-and-infiltration-of-the-catholic-priesthood.

Terkel, Studs. Interview with Bricktop. WFMT, radio broadcast, May 6, 1975.

"Testimony of Bella V. Dodd". In *Hearing before the Committee on Un-American Activities, 83rd Cong. (First Session)*, 1750–51. Washington, D.C.: United States Government Printing Office, 1953.

Thoreau, Henry David. "Walden". In *A Week on the Concord and Merrimack Rivers; Walden, or Life in the Woods; The Maine Woods; Cape Cod*. New York: Library of America, 1985.

Threshold of Hope. Aired June 30, 2015, on EWTN. https://www.youtube.com/watch?v=vReHEgsyGYo.

Trouvé, Marianne Lorraine, ed. *The Sixteen Documents of Vatican II*. Boston: Pauline Books and Media, 1999.

United States Council of Catholic Bishops Committee on Divine Worship. *Ordination of a Bishop, of Priests, and of Deacons*. Washington, D.C.: United States Council of Catholic Bishops, 2021.

Watson, Mary Ann. "And They Said Uncle Fultie Didn't Have a Prayer ...". *Television Quarterly*, no. 26 (1992).

Yablonsky, Sr. Mary Jude. "A Rhetorical Analysis of Selected Television Speeches of Archbishop Fulton Sheen." Ph.D. diss., Ohio State University, 1974.

INDEX

273